Sexual Abuse in the Catholic Church

Recent Titles in
Abnormal Psychology

Mental Disorders of the New Millennium, Volumes 1–3
Thomas G. Plante, editor

Bleeding to Ease the Pain: Cutting, Self-Injury, and the Adolescent
Lori G. Plante

Understanding and Treating Depression: Ways to Find Hope and Help
Rudy Nydegger

The Praeger International Collection on Addictions, Volumes 1–4
Angela Browne-Miller, editor

SEXUAL ABUSE IN THE CATHOLIC CHURCH

A Decade of Crisis, 2002–2012

Thomas G. Plante and
Kathleen L. McChesney, Editors

Abnormal Psychology

Thomas G. Plante, Series Editor

PRAEGER

AN IMPRINT OF ABC-CLIO, LLC
Santa Barbara, California • Denver, Colorado • Oxford, England

Copyright 2011 by Thomas G. Plante and Kathleen L. McChesney

Library of Congress Cataloging-in-Publication Data

Sexual abuse in the Catholic Church : a decade of crisis, 2002–2012 / Thomas G. Plante and Kathleen L. McChesney, editors.
    p. cm. — (Abnormal psychology)
    Includes bibliographical references and index.
    ISBN 978–0–313–39387–7 (hard copy : alk. paper) — ISBN 978–0–313–39388–4 (ebook)
1. Catholic Church—Clergy—Sexual behavior—United States. 2. Child sexual abuse by clergy—United States. I. Plante, Thomas G. II. McChesney, Kathleen, 1950–
BX1912.9.S387   2011
261.8′3272′088282—dc22   2011028861

ISBN: 978–0–313–39387–7
EISBN: 978–0–313–39388–4

15 14 13 12 11   1 2 3 4 5

This book is also available on the World Wide Web as an eBook.
Visit www.abc-clio.com for details.

Praeger
An Imprint of ABC-CLIO, LLC

ABC-CLIO, LLC
130 Cremona Drive, P.O. Box 1911
Santa Barbara, California 93116-1911

This book is printed on acid-free paper ∞

Manufactured in the United States of America

For all those who have suffered from the tragedy of clergy sexual abuse in the Catholic Church: the victims, their families, the disturbed perpetrators, the innocent clergy, and the faithful.

Contents

PART III: CHURCH CULTURE

PART IV: REFLECTIONS FROM THE FAITHFUL, THE VICTIMS, AND THE CLERGY

PART V: CLERGY SCREENING, FORMATION, AND TREATMENT

PART VI: CONCLUSION

Preface

Few topics during the past decade have received the kind of constant media attention, heated debate, and expression of such strong viewpoints and emotions as that of sexual abuse in the Catholic Church. Yet behind the media frenzy are thousands of personal stories of vulnerable children and teens who were sexually violated by members of the clergy and thousands of astonishing stories of how bishops and other religious superiors often failed to protect victims and attempted to avoid scandal by covering up, denying, and minimizing these crimes.

The clergy abuse story is about too many bishops and priests behaving badly when they claim to be and are viewed as the moral, religious, and ethical mentors and leaders of society. It is a heartbreaking story indeed—one that has been the subject of movies, plays, and endless op-ed pieces in all of the leading newspapers across the land during the past decade. However, it is also a highly complex story that has received remarkably little thoughtful, civil, and data-driven scholarship and discourse.

The purpose of this book is to bring together some of the best minds on this topic—individuals who have been personally or professionally involved with the issue—in order to offer reflections about where we are 10 years after the clergy abuse crisis unfolded in America. The book is a companion to two earlier edited books on this topic published by Praeger/Greenwood Press: *Bless Me Father for I Have Sinned: Perspectives on Sexual Abuse Committed by Roman Catholic Priests* (1999) and *Sin Against the Innocents: Sexual Abuse by Priests and the Role of the Catholic Church* (2004).

Clergy sexual abuse in the Catholic Church is a multilayered and complicated issue with many unknowns and too few simple and straightforward explanations. Nonetheless, the past decade has been a time of great learning about the national and international scope of the problem, some of the causes behind it, and the development of ways to prevent future abuse in church environments and elsewhere. We hope that this book will enable others to better understand and deal with clergy sexual abuse and to find ways to make this a problem of the past and not of the future.

Acknowledgments

Many people other than the authors or editors assist in the completion of a book project. Some contribute in a direct way, while others help in a more supportive manner. We would like to acknowledge the assistance of the people who worked to make this book idea a reality.

First and foremost, we would like to thank the contributors to this volume, especially those who have been victims of sexual abuse. Their courage in writing about their experiences helps other victims to know that they can come forward and find support and compassion. We are also grateful for our writers whose professional lives have been involved with the scandal described in these pages. They are the experts—individuals uniquely suited to provide their wisdom gained from dealing with victims of abuse, prevention of abuse, and conducting research and analysis of the myriad issues that comprise this enormous crisis. Their tireless efforts are the result of their deep concern for helping the Church to keep children safe.

It is important to recognize the wonderful people at ABC-CLIO who published this book. Most especially, many thanks go to our editor, Debbie Carvalko, for her enthusiasm and vision.

Last, we would like to thank our families, Lori and Zach Plante and Richard and Louisa McChesney as well as our friends and colleagues. We are grateful to all of them for encouraging us to document the personal observations of the men and women who were impacted by the most devastating events to ever occur in the history of the Catholic Church in the United States.

Part I

WHERE ARE WE NOW?

A Victim's Journey

Anonymous

I wonder if anyone can see that I am dead. Do they notice? I act like other people so that no one will know. I am between worlds, neither here nor there. It doesn't matter what happens. It doesn't matter . . . I am nothing . . . It is 1970 and I am 14.

A victim of clergy sexual abuse

It is impossible to talk about my journey to healing and my meeting with the Holy Father without understanding what I lost as a result of my abuse.

In the years before I was abused, I was baptized, made my First Communion and First Penance. My mother and father knelt down with my brother and me every night to pray. We attended Mass together, I sang in the choir and even went to daily Mass with my grandmother during the summer months. One year before my abuse began, I was confirmed by the bishop as my future abuser stood beside him. I loved being Catholic, in fact, it was my love of Catholicism that placed me in the path of the one who would hurt me.

I graduated from college, embarked on a fulfilling professional career, married a compassionate man, had three loving children and continued to be involved in the life of the Church. Some years later I returned to my own parish and was distressed to discover that my abuser was now a fixture at the school. Our relationship now appeared to resemble an adult one although in his presence I became the frightened 14-year-old child that I had been when he first molested me.

After my abuser was safely out of my life, I nearly had an emotional break-down. Whatever the trigger, the images of the past flooded my mind. I felt as though there were parts of me scattered all around. I was picking up pieces of myself, examining them and then keeping them or discarding them. I reported the priest to Chancery in the Boston Archdiocese in January, 1999 and accepted the therapy that was offered. This offer came with a letter that was really a dis-claimer. "Nothing happened," they said, and "no one was responsible."

My psychiatrist, a Catholic and father of five children, was without ques-tion Christ for me. His compassion, kindness, and empathy made it possible for me to face the past and reconstruct my life. He helped me to determine which parts of my life were really me and which parts were the manifestations of the childhood abuse. I also received a tremendous amount of support from Barbara Thorp, the director of the Office of Pastoral Support for the Archdiocese of Boston. After my initial negative experience with Archdiocese, it was Barbara and her colleagues who helped me to see that there were kind and caring people in the Church who treated victims with dignity and respect.

It took months for me to go beyond the rage and the feelings of hopeless-ness, depression, and anger. One day, a kind and understanding parish priest (unlike my abuser) offered me the Sacrament of the Sick. Puzzled, I gave my consent and felt a flooding of God's love and grace. About this same time, I asked him for Penance. He seemed puzzled as I continued to confess my guilt for several months. Like some other survivors, I believed that because the perpetrator had been a priest, it must mean that he was blameless and I was guilty. He couldn't be guilty. He was a priest—good, holy, and loved by many. So I absorbed the shame and the guilt for the one who had victim-ized me. With patience, my parish priest continued to absolve me, even as he told me there was nothing for which I should feel guilt. But I was becoming "unbound . . . I was becoming free."

As I began to reach some measure of healing, I also came face to face with another level of betrayal. The "crisis" of clergy sex abuse erupted in Boston and I became aware that I had not been the only victim of this man. My abuser had "replaced" me with some of the students at the parish school. I wondered if I had unknowingly facilitated some of the crimes against these children by not coming forward sooner. I began to bear their grief and their pain.

I learned, too, that my abuser had not been the only priest to harm a child. A number of priests had preyed on children, many younger than I had been. Many bishops didn't seem to recognize that wolves disguised as priests had attacked the sheep within their flocks, and some bishops covered up their offenses. I was devastated, enraged, hurt, and disgusted, but I did not let this crisis impede my healing. I accepted a position where I work with children and families. As I began to serve, and love, those in my care, I started to become the person I believe God always meant me to be.

Several years later, Barbara Thorp and Fr. John Connolly came to visit me. Pope Benedict was coming to the United States, and only five victims would be allowed to meet with him. They asked if I would be one of the five. Initially I felt that I had nothing more to say to anyone. I was healing and serving God. I was certain there was nothing the Holy Father could say to me that would matter. Barbara pointed out that maybe it wasn't something I needed to hear, maybe the point was that I had something to say that the Pope needed to hear. After a few days of prayer and reflection, I decided to accept the honor of having the opportunity to meet the person in charge.

Before the meeting, Fr. John spoke to me about the Gospel of the five loaves and two fish. Perhaps he and Barbara and the five survivors would, through God's Grace, feed the multitudes through this meeting. Many victims hunger for the Vicar of Christ on earth to understand the extent of the damage done to the Body of Christ. The stories of our abuse might make him see the depth of our pain and the agony of the thousands of other survivors whom he would never meet.

On the morning of the historic meeting, I choose to attend Mass alone. Surrounded by statues of the saints, I truly felt that I was not alone. The saints had been with me and would give me the strength and courage I needed to speak. They would be with me as the Holy Father heard my voice.

Later, I sat with the others in the small chapel of the Papal Nuncio. I had already asked that no photographs be taken—I only wanted the chance to lay the lives of myself and my former students at the feet of the one in charge. It was an emotional moment when the Holy Father took my hands in his and I told him I was there for so many others. I asked him to make certain that the cardinals and bishops understood that we are part of the Body of Christ . . . not ugly stepchildren . . . but rightful heirs to the same faith that they themselves professed. He looked into my eyes and nodded. He seemed to understand the pain, but I am not sure if he understood the empathy required of the hierarchy.

Meeting with Pope Benedict changed me. I was a still a survivor, but I had been given the opportunity to bring the hurt, the pain, the anger and resentment to the Shepherd. Now I was certain that he knew firsthand what an abused child endures. With this knowledge comes responsibility to care for us and protect the children. When he accepted the responsibility, he lightened my own burden.

All of the victims of clergy abuse belong to the Holy Father. They are his to hold, to comfort, and to heal. He must provide for the wounded members of the Body of Christ. He must reach the cardinals, the bishops, and the priests to help them understand that we are one. Our pain, our hurt, and our shame belong to them—and us. As a Church, we are responsible to each other; we must also be Christ for one another.

Although not all victims will respond to outreach in this way, and only a few will ever meet with the pope, the profound impact of this type of sincere interaction can surely be replicated by others who represent the Church and bring healing to those who seek it.

This past spring has been difficult for me as stories of clergy sexual abuse from around the globe come to light. Revelations about bishops, cardinals, and the pope himself are disturbing and upsetting. It is all too real and all too familiar. The inability of many cardinals and bishops to stand up for children demonstrates once again how removed these men are from the reality of our lives and their inability to see the wounded Christ in us.

Nonetheless, there are many good and holy priests and bishops who do understand our pain and our spiritual needs. They know that I need to receive Christ in the Eucharist. They know that I love my sacred home, my faith, and my Church. These good men have supported me and other victims. They have used their gift of the priesthood to promote healing and to put an end to pain and separation.

* * *

As a child, I loved the story of Our Lady of the Rosary. During grammar school, I devoured every book I could find, but in many ways, I felt that Our Lady had abandoned me when I needed her most. I could not feel her presence, and I felt so alone. In recent years, through the witness of others, I began to draw closer to her and understand that she is the Mother of Sorrow, weeping for her children. As she had witnessed Christ's passion and death, she had witnessed my own spiritual death. I began to realize that she had never left me and, with her Son, she was leading me to life all along.

I went to Fatima last year where, every night from May until October, there is a procession. People from all over the world come together to pray the Rosary and honor the Mother of Our Lord and Savior. The prayers are said in five languages and one night, I was chosen to recite the five Hail Marys in English.

As I stepped to the microphone, I remembered that fateful night in 1970 when I was first abused.

Holy Mary, Mother of God . . .

Where are you? I want my mother. I am 14, but I am hurt and crying and helpless and small and I want my Mother to wrap her arms around me and protect me. I am alone and afraid, and she's not coming. No one is coming.

But I am healed now . . . I am safe . . . I feel your arms around me . . . I see you gaze at the tabernacle in Fatima and am reminded that I am loved beyond measure.

"Hail Mary, full of grace . . ."

You are with me now, as you were with me then. You have never stopped loving me or caring for me. You have never stopped praying for me or being my Mother.

"Blessed are you among women . . ."

In your heart you have carried my pain and the pain of so many others. Our suffering has pierced your heart, and you are blessed.

"Now, and at the hour of our death . . ."

You were there then, you are here now, and you will be with me when I finally pass over from this life to New Life. You are my Mother, my Friend, and my Guide in this world and the next.

"Holy Mary, Mother of God . . ."

You have brought me back to your Son, Jesus. It is all you ever wanted, and you knew it was all I ever needed.

Chapter 1

Tragedy and Travesty: The Sexual Abuse of Minors by Catholic Clergy

Thomas G. Plante and Kathleen L. McChesney

The past decade has been exceedingly difficult for the Roman Catholic Church in the United States, perhaps representing the most tumultuous period ever in its in America. The "crisis" of sexual abuse of minors by Catholic clergy began on January 6, 2002, the Feast of the Epiphany, with the publication of a devastating investigative report in the *Boston Globe*[1] reporting hundreds of allegations of child sexual abuse perpetrated by Catholic priests and brothers over several decades. Even more shocking were assertions that bishops and other religious superiors had done little to stop the abuse.

The case of Fr. John Geoghan, accused of sexually violating 138 children over many years while being moved from parish to parish, and the administrative decisions by Cardinal Bernard Law of Boston allowing Fr. Geoghan to continue in ministry even after his sexual victimization behavior, became known as the most egregious. The *Boston Globe*'s report was quickly followed up by articles in every major newspaper, newsmagazine, and television news program across the country as well as the international media, highlighting what appeared to be an endless number of additional cases of Catholic clergy who sexually violated children and teens during the current and previous decades. Few stories have ever held this kind of media attention for so long. In fact, the *New York Times* published reports on cases of abuse or cover-up by Church leaders on its front page for 41 days in a row.

People within and outside of the Catholic Church were outraged. Many demanded the resignation and defrocking not only of those clergy accused of sexual misconduct but also of members of the Catholic Church hierarchy—most especially the bishops who were responsible for these men and assigning them to their duties. Without a doubt, this was the worst scandal to ever face the Catholic Church in America.

In the unfolding weeks and months that followed, victims quickly filed numerous lawsuits. Criminal and civil laws were changed in several states to extend the statutes of limitations so that additional victims could come forward. The resulting judgments against the Church amounted to well over a billion dollars and caused several Catholic dioceses to file for bankruptcy and Chapter 11 protection.

In June 2002, the United States Conference of Catholic Bishops (USCCB) responded to the crisis by publishing a document, the *Charter for the Protection of Children and Young People (Charter)*, more commonly known the *Dallas Charter*,[2] that provides specific guidelines and instructions for bishops on dealing with clergy sex offenders and their victims. The *Charter* mandates a zero-tolerance policy for the perpetrators, outlines efforts to reach out to victims and their families, requires regular audits of each diocese's compliance with the *Charter* and, among other directives, calls for research to determine the nature, scope, causes, and context of the abuse crisis in the Church. The USCCB promptly established the Office of Child and Youth Protection, hired a high ranking-female FBI executive to be its first executive director, and put together an impressive National Review Board of leading lay Catholics to provide advice, guidance, and oversight to the USCCB in the implementation of the *Charter*.

In 2003, audits were conducted of all dioceses throughout the country to verify implementation of the *Charter*. Hundreds of safe-environment training programs were established for children, clergy, and Church employees and volunteers. The USCCB hired researchers from the John Jay College of Criminal Justice in New York to conduct several comprehensive research projects to determine how and why the clergy abuse problem emerged in the Church.[3] Unlike before the crisis began, the USCCB was now engaged in a full court press to address the problem.

The critical question now, 10 years after the Dallas *Charter* was adopted by the USCCB, is how well has the Church dealt with the distressing problem of sexual abuse of minors? Are children safer in the Catholic Church now than before? Are there any sex abusers still in ministry? Were individuals who knowingly failed to protect children held accountable for their inaction? This book, written by a group of professionals intimately involved with these issues, is a reflection on this past decade of crisis in the Church and addresses these questions and poses some new ones.

To better understand the context of the (sometimes disparate) perspectives that follow in these chapters and to dispel several myths, it is important to consider four important facts.

First, many laypeople and priests were well aware of the problem of clergy sexual abuse well before 2002. The news media had reported on this topic many years earlier (e.g., reports published in the 1980s regarding Fr. James Porter in New England, Fr. Gilbert Gauthe in Louisiana, and the Santa Barbara Seminary School of the Franciscans), and the USCCB had published several well-known documents about the issue.[4] Some of these reports, articles, and even books stated that between 2 and 6 percent of Catholic priests in the United States had sexually abused a minor (typically a teenage boy), citing estimates derived from clinicians who evaluated and treated these men in hospital and outpatient settings.[5] Later, a national research study by the John Jay College of Criminal Justice confirmed this percentage of clergy offenders.

Thoughtful and insightful comments about clergy sexual abuse were recorded as far back as 1,700 years ago when St. Basil (330–379) wrote, "A cleric or monk who seduces youths or young boys . . . is to be publicly flogged . . . For six months he will languish in prison-like confinement, . . . and he shall never again associate with youths in private conversation nor in counseling them." St. Basil wisely foretold the zero-tolerance policy of today's *Charter* by maintaining that no clergy member who sexually violates a minor should ever be allowed to associate with youth again. Notwithstanding St. Basil's admonitions over a century ago, various members of the clergy continued to sexually abuse children and Church leaders were aware that the problem existed.

Second, no evidence yet exists to suggest that Roman Catholic priests and brothers are more likely to sexually violate minors than are men in the general population[6] or non-Catholic clergy. Sexual abuse of minors is committed by male clergy of Protestant, Jewish, Muslim, and other religious traditions,[7] as well as some men who have access to and are generally trusted with minors, including doctors, school teachers, scout leaders, coaches, and school bus drivers. In fact, research indicates that school teachers are more likely to sexually violate children than Catholic priests.[8]

Tragically, sexual exploitation of children by adults is fairly common in society. It is well established through sociological research that about 17 percent of American women and 12 percent of American men report that they were victimized by an unwanted sexual encounter with an adult while they were minors.[9] Their abusers come from all walks out life and all religious traditions and can be family members, acquaintances or strangers.

The third fact is that because Catholic clergy are no more likely to sexual violate children than clergy from other traditions or from the general population of men, one cannot blame the problem of sexual abuse in the Church on the unique qualities of Roman Catholic clergy such as celibacy or an all-male clergy.

Many have tried to argue that if priests could marry or if women were allowed to become priests, the clergy abuse scandal would not have occurred. While there are a variety of thoughtful reasons why the Church may wish to expand its pool of clergy to include married men and women, the argument that celibacy or an all-male priesthood *caused* these men to sexually violate children is not supported by the facts. Child sexual abuse occurs in the general population at levels even higher than in the Catholic Church, and some married clergy from other religious traditions sexually exploit children. Furthermore, there are many celibate men who are not Catholic clergy. Whether the celibacy is the result of personal choice, lack of a suitable sexual partner, or a physical/emotional difficulty, these men are not at higher risk for sexual abusing children than non-celibate men.[10]

The fourth point to consider is that researchers and clinicians argue that homosexuality is not, in and of itself, the cause of clergy sex abuse. However, because 81 percent of victims of clergy sexual abuse are post-pubescent teens,[11] many argue that homosexuality is to blame for the crisis. The Church has made clear that homosexual men should not become priests,[12] although current estimates suggest that between 22 and 50 percent of priests in America are homosexual.[13]

Studies show that being homosexual does not put men at higher risk for sexually violating minors and homosexuality is not associated with psychopathology or committing crimes.[14] More important, issues such as lack of human formation in the seminary prior to the 1980s and easy access to young boys may have contributed to the large percentage of male victims.[15]

* * *

For many rank-and-file Catholics who may have had the tendency to put priests on a pedestal, it was shocking to hear that some of their priests sexually harmed anyone, let alone children. The decade-old crisis in the Catholic Church is one of priests behaving badly, but it is equally about their superiors who made poor decisions in dealing with wayward priests.[16] Moreover, in some cases, Church leaders failed to treat victims and their families with understanding and compassion. Many Catholics as well as non–Catholics are now justifiably outraged by the behavior of Church leaders, whom they consider to be especially defensive and arrogant regarding this issue.

The Church has tried to be an ethical voice of moral authority for centuries. The Church's standards associated with sexual behavior such as masturbation, contraceptive use, sexual activity among unmarried persons, homosexuality, and divorce make sex crimes committed by priests seem even more scandalous and outrageous.[17] The secrecy, otherworldliness, and inner workings of the Catholic Church also contribute to a narrative of child sexual abuse committed by priests that interests and fascinates the media and the general population.[18]

Many of the 23 percent of Americans who state that they are Catholic had ambivalent feelings about their Church even before the clergy abuse crisis occurred. Some of those who were raised in the Church, especially in the 1960s prior to Vatican II, tell deeply emotional stories of priests and nuns who set impossibly high standards for student thought and behavior. That type of dogma makes stories of clergy sexually violating children seem especially hypocritical. Perhaps the gospel verse attributed to Jesus—"he who is without sin may cast the first stone"—from John 8:7 sums up this sentiment.

The purpose of this book was to examine the problem of clergy sexual abuse and the bishops' response to it during the past decade. The authors represent a variety of disciplines and perspectives and are some of the leading experts in the field of clergy sexual abuse. They include abuse victims, academics and canon lawyers, as well individuals who helped draft and edit the Dallas *Charter*, founded and managed victim advocacy and lay leadership groups, and provided psychological services to offenders.

The sexual abuse crisis in the Catholic Church has impacted countless people across the United States and in other countries as well. Those affected include the victims as well as their families, clergy, and religious and faithful Catholics who are demoralized about what has happened to their Church. The best available data, reason, and compassion can help to avoid hysteria about this issue. Steps taken to minimize this problem in the future must be increased. Joint efforts among the Church leadership, laity, and appropriate professionals are needed to avoid future sin and the victimization of innocent children.

In 2002, the Catholic Church in the United States experienced a major earthquake with Boston at its epicenter.[19] Ten years later, the earth around the Catholic Church still shakes violently with the aftershocks and the ripple effects of foreseen and unforeseen consequences. Considerable progress has been made by the American bishops toward recovering and moving forward by providing safe environments for the young and the vulnerable. However, has the Church done all that is necessary to deal with this problem, or is there more to be done?

This book seeks to answer by providing a historical accounting of what the Church has accomplished thus far. As important, we hope that our insights help to support the important processes of healing, reconciliation, and change for a better, stronger, and more Christ-like Church.

NOTES

1. Boston Globe Investigative Staff, *Betrayal: The Crisis in the Catholic Church* (New York: Little, Brown, 2002).

2. United States Conference of Catholic Bishops, *Charter for the Protection of Children and Young People* (Washington, DC: Author, 2002). United States Conference of Catholic Bishops, *Essential Norms for Diocesan/Eparchial Policies Dealing with Allegations of Sexual Abuse of Minors by Priests or Deacons* (Washington, DC: Author, 2002).

3. John Jay College of Criminal Justice, *The Nature and Scope of the Problem of Sexual Abuse of Minors by Catholic Priests and Deacons in the United States* (New York: Author, 2004). John Jay College of Criminal Justice, *The Causes and Context of the Problem of Sexual Abuse of Minors by Catholic Priests and Deacons in the United States* (New York: Author, 2011).

4. United States Conference of Catholic Bishops, *Canonical Delicts Involving Sexual Misconduct and Dismissal from the Clerical State* (Washington, DC: Author, 1995).

5. J. A. Loftus and R. J. Camargo, "Treating the Clergy." *Annals of Sex Research* 6 (1993): 287–303. T. G. Plante, (Ed.), *Bless Me Father for I Have Sinned: Perspectives on Sexual Abuse Committed by Roman Catholic Priests* (Westport, CT: Praeger/Greenwood, 1999). T. G. Plante, "Sexual Abuse Committed by Roman Catholic Priests: Current Status, Future Objectives," in *Bless Me Father for I Have Sinned: Perspectives on Sexual Abuse Committed by Roman Catholic Priests*, edited by T. G. Plante (Westport, CT: Praeger/Greenwood, 1999), 171–178. A. W. R. Sipe, *Sex, Priests, and Power: Anatomy of a Crisis* (New York: Brunner Mazel, 1995).

6. P. C. Francis and N. R. Turner, "Sexual Misconduct within the Christian Church: Who Are the Perpetrators and Those They Victimize?" *Counseling & Values* 39 (1995): 218–27. J. L. Young and E. E. H. Griffith, "Regulating Pastoral Counseling Practice: The Problem of Sexual Misconduct." *Bulletin of the American Academy of Psychiatry & the Law* 23 (1995): 421–32.

7. Francis and Turner, 218–27.

8. C. Shakeshaft, *Educator Sexual Misconduct: A Synthesis of Existing Literature* (Washington, DC: U. S. Department of Education, 2004).

9. E. O. Laumann, J. H. Gagnon, R. T. Michael and S. Michaels, *The Social Organization of Sexuality* (Chicago: University of Chicago Press, 1994). S. J. Rossetti, "The Catholic Church and Child Sexual Abuse." *America* 186 (2002): 8–15.

10. E. O. Laumann, J. H. Gagnon, R. T. Michael and S. Michaels, *The Social Organization of Sexuality* (Chicago: University of Chicago Press, 1994).

11. John Jay College of Criminal Justice, *The Causes and Context of the Problem of Sexual Abuse of Minors by Catholic Priests and Deacons in the United States* (New York: Author, 2011).

12. Congregation for Catholic Education, *Instruction Concerning the Criteria for the Discernment of Vocations with Regard to Persons with Homosexual Tendencies in View of Their Admission to the Seminary and to Holy Orders* (Vatican City, Author, 2005).

13. T. G. Plante, "Homosexual Applicants to the Priesthood: How Many and Are They Psychologically Healthy?" *Pastoral Psychology* 55 (2007): 495–498.

14. American Psychological Association Division 44/Committee on Lesbian, Gay, and Bisexual Concerns Joint Task Force on Guidelines for Psychotherapy with Lesbian, Gay, and Bisexual Clients, "Guidelines for Psychotherapy with Lesbian, Gay, and Bisexual Clients." *American Psychologist* 55 (2000): 1440–1451. R. E. Fox, "Proceedings of the American Psychological Association, Incorporated, for the Year 1987: Minutes of the Annual Meeting of the Council of Representatives." *American Psychologist* 43 (1988): 508–531.

15. John Jay College of Criminal Justice, *The Causes and Context of the Problem of Sexual Abuse of Minors by Catholic Priests and Deacons in the United States* (New York: Author, 2011). F. Barry and T. G. Plante, "Homosexual Candidates, the Seminary and the Priesthood." *The Priest* 62 (2006): 14–16.

16. Boston Globe Investigative Staff, *Betrayal: The Crisis in the Catholic Church* (New York: Little, Brown, 2002). John Jay College of Criminal Justice, *The Nature and Scope of the Problem of Sexual Abuse of Minors by Catholic Priests and Deacons in the United States* (New York: Author, 2004). John Jay College of Criminal Justice, *The Causes and Context of the Problem of Sexual Abuse of Minors by Catholic Priests and Deacons in the United States* (New York: Author, 2011). T. G. Plante, (Ed.), *Bless Me Father for I Have Sinned: Perspectives on Sexual Abuse Committed by Roman Catholic Priests* (Westport, CT: Praeger/Greenwood, 1999). S. J. Rossetti, "The Catholic Church and Child Sexual Abuse." *America* 186 (2002): 8–15.

17. D. Cozzens, *Sacred Silence: Denial and the Crisis in the Church* (Collegeville: MN: Liturgical Press, 2002).

18. G. Wills, *Papal Sin* (New York: Doubleday, 2000).

19. T. G. Plante, "After the Earthquake: Five Reasons for Hope after the Sexual Abuse Scandal." *America* 190 (2004): 11–14. T. G. Plante, "Another Aftershock: What Have We Learned from the John Jay College Report?" *America* 190 (2004): 10–12.

Chapter 2

Incidence of Clerical Sexual Abuse over Time: Changes in Behavior and Seminary Training between 1950 and 2008

Karen J. Terry, Katarina Schuth, and Margaret Leland Smith

In June 2002, the United States Conference of Catholic Bishops (USCCB) signed the *Charter for the Protection of Children and Young People* (the *Charter*). As part of their broad mission to protect children, the bishops agreed in this *Charter* to support two studies aimed at understanding the problem of child sexual abuse by Catholic priests. The Office of Child and Youth Protection (OCYP) and the National Review Board (NRB), two entities formed as a result of the *Charter*, commissioned researchers at John Jay College to conduct these studies. The first was a descriptive study assessing the nature and scope of the problem in the United States from 1950 through 2002 (the *Nature and Scope* study). The second was an in-depth assessment of the causes and context of the problem from historical, sociological, psychological, and situational perspectives (the *Causes and Context* study).

The topic of child sexual abuse by Catholic priests came to the forefront in 2002 largely as a result of the case of John Geoghan, a priest in the Boston Archdiocese. Geoghan was accused of abusing more than 130 children over three decades, and reports about his abuse and the cover-up of his actions by officials of the Catholic Church were the catalyst for an ensuing media frenzy that would trigger an unprecedented cascade of reports of sexual abuse of minors by priests.[1] As Catholic communities, survivors' groups, victim advocates, and the general public were seeking an explanation of how and why this could happen, so was the Catholic Church. In 2002, they did not know the extent of the crisis or its causes.

The sexual abuse crisis in the Catholic Church is an incredibly complex phenomenon. A crucial fact that was not understood as the crisis was emerging in 2002 was the delay in reporting of abuse cases. Although the news was full of the almost-daily reports of abuse, most cases being reported had occurred decades earlier. If all the incidents of child sexual abuse by priests reported between 1950 and 2009 are counted, more than 93 percent took place before 1990. Incidents of sexual abuse by priests continued to occur in the last 20 years, but the *Nature and Scope* data show this phenomenon to be in large part a historical problem—concentrated between 1965 and 1985. This chapter outlines the key findings from the *Nature and Scope* study, including the longitudinal patterns of incidence and reporting and the characteristics of abusers and victims. It also reviews the key conclusions of the *Causes and Context* study that relate to the patterns of abuse. Finally, the chapter provides a discussion about changes in seminary education between 1950 and the present and the implications for the study of sexual abuse by priests.

NATURE AND SCOPE STUDY

The *Nature and Scope* study was based on data from diocesan records for all priests and deacons in the United States from 1950 to 2002. The aim of the study was to provide a thorough analysis of the extent of the problem with a specific focus on the abusers, those they abused, in what situations the abuse occurred, types of abuse incidents, and the financial impact on the Church. Researchers at John Jay College collected information from 97 percent of Catholic dioceses (representing 99% of the Catholic population) and 64 percent of religious communities (representing 83% of religious priests) and released the report of the *Nature and Scope* study in February 2004.[2] In the two years that followed, the John Jay researchers conducted further analyses of that data, and a supplementary report was released in 2006.[3] The supplemental report focused on the estimation of the overall problem of abuse in the Church, patterns of abuse, duration of abusive behavior, a comparison between subgroups of priests with allegations of abuse, and the institutional response to the abuse problem. Some of the key findings from this study are as follows.

Scope of the Problem

Data collected by the end of 2003 showed that 4,392 priests—or 4 percent of priests in ministry in that time period—had allegations of abuse between 1950 and 2002, and 10,667 individuals made allegations of child sexual abuse against priests known to dioceses during that time period.

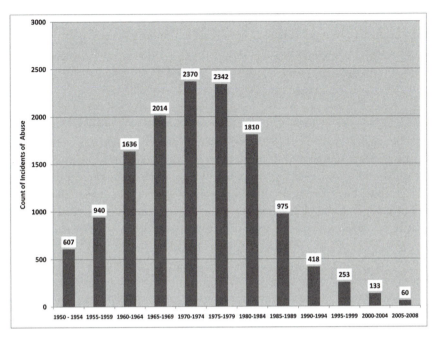

FIGURE 2.1 Distribution of incidents from 1950 to 2008, counted in the year the abuse began.

Distribution of Cases by Year, Region, and Size of Diocese

The number of incidents of sexual abuse peaked in the 1970s. There was an increase in abuse cases in the 1960s, with a sharp decline by the mid-1980s. This pattern was consistent across all regions of the Catholic Church in the United States, and it was also consistent in dioceses of all sizes. Figure 2.1 shows the distribution of incidents of sexual abuse between 1950 and 2008, counted in the year of occurrence and clustered in five-year increments. This chart includes both the 10,667 allegations of abuse from the *Nature and Scope* study and the reports made to dioceses between 2004 and 2008. The post–2002 data document a total of 3,863 new reports, as collected by the Center for Applied Research in the Apostolate (CARA) between 2004 and 2008.

Abusers

The majority of abusers were diocesan priests who were pastors or associate pastors at the time of the abuse. The abusers' age range at the onset of abuse was 30–39, and most known abusers had one victim. However, a small number of abusers (3.5%) were responsible for abusing more than a quarter of the youth who were victimized. This research finding is consistent with the criminological scholarship that has documented that a small percentage of offenders account for a disproportionate number of crimes.

Victims

The majority of victims (81%) were male. Most of the victims were pubescent or postpubescent, and approximately half were between the ages of 11 and 14. One in five victims was under the age of 10 at the time of the abuse. Thus, while the media often dubbed the priest abusers "pedophile priests," this is a misnomer; a pedophile is someone who is diagnosed with a mental disorder that is consistent with sexual urges and fantasies about *prepubescent* children.

Types and Location of Offenses

Priests were accused of committing more than 20 types of offenses, ranging from touching outside the clothes to genital penetration. The majority of priests committed multiple types of abuse, and few priests committed only the most minor acts of abuse. The most common place for the abuse to occur was in the home of the priest (41%), though it also occurred in high frequency in the Church (16%), the victim's home (12%), in a vacation house (10%), in school (10%) and in a car (10%).

Reporting of Abuse

Although the majority of abuse incidents had occurred by 1985, most cases were not known to the dioceses at that time. Data now show that more than 11,000 incidents of abuse had occurred by 1985, but only 840 reports had been made to dioceses by that time. Many victims of abuse would wait 30 or 40 years before making a report; one-third of all incidents known by the end of 2002 were reported in that year alone. See Figure 2.2 for reporting trends through December 2008.

CAUSES AND CONTEXT STUDY

A primary focus of the *Causes and Context* study, given the findings from the *Nature and Scope* study, was to determine what caused this rise in abuse cases in the 1960s and decline in the 1980s. To understand more about the distribution of offending, it was necessary to ask two questions:

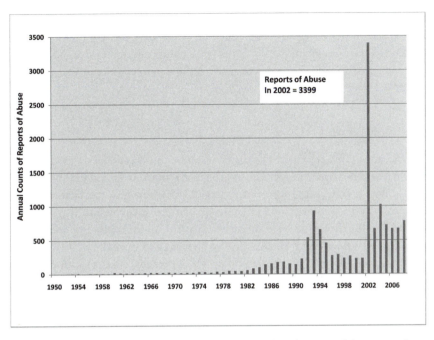

FIGURE 2.2 Distribution of reports of abuse, counted in the year of the report, from 1950 through December 2008.

(1) Is the shape of the distribution of abuse cases stable? In other words, will the peak of the abuse cases remain where it is, or will the peak of cases shift forward in time as more victims come forward to report offenses in the future?
(2) If this distribution of cases is accurate, what factors are associated with the rise and subsequent decline in abuse cases over this time period?

Distribution of Abuse Cases

An observed lag in the disclosure of sexual abuse is generally common, not simply specific to the Catholic Church, so it was clear that more victims would come forward to report acts of abuse by clergy after 2002. The questions were: Would these victims be reporting abuse cases that occurred many years ago, during the peak of the abuse crisis observed in the *Nature and Scope* study? Or would the newly reported abuse cases have occurred more recently? To test whether the distribution of cases over this time period was stable, the researchers used mathematical models to estimate the distribution of unknown cases. The estimation modeling confirmed that the peak is stable, that the incidence of abuse was highest in the late 1970s and was fairly low and stable by the early 1990s. Thus, the data illustrated in Figure 2.1 are a true picture of the abuse crisis, and the peak of cases in the 1970s and early 1980s is real.[4] Subsequent data collected by CARA for the USCCB have confirmed the conclusion of the John Jay College researchers: and although new reports are made each year, the longitudinal pattern in each year matches Figure 2.1 very closely.

Causes of the Abuse Crisis

Once it became clear that the distribution of abuse incidents over time was stable, it was necessary to ask why abusive behavior peaked and declined when it did. Was this peak the result of individual differences in the character and composition of the priesthood in these years? Was it the result of changes in seminary education? Or were larger sociocultural influences responsible for the pattern? The focus of the inquiry was whether priests who abused minors were primarily driven by pathological or developmental factors or, in contrast, situational, organizational, or social factors.

Individual Differences in Priests

Data from the *Causes and Context* study showed that few priests were driven to commit acts of sexual abuse against minors because of serious psychological disorders. Abusive priests were not significantly more likely to have personality or mood disorders than priests who did not have abuse allegations, and there were no statistically significant differences between the two groups on psychological inventories or IQ tests.[5] Importantly, very few of the priest-abusers were diagnosed with or exhibited behaviors consistent with pedophilia. Pedophilia is a diagnosable sexual disorder characterized by sexual urges, fantasies, or behaviors about prepubescent children; most priests-abusers had allegations against minors who were pubescent or postpubescent. In fact, most priests who had allegations of abuse were "generalists" who did not target victims of a particular age and/or gender. Many of the priests who sexually abused youths had also violated their vows of celibacy with adults. Individual differences did not distinguish those priests with a history of behavior involving child abuse from priests with no history of such behavior.

Onset, Persistence, and Desistance of Abuse

The data suggest that a combination of factors played a role in the onset, persistence, and desistance of abuse behavior by priests. Priest-abusers showed patterns of behavior consistent with the four-factor model of offending proposed by David Finkelhor, which includes: (1) motivation to abuse (often emotional congruence with the minor, as well as a blockage to [nonsexual] intimate relationships with adults); (2) overcoming internal inhibitions to abuse (through the excuses and justifications that alleviate their sense of responsibility for the behavior); (3) overcoming external factors (by creating opportunities for abuse to occur); and (4) overcoming the child's resistance (through grooming techniques). Many priest-abusers created opportunities to be alone with minors in order for abuse to occur, and they often integrated themselves into the families of the victims. Most victims of abuse did not disclose their victimization for many years, and the signs of abuse were not detected by those close to them. Detection and an official report were rarely the reason for the end of an abuse incident, as reports of abuse were often made decades after the abuse occurred.

Organizational Factors

Although most of the incidents of abuse occurred before the precipitous decline in abuse cases in 1985, only 810 cases of abuse had been reported by then. In 2002, at the height of the media attention on the sexual abuse by priests, and in every year thereafter, victims have come forward to report abuse that occurred decades earlier. Prompted by the high-profile case of Gilbert Gauthe, bishops began discussions about abuse in 1985. The predominant response in the 1990s to reports of abuse was to focus on the priest-abusers rather than on the victims.

By 1992, the understanding of the harm to victims of sexual abuse by an adult was increasing. The bishops endorsed the "Five Principles," which stated that diocesan leaders should: (1) respond promptly to all allegations of abuse where there is reasonable belief that abuse has occurred; (2) relieve the alleged offender promptly of his ministerial duties and refer him for appropriate medical evaluation and intervention if an allegation is supported by sufficient evidence; (3) comply with the obligations of civil law regarding reporting of the incident and cooperating with the investigation; (4) reach out to the victims and their families and communicate sincere commitment to their spiritual and emotional well-being; and (5) deal as openly as possible with the members for the community within the confines of respect for privacy of the individuals involved.

Though many diocesan leaders responded to allegations of abuse, they responded through internal mechanisms such as investigation, evaluation, and administrative leave rather than through the external mechanisms of the criminal law. Additionally, few bishops utilized the formal canonical responses such as laicization, or dismissal from the clerical state, finding them complicated, time consuming, and often confusing. The reliance on "insiders" and insistence on private agreements with victims led to frustration with the lack of transparency by many Catholics and advocates for victims.

Social and Cultural Changes in Society

To understand changes in an organization, it is first necessary to understand social changes in society. The *Causes and Context* study evaluated changes in cultural, social, and psychological factors in American society and the Catholic Church that may have contributed to the likelihood of sexual abuse of minors, particularly during the 1970s. These factors include changes in social behavior (e.g., marriage and divorce rates, rates of single parents); criminal behavior (e.g., crimes rates for robbery); "deviant" behavior (e.g., drug use), legal changes (e.g., new definitions of sexual abuse, increases in the number of laws regulating child abuse); and demographic changes (e.g., economic development). Data show that these overall changes in American society, or "social indicators," increase and decrease over time in a way that is consistent with the observed changes in the incidence of abuse by Catholic priests. The peak years of abuse by Catholic priests are also peak years for other types of "deviant" behavior, including divorce, drug use, and criminal behavior. Thus, the pattern of abuse by priests in the Catholic Church was consistent with other types of deviant behavior during this time period. Because individuals within institutions are necessarily influenced by broader social factors, it is not surprising that the patterns of abuse are consistent with other types of deviant behavior generally.

Preparation for Priesthood

Given these social and cultural changes, we sought to understand how the shift in priestly formation could have affected the development of priests ordained in different periods. The incidence of abuse peaked in the 1970s: the priests responsible for the abusive behavior were ordained prior to the 1970s—in the 1940s, 1950s, and 1960s, when almost no attention was paid to human formation. However, during the decades under discussion, especially from the 1960s to the 1980s, significant changes in preparation for priesthood were incorporated in many seminaries. In the earlier decades, education for the

Catholic priesthood was more likely to begin during high school or college years. Since the 1980s, a pretheology program of one or two years often supplanted the longer period of studies. In many other ways, seminary education underwent major change and development between the postwar period and the present. Ordination to ministry, however, almost always followed four years of postgraduate preparation in a theological seminary, called "the program of priestly formation."

Especially in the area of human formation, theological seminaries made considerable changes in the models and content in the past 25 years. In comparing the information available in diocesan seminary catalogs from the mid-1980s, the mid-1990s, and current catalogs (2008–2011), it is evident that almost every seminary responded to pressing problems in the Church related to clerical sexual abuse and to directives from the Vatican and the USCCB regarding seminary formation. During the first period, virtually none of the programs described in catalogs referred to human formation, but, rather, under the banner of spiritual formation, they mentioned the need for growth in maturity and balance in daily life. These directives were intended to prepare seminarians more effectively for the sake of the people they would eventually serve. By the middle period, many seminaries adopted the language of personal development, and some described the formation associated with it as a separate component. During that period, more than a few seminaries adopted the practice of providing a formation advisor for each student to monitor growth in all areas of formation. This development is consistent with the late-twentieth-century emphasis on the importance and value of the individual person.

Only in the third period, beginning significantly by about 2005, did seminaries adopt the four-fold model of formation identified by Pope John XXIII in *Pastores dabo vobis* (1992). He proposed the necessity of including these four dimensions of formation: human, spiritual, intellectual, and pastoral.[6] The five editions of the *Program of Priestly Formation*, initiated in 1971 and revised periodically up to 2005, began with scant mention of human formation, celibacy, or sexuality until the last two editions, especially the most recent. What follows are details of the evolution of the priestly formation program, eventually resulting in separate human and spiritual components that responded to hierarchical directives and changing dynamics in the Church and society.

1980s Formation Programs

In the mid-1980s, almost all seminary catalogs described priestly formation as comprised of three basic elements: spiritual, academic, and pastoral.

The focus during this period was on the content and organization of the spiritual dimension of some 30 diocesan seminaries whose main mission was to prepare men for priesthood. Almost all of the descriptions contained at least some mention of personal formation; half the programs are called simply "spiritual formation." The other half specifically includes aspects of both spiritual and personal formation in their titles.[7] Clearly, human formation and its associated topics were not in the forefront of the minds of seminary personnel during the 1980s and before.

Several elements were common to most of the programs during this time, regardless of the title, but for those called "spiritual formation," the emphasis, as expected, was on spirituality, with minimal elaboration of other areas of formation. First among the common elements was spiritual direction, in which almost all seminarians were specifically required to participate. They were to see a spiritual director every two weeks or, in a few cases, at least once a month. Many emphasized the confidential nature of the relationship, which was to be characterized by trust and openness. Terms like *complete confidentiality* and *strict secrecy* were used to indicate that this practice was entirely in the "internal forum," the content of which was not to be revealed except under a few rare circumstances.

To balance this practice, in nine seminaries each student was guided also by a formation advisor who was to assist him with all areas of formation. This relationship was not confidential in the sense that the material covered in the conversations between advisor and student was understood to be in the "external forum" and thus, with the advisor using prudence about what to reveal, was to be included in evaluations. A third form of consultation mentioned by almost every seminary was psychological counseling. This arrangement would not be compulsory, but the service was available through the seminary. Accurate self-knowledge was the broad goal of all three forms of consultation.

A second common element in the spiritual/personal formation programs was an emphasis on the importance of solidifying the vocation or commitment to lifelong ministerial service on the part of seminarians. Part of this task was to be achieved by developing spiritual and emotional maturity: development of the mature person was for the sake of the people they would eventually serve in ministerial positions. They were to cultivate a deep prayer life, consisting of many required spiritual exercises, so that they could be prepared "to accept priestly burdens, particularly celibacy," as one seminary expressed it.

Less common were several other themes, most often included by seminaries whose understanding of spiritual formation was broader and involved a more developed program of personal formation, later to be called "human formation" by Pope John Paul II in *Pastores dabo vobis*. Of particular interest was the inclusion of program elements dealing with sexuality and preparation for celibacy. Only about half the seminaries mentioned workshops, formation sessions, and/or courses dealing with these topics. They described the programs as necessary for the seminarian to develop "a mature attitude toward his own sexuality and the celibate life," to learn about "the meaning of celibate chastity" and how to deal with it in ministerial situations, as well as to understand "sexuality, intimacy, and generativity" and "the many facets of celibacy." Less directly, they talked about "the ability to live a moral and virtuous life" and "social maturity." Often these expressions were followed by the comment that this development was for the sake of the "quest to be more fully human and fully Christian for the sake of the people." Certainly other seminaries may have discussed these matters, but catalogs did not refer to them until years later.

Responsibility for the evaluation process usually fell to the spiritual formation team, consisting mainly of faculty members. Components of the evaluation also involved peer evaluators, a practice in about 10 of the seminaries. The explanation of the purpose of annual, or occasionally more frequent, evaluations was to assess the readiness of the seminarian for pastoral ministry. His personal qualifications and attributes were to be judged largely on the basis of how effectively he would be able to serve as a priest.[8]

1990s Formation Programs

By the mid-1990s, some shifts in the content of catalogs relative to spiritual and personal formation were evident. More seminaries identified personal formation as a component, but only one or two mentioned "human formation." The descriptions of the human dimension of formation were relatively meager in most cases, and the emphasis was still strongly on spiritual formation. Although none of the seminaries had established distinct programs in human formation, personal formation and affective maturity received more attention than earlier. At least half the seminaries included some programs related to celibacy and described them at least briefly in a paragraph or two. These were often special workshops, class conferences, and discussions.

Notable in this period was the introduction of formation advisors in almost all seminaries, compared with only nine using this structure 10 years earlier. The practice allowed for information about seminarians to move from the confidential internal forum of spiritual direction to the communal external forum of faculty evaluations. Certainly program development related to personal formation was expanded in the 1990s, but only by the mid-2000s and later did the content of the formation programs change significantly in seminary catalog descriptions.[9]

Post–2000 Formation Programs

From about 2006 to 2010, immense changes were recorded demonstrating greater awareness of the need for human formation, including education about the role of sexuality and celibacy in the life of a priest. Separate programs for human formation and spiritual formation were documented in 20 of the 31 seminary catalogs, and most others made at least mention of the two areas. The term *human formation*, taken from John Paul II's *PDV*, replaced *personal development* and similar phrases used in the past. The remaining 11 seminaries titled their programs in different ways and usually combined the content of human and spiritual formation. About a third of the seminaries described the content of the programs in substantial detail, including considerable information about how the seminaries contend with the topics of sexuality and celibacy.

The effects of the sexual abuse scandal from 2002 and the Vatican-initiated visitation of seminaries in 2005 to 2006 undoubtedly influenced the considerable attention paid to these topics. The 2005 *Program of Priestly Formation* (PPF) included a chapter titled "Human Formation" for the first time and contained numerous other references to this dimension of formation. In particular, the document provided extensive explanations and directives concerning the role of seminaries in preparing men to live a life of celibate chastity. Relative to admissions, for example, the *PPF* states, "For the seminary applicant, thresholds pertaining to sexuality serve as the foundation for living a lifelong commitment to healthy, chaste celibacy. As we have recently seen so dramatically in the Church, when such foundations are lacking in priests, the consequent suffering and scandals are devastating" (# 41).

Of particular interest is the shift in vocabulary that accompanied the new approaches to formation. To begin with, almost all seminaries discussed the importance of integration of the four aspects, or "pillars," of formation—human, spiritual, intellectual, and pastoral. These are not to be considered discrete or layered dimensions of seminary formation but, rather, are to be interrelated. Human formation is the foundation for all the others; spiritual formation enhances the capacity of the individual to develop a relationship with God and others; intellectual formation provides an understanding of all areas; and pastoral formation is the expression in ministry of the other dimensions of formation. An emphasis on developing positive relationships characterizes the role human formation is to play.

Another approach emphasized anew in the human formation program is the personal responsibility each seminarian must take in preparing for priesthood. In this regard, development of moral virtues is considered necessary to the life of a priest—self-knowledge, self-discipline, integrity, justice, and prudence among them. The practice of these virtues is to lead to development of a moral conscience, a proper ordering of the passions, and maintaining boundaries in order to achieve good and avoid evil. Acquiring these qualities is to result in the seminarian taking on habits that will make it possible for him to build his capacity to become emotionally mature, to live a chaste celibate life, and thus enable him to meet the expectations of the Church. Spiritual directors and formation advisors assist the seminarian in this growth; periodic evaluations enable him to recognize the shortcomings he still must overcome. The interconnected areas heightened in recent seminary programs, more than ever before, have to do with integration, relationships, and personal responsibility for moral behavior.

As is evident from the evolution of formation programs from the 1980s to the 2000s, seminaries responded to societal changes and reports of clergy sexual abuse by incorporating significant elements related to celibate chastity. Most seminaries have added a separate program in human formation that clearly defines the nature of appropriate relationships and the meaning of moral behavior for a priest.

CONCLUSION

The *Causes and Context* study examined developmental, behavioral, and psychological characteristics in detail in order to understand whether any of these individual-level factors predict future sexual abuse of a minor by a priest. We did not find any such predictor; however, the influence of social and cultural factors was apparent throughout the study period of 1950 to 2010. If individuals who are vulnerable or at risk for future abuse cannot be identified in advance, then careful preparation in seminary for the demands of the priesthood is required.

The role that priestly formation played in the sexual abuse crisis is crucial. In particular, the cohorts of priests with the most allegations of abuse are those who were educated in seminary prior to the peak years of the abuse crisis (the 1970s). These priests, who were vulnerable to commit acts of abuse, had little training in human formation and were ill-prepared to resist the influences of the social culture of the times. Studies of victimization were nascent and little was understood about the extent of the harm caused by sexual victimization of youths. This lack of attention to the human development of candidates for the priesthood, combined with the lack of understanding of victimization and the minimal oversight of individual priests in positions of power in parishes (as pastors or associate pastors), allowed the crisis to escalate as it did. Though the sexual abuse "crisis" is an historical problem, it is critical that we understand the causes of this crisis so as to prevent another in the future. Implementing periodic systems of review and evaluation for priests would help to ensure that the Church take responsibility for preparing men for the priesthood but also that priests continue to build upon their capacities to live emotionally mature, chaste celibate lives.

NOTES

1. Boston Globe Spotlight Team, "The *Boston Globe* Spotlight Investigation: Abuse in the Catholic Church." *Boston Globe*, retrieved May 1, 2011 from http://www.boston.com/globe/spotlight/abuse/.
2. John Jay College, *The Nature and Scope of Sexual Abuse of Minors by Catholic Priests and Deacons in the United States, 1950–2002* (Washington, DC: United States Conference of Catholic Bishops, 2004).
3. John Jay College Research Team, *The Nature and Scope of Sexual Abuse of Minors by Catholic Priests and Deacons in the United States, 1950–2002: Supplementary Data Analysis* (Washington, DC: United States Conference of Catholic Bishops, 2006).
4. For more information about the estimation modeling, see: M. L., Smith, A. Rengifo and B. Vollman, "Trajectories of Abuse and Disclosure." *Criminal Justice and Behavior* 35, no. 5 (2008): 570–582.
5. Personality test data included the Minnesota Multiphasic Personality Inventory and the Millon Clinical Multiaxial Inventory. Intelligence scores were based on the Wechsler Adult Intelligence Scale.
6. Other major documents influencing seminary programs included: *Optatam totius* (Decree on Priestly Formation), Document of Vatican II, 1965; *Ratio fundamentalis institutionis sacerdotalis* (Spiritual Formation in Seminaries), Sacred Congregation for Catholic Education, 1980; and five editions of the *Program of Priestly Formation:* 1971, 1976, 1981, 1992, and 2005, United States Conference of Catholic Bishops (under various names).
7. Eight use just that title, five others use a broader title of "Priestly Formation," and two others are unique, one being "Growth in Life and Ministry" and the other "Student Life and Formation."
8. For a fuller explanation of formation programs in the 1980s, see Katarina Schuth, "Personal and Spiritual Formation," in *Reason for the Hope: The Futures of Roman Catholic Theologates* (Wilmington, DE: Michael Glazier, Inc., 1989), 137–165.
9. For a fuller explanation of formation programs in the 1990s, see Katarina Schuth, "Human and Spiritual Formation in Theologates," in *Seminaries, Theologates, and the Future of Church Ministry* (Collegeville, MN: Liturgical Press, 1999), 131–153.

Part II

THE "DALLAS" CHARTER

Chapter 3

Journey to the *Charter*

Mark E. Chopko, J. Cletus Kiley, and Francis J. Maniscalco

The journey to the *Charter for the Protection of Children and Young People*[1] *(Charter)* began nearly 30 years ago with heartbroken parents challenging dioceses to provide justice for their children who had been sexually abused by Catholic priests. Adults who had been victimized as children started to speak out as well, expressing their outrage not only at their abusers but also at church authorities who appeared unresponsive to their pain.

Concern about clergy who abused minors was one aspect of a growing social awareness of the vulnerability of children to abuse by adults. Society was open to hearing the victims' stories and responding to them. Those years also saw an increase in the media's willingness to report this misconduct and the strengthening of state and federal laws dealing with sexual abuse of children.

From the study produced by the John Jay College of Criminal Justice in 2004, *The Nature and Scope of Sexual Abuse of Minors by Catholic Priests and Deacons in the US 1950–2002,*[2] we now know that the sexual abuse of minors by clergy was at its height in the 1970s without its being apparent even to expert observers.[3] This was the same timeframe in which abuse cases in general were coming to the attention of the public, media, legislators, and the justice system.

Catholic Bishops of the United States were to find in the second half of the 1980s that the plague of sexual abuse of minors was becoming a crisis for the Church, as well as society, due to clergy-related cases that began to receive widespread attention at that time. They turned to their Bishops' Conference,[4] as well as to experts known to them locally, to help piece together an understanding of this heinous misconduct and to develop a response to it. This chapter, written by some of us who were directly involved in developing the response of the Bishops' Conference, tells the seldom-acknowledged story of the years-long journey to the *Charter* from the bishops' initial collective response through the development of the *Restoring Trust* reports and the other efforts of the Ad Hoc Committee on Sexual Abuse (AHCSA).[5]

THE BISHOPS' RESPONSE: MID-1980s TO EARLY 1990s

Pastoral, legal, canonical, and communications concerns all played a part in the bishops' response to the problem of sexual abuse of minors, as did media coverage. Between 1984, when the Bishops' Conference first focused on the issue, and 2002, when reports of the criminal trial of Boston priest John Geoghan sparked a national crisis, the media alternated between a few periods of intense coverage and longer periods of relative inattention. The avalanche of coverage of clerical misconduct that accompanied and followed the Geoghan trial often failed to recognize that even when the media paid limited attention to the problem, the bishops were still responding to allegations of victims who continued to come forward.

The bishops' response took into account the perspective of therapists. From the mid-1980s, the bishops were updated about developments in therapy by professionals who were treating perpetrators of sexual abuse of minors. Diagnoses of the causes of this abusive behavior and protocols for treatment were undergoing improvement, providing the bishops with a more complete understanding of this psychosexual dysfunction and whether it manifested, in individual cases, an incurable condition or one for which something like a cure was available.

During this time, some state Catholic conferences and/or individual dioceses, notably the dioceses in Florida and New Jersey and the archdioceses of Chicago, St. Paul-Minneapolis, and Seattle, developed policies on the sexual abuse of minors that received local and even national media attention. At the Bishops' Conference level, the discussions of this painful and demoralizing issue were held in executive session and, consequently, were below the public's radar. Although *Time* and other media outlets reported that discussions were taking place, their contents were not publicized. Only a limited number of statements on the matter were issued publicly by the bishops before 1992.

Even then, some bishops disliked open discussion of this egregious violation of priestly commitment and their response to it. As a result, the efforts of the

Bishops' Conference and its staff to develop policies in conjunction with dioceses based on their actual experience with abuse allegations were not well known.

Apart from the work of the Conference staff, a document was being drafted that was variously described as a "report," "manual," or "project" by three concerned parties: Father Thomas Doyle, O.P., a canon lawyer working for the papal nuncio to the United States; Ray Mouton, a trial lawyer who had represented a priest-abuser; and Father Michael Peterson, a psychiatrist who was then president and CEO of the St. Luke Institute, a treatment facility in Maryland for clergy and religious with psychological problems. Titled *The Problem of Sexual Molestation by Roman Catholic Clergy: Meeting the Problem in a Comprehensive and Responsible Manner*, the document was often referred to by the names of its authors and contained information about the types and likely outcomes of clinical treatment of priest-abusers, a summary of the canon law related to this matter and a description of the financial threat posed to the Church through civil litigation initiated by victims.[6] The report recommended that a team made up of a psychiatrist, a canon lawyer, and a civil lawyer be hired on a contract basis by the Bishops' Conference and individual dioceses to deal with these cases.

When the bishops met in Collegeville, Minnesota, in June 1985, numbered copies of the Doyle-Mouton-Peterson report were given, confidentially and in draft form, to the Conference's executive officers and several committee chairmen, asking in the text "that each reader return [it] to the person from whom they received same, without copying." The authors urged these few bishops to exercise "an abundance of caution" with the material due to the "active interest" of the "national press."[7]

Several months after the bishops' meeting in Collegeville, Father Peterson mailed a copy of the Doyle-Mouton-Peterson report to the diocesan bishops attached to one of his own creation that carried the disclaimer that his report was not to be considered a "national plan" for the Bishops' Conference. It was in this context that the vast majority of bishops received the Doyle-Mouton-Peterson report. Despite the report's original, narrow, and confidential distribution and the fact that the bishops never received it as a body or discussed it as such, since becoming public, it has attained iconic status as the "plan" that the bishops ignored to their detriment.

However, the bishops did address the abuse of minors by priests while meeting in Collegeville. They heard from and questioned experts in psychiatry and the law. One bishop, well acquainted with the situation as it then was, urged his fellow bishops to educate themselves about the issues and to respond responsibly to victims. Many bishops did as suggested, establishing rudimentary abuse response and prevention policies, handling complaints accordingly, and following the paths marked out by their respective state laws. That the bishops' response was not sufficient to solve the problem was not yet apparent to the bishops or their advisers.

In 1992, the case of James Porter, a former priest of the Fall River Diocese in Massachusetts who abused a large number of children, came to light and was extensively reported in the media. The bishops renewed their determination to deal with the problem. They discussed it during the executive session of their general meeting in June of 1992. Following that discussion, the Conference president, Cincinnati Archbishop Daniel E. Pilarczyk, issued a statement to the media in which he described the *Five Action Principles*[8] that had formed the basis of advice given by the Conference legal staff to the bishops since the mid-1980s but that had not been made public before:

1. Respond promptly to all allegations of abuse where there is reasonable belief that abuse has occurred.
2. If such an allegation is supported by sufficient evidence, relieve the alleged offender promptly of his ministerial duties and refer him for appropriate medical evaluation and intervention.
3. Comply with the obligations of civil law as regards reporting of the incident and cooperating with the investigation.
4. Reach out to the victims and their families and communicate our sincere commitment to their spiritual and emotional well-being.
5. Within the confines of respect for privacy of the individuals involved, deal as openly as possible with the members of the community.

A WATERSHED MOMENT: NOVEMBER 1992

As the bishops' fall general meeting in November 1992 was beginning, a group of bishops led by Cardinal Roger Mahony of Los Angeles met with several victims/survivors of clergy sexual abuse. Cardinal Mahony reported the outcome of this emotional meeting to the full body of bishops, who reacted by recommitting themselves to return to their dioceses and take action to prevent and eliminate sexual abuse of minors. The full body of bishops also affirmed the *Five Action Principles* as those that their dioceses should take with regard to child sexual abuse.[9]

These events marked a watershed moment in the bishops' response to the crisis. Dioceses either revised their abuse policies to increase their effectiveness or developed policies if they did not have them. Many dioceses also reviewed personnel files to make sure that clergy perpetrators had been adequately dealt with. A subcommittee on sexual abuse of minors of the Conference's

Committee on Priestly Life and Ministry was established, chaired by Father Canice Connors, OFM Conv., who became president and CEO of the St. Luke Institute after Father Peterson died. The following February, the subcommittee convened a think tank in St. Louis, Missouri, including experts in the sexual abuse problem, theologians, victims of abuse, and even a priest "in recovery" from this behavior. The participants formulated recommendations to be presented to the bishops.

THE AD HOC COMMITTEE ON SEXUAL ABUSE

In March 1993, partially in response to the think tank recommendations, the Conference's Administrative Board—a group of about 50 bishops that acts as a board of directors to oversee Conference activities between general meetings—recognized the need for a special committee, separate from the Committee on Priestly Life and Ministry, to be devoted solely to the issue of sexual abuse of minors and the multiple dimensions of the problem.

At the June general meeting that year, Father Connors reported the think tank results in public session,[10] and the Conference president, Baltimore Archbishop William H. Keeler, announced the establishment of the Ad Hoc Committee on Sexual Abuse (AHCSA) to be chaired by Bishop John F. Kinney of Bismarck, North Dakota. The committee was given a comprehensive mandate:

+ To look at assisting the membership in effectively dealing with priests who sexually abuse minors and others
+ To examine what the [the Bishops' Conference] can do pastorally nationwide to assist in the healing of victims and their families
+ To address the issue of morale of bishops and priests burdened with the terrible offenses of a few
+ To assist bishops in screening candidates for ministry and assessing the possibility of reassignment of clergy found guilty of sexual abuse of minors
+ To recommend steps to safeguard against sexual abuse of minors by employees or volunteers of the Church
+ To address the national problem of sexual abuse of children, coming from many directions, especially from within families

Like Congress, much of the Conference's work is done in committees. The establishment of the AHCSA guaranteed the Conference a more proactive, consistent role in addressing the problem. This included discussing it openly at the public sessions of all of the bishops' general meetings. While not every bishop was completely at ease with this, most recognized that they had in the AHCSA, and especially in its chairman, Bishop Kinney, something they had long needed—fellow bishops who could give public voice to the bishops' concerns and convey their spirit of commitment to deal with these offenses.

The AHCSA's first action was to bring the bishops up to date with an overview of the Conference's involvement in responding to the problem.[11] The AHCSA, whose membership was made up solely of bishops, was open to hearing from all concerned, especially victims and their advocates. Outside consultants were invited to join in its deliberations, including the parent of a victim and experts in treating sexual paraphilias. It surveyed the 194 existing Catholic dioceses and eparchies[12] to make certain that each one had established a policy on the sexual abuse of minors. The AHCSA also contacted centers that treated clergy for psychological disorders to determine how they interacted with dioceses and what specific therapies they offered.

ASSISTANCE FROM ROME

All bishops are required to report personally to the Holy Father on their dioceses every five years in the form of an *ad limina* visit. During their visits in the early 1990s, the U.S. bishops shared the problem of sexual abuse of minors by clergy with curia officials and sought their assistance, since a few provisions of the Church's canon law made it difficult to discipline some of the priests who had engaged in this misconduct. In June 1993, Pope John Paul II wrote to the bishops responding to their discussions during the *ad limina* visits and other interventions. The Pope promised to assist them in dealing with the terrible problem of abuse and announced that he had appointed a commission made up of curial and U.S. experts in canon law to develop recommendations as to "how the universal canonical norms can best be applied to the particular situation of the United States."[13] Eventually, the commission made several recommendations, including the extension of the statute of limitations under canon law for the crime of sexual abuse of a minor to 10 years past the victim's 18th birthday. The Commission's recommendations were accepted by the Conference and received papal approval.[14]

RESTORING TRUST

In November 1994, the AHCSA issued its first public report, *Restoring Trust*. It included proposals, based on the survey of diocesan policies, for writing or strengthening these policies.[15] It offered descriptions of 10 treatment centers, advice on what dioceses should look for in treatment centers, and information as to what treatment centers might expect of dioceses. It also contained articles on topics such as pedophilia, parishes as victims, and expectations of treatment.

This first report was followed by *Restoring Trust, Volume II*, issued in November 1995. It included information on an additional eight treatment centers, a 42-page presentation on care and concern for victims/survivors, and articles on topics ranging from the effectiveness of treatment to insurance matters. *Restoring Trust Volume III* was released in November 1996 and provided a review of the Conference's efforts to that point and noted areas that still needed to be addressed.

The AHCSA also provided educational opportunities for the bishops, including conducting a symposium before the June 1998 general meeting on working with victims, communications, civil law, and canonical issues, especially as the latter related to reassignment of abusers or their permanent dismissal from the clerical state. The chairman of the Bishops' Committee on Priestly Life and Ministry, who served *ex officio* on the AHCSA, directed his Committee to draft a *Basic Plan for the Ongoing Formation of Priests*[16] that would include attention to human formation as well as to other traditional areas of ongoing education. That plan was promulgated by the bishops in 2000. The AHCSA also asked the National Organization for Continuing Education of Roman Catholic Clergy (NOCERCC) to develop a video for priests on boundary violations. This instructional video focused on intimacy, sexuality, and the development of skills in interpersonal relations and was promoted by AHCSA.

The AHCSA also strongly recommended dialogue with victims. Bishop Kinney and the Committee staff participated in a series of sessions with victims organized in cooperation with the victim advocacy groups Search for Higher Ground and The Link-Up. These interactions, which also included representatives of the Survivors Network for those Abused by Priests (SNAP), provided access to and communication with an outspoken group of victims. These meetings were aimed at promoting discussions of how to heal, how to reconcile, and how to move forward with faith, which was not always easy to achieve when bishops and victims found themselves at variance in litigation.

WAS THE CRISIS ABATING?

From the early 1990s, a significant shift in the demographics of victims took place. Relatively few allegations of abuse of persons who were still minors were being made—in contrast to the 1980s, when most of the cases involved parents reporting abuse of minor children. The overwhelming majority of allegations now came from victims who were alleging misconduct that occurred more than a decade before.

As the AHCSA reached the conclusion of its third year, the crisis appeared to be abating. Dioceses seemed to have developed effective responses to the victims who came forward and the media no longer seemed to take much notice. Because the AHCSA was an ad hoc committee, under the Conference's by-laws it would have to sunset after three years unless specifically reauthorized. Despite the diminishing number of allegations, the Conference determined that the sex abuse problem continued to deserve serious attention and reauthorized the existence of the AHCSA. Its mandate was to concentrate on the healing of victims, on the education of clergy regarding sexuality and abuse issues, and on finding ways for dealing with priest-offenders.

Moving forward on these matters, the AHCSA, the Conference's Committee on Priestly Formation, and the National Catholic Educational Association (Seminary Department) conducted a survey in 1994 of major seminaries (which provide the immediate preparation for priestly ordination) and college seminaries (which prepare candidates to enter the major seminary). The purpose of the survey was to identify the psychological screening and formation procedures used relating to the candidates' sexuality. Responding major seminaries indicated that their pre-acceptance interviews included specific inquiry about sexual history and experience in relationships. Both the major and the college seminaries identified "growth in sexual maturity" and "questions of relationships" as formation issues.

The AHCSA continued to study future options for dealing with priest offenders, that is, to find ways to assist bishops in assessing possible reassignment. The members discussed such issues as the need for community consultation and disclosure in considering reassignment. The AHCSA did not formulate any specific guidelines on this matter, which came to the fore in 2002 as the most contentious issue for priests.

THE 2002 CRISIS

Though the predatory activity of Boston priest John Geoghan had been in the news in 1998 when the Archdiocese settled with some of his victims, the coverage of his criminal trial in January 2002 by the *Boston Globe* precipitated a crisis that overshadowed the period in the 1990s just described. In March 2002, the Conference's Administrative Committee charged the AHCSA with reviewing the matter and making recommendations leading to "a comprehensive response on the national level" to ensure "the safety of children and the healing of victims and their families."[17]

The AHCSA began drafting the document that would eventually become the *Charter*. It developed a series of questions to be presented to bishops in regional meetings to obtain feedback on the most significant issues that the *Charter* would have to include. Persons responsible for responding to victims' concerns were included among the AHCSA's consultants in the drafting process.

The outpouring of public response to the widespread reports of misconduct and cover-up that appeared daily in the media had an impact on the actions of the AHCSA and the Conference. There were also international repercussions and the Roman Curia summoned the United States Cardinals and Conference officers to a meeting on April 23, 2002, to discuss the situation with the heads of the relevant offices.

Pope John Paul II personally conveyed his concerns in his address to the group:

> The abuse which has caused this crisis is by every standard wrong and rightly considered a crime by society; it is also an appalling sin in the eyes of God. To the victims and their families, wherever they may be, I express my profound sense of solidarity and concern.

He also affirmed that "there is no place in the priesthood or religious life for those who would harm the young."[18]

The meeting's final communiqué stated that, "as part of the preparation for the June meeting of the American Bishops," which was scheduled to take place in Dallas, Texas, the U.S. participants would send a set of "national standards" to the relevant Holy See congregations containing "the essential elements for policies dealing with the sexual abuse of minors in dioceses and religious institutes in the US." The Holy See would then review them with a view to granting its *recognitio* (approval) for these standards.[19]

THE *CHARTER*: "A COMPREHENSIVE RESPONSE"

Shortly before the Dallas meeting, and consistent with Conference practice, the AHCSA chairman, Archbishop Harry Flynn of St. Paul and Minneapolis, publicly released a draft of the *Charter*[20] at a news briefing in Washington, DC. Archbishop Flynn proved as great an asset to the Bishops' Conference as Bishop Kinney had been. Archbishop Flynn guided the AHCSA as its members considered 850 possible modifications to the *Charter* and a companion document, the *Essential Norms (Norms)*,[21] submitted by their fellow bishops. Both documents contained provisions that needed the approval of the Holy See to be binding in the United States. The AHCSA also considered the many comments offered by concerned individuals and groups, and before the meeting began in Dallas, the members and several cardinals met with victim representatives to hear their concerns.

At the meeting's opening session, four victims shared their experiences with the bishops, and Catholic lay leaders and a psychologist also addressed the group. After intense debate, especially over the issue of permanent removal from ministry, the Conference adopted the *Charter* by a vote of 239–13.[22] The accompanying *Essential Norms* was passed by a similar majority but required some further work by a joint commission of U.S. bishops and curia officials. A revised version of the *Essential Norms* was ultimately adopted by the bishops in November and received the *recognitio* (approval) of the Holy See in December 2002.[23] Several procedural steps were specified in the revised *Norms*, but the principles remained as adopted by the bishops the previous June. To reflect changes in the *Essential Norms*, the *Charter* was also slightly revised.[24]

As previously pointed out, the *Charter* and *Essential Norms* were drafted and adopted with relative speed because a firm foundation had been laid for them in the *Five Action Principles* formulated in the late 1980s. Furthermore, the actual experience of dioceses in dealing with allegations throughout the late 1980s and 1990s and the material developed by the AHCSA provided significant resource material for the development of these important documents.

Despite the persistence of claims that the 2002 crisis was a result of the bishops' neglect, the bishops had been in almost continuous dialogue about this terrible misconduct and its repercussions for nearly two decades. Bishop Wilton Gregory, the Conference president at the time, pointed out in his keynote talk at the Dallas meeting that the bishops' image had been distorted

> to an extent which I would not have thought possible six months ago. Sad and disturbing facts, often long in the past, have been readily presented in ways that create an erroneous image of the Church in 2002 as neglectful and uncaring in a matter about which we bishops have cared a great deal for many years now.[25]

Bishop Gregory was credible with the clergy and the public because he had dealt firmly with the problem of sexual abuse when he became the bishop of Belleville in 1994. He was also eloquent and empathetic in his expressions of regret for the misconduct of priests.

Unfortunately, the advice proffered by the Bishops' Conference before 2002 for dealing with sexual abuse had not been applied uniformly across the country. The *Charter* and *Essential Norms* were designed to address the question of consistent application. The *Charter* now provided the "comprehensive response" to the sex abuse crisis that the Administrative Board had called for, confirming, building on, and strengthening important practices embodied in the original *Five Action Principles*, such as reporting abuse of minors to and cooperating with civil authorities. The *Charter* contained a pledge to report allegations in all instances in which the victim was still a minor, regardless of legal requirements. Bishops also pledged to come to an agreement with public authorities on reporting cases in which the victim was no longer a minor.

The *Charter* provided a far more detailed framework for responding to victims than the *Five Action Principles*. It included provisions for each diocese to place a priority on healing victims, for example, by having a victims' assistance coordinator, and to take steps to prevent abuse from happening in the first place. These steps included screening candidates for the priesthood, conducting background checks on employees who had regular contact with children, and promoting "safe environments." Safe environments were to be established by educating parents, young people, ministers, employees, and volunteers about the existence of the abuse problem, its warning signs, the situations in which it is manifested, and the possible perpetrators—who are not confined to the people often stereotyped as abusers. Furthermore, anyone, including minors, who suspected abusive behavior, was to be instructed in the necessity to report it at once.

The *Charter* also provided for external and verifiable accountability, an issue not addressed in the original *Five Action Principles*, in the form of diocesan review boards, a National Office for Child and Youth Protection and annual diocesan audits. Diocesan review boards, "the majority of [whose] members are to be laypersons not in the employ of the diocese," existed in many dioceses before the *Charter* was approved but were now the norm. Nationally, a new Office for Child and Youth Protection was established at the Conference to assist dioceses in implementing the *Charter* and to provide an annual report on diocesan compliance with the *Charter*. The first director, Kathleen McChesney, developed an annual audit process that was then carried out in the dioceses by an independent auditing firm.

It was clear during the 2002 crisis that without hard data, the Conference was hamstrung in trying to refute charges by media and others that the bishops had done little or nothing in response to sexual abuse by clerics or that their efforts were confined solely to the realm of public relations. The newly mandated annual reports were aimed at preventing a repeat of the situation. The reports served to ensure accountability on the part of the bishops and provided a comprehensive, public overview of diocesan actions to prevent abuse.

Within the *Charter*, the bishops established a national review board and authorized studies of both "the nature and scope of the sexual abuse of minors by Catholic clergy" and "the causes and context of the crisis." The former study, conducted by John Jay College,[26] provided the previously uncollected data about the extent of the problem. This study found that nearly 4,400 priests (more than 4 percent of the clergy) had been accused by approximately 11,000 victims during the 52-year period of the study, indicating that the problem was more widespread among the clergy than previously assumed— but not as great as speculations by the media and others. These data served to rebut charges, which still occasionally persist in some quarters, that abusive priests have preyed on hundreds of thousands of victims and that the priesthood has been thoroughly infested with sex offenders in ways that other occupations, such as coaching and teaching, have not been. As described in Chapter 2 these studies have provided some positive outcomes of this crisis by contributing to an awareness of the sexual abuse problem and identifying what needs to be done to prevent abuse in various types of organizations, not merely in the ministries of the Catholic Church.

"ZERO TOLERANCE"

The most difficult discussion for the bishops during the drafting of the *Charter* had to do with their priests who had perpetrated abuse in the past. Transferring a priest to another assignment as a "cure" for misconduct certainly happened in an earlier period when the bishops were less sophisticated about psychosexual disorders. However, that time was long past. "Reliev[ing] the alleged offender promptly of his ministerial duties and refer[ring] him for appropriate medical evaluation and intervention" was one of the *Five Action Principles* the bishops formally adopted in 1992. By the time the *Charter* was developed, pedophilia was clearly recognized as a mental illness that could never be cured, though the pedophile might learn to control his behavior. The true pedophile was never again going to be allowed to minister in any position that allowed him unsupervised contact with children.

However, many (some would even say most) priests who had perpetrated abuse were not afflicted with an incurable mental illness. They had acted out in times of personal crisis, perhaps because they were also suffering from other conditions such as alcoholism, which, once treated, removed the impulse toward sexual misconduct. Priests who had willingly undergone treatment were once again serving, it was believed, without being a danger to anyone. Indeed, the John Jay study confirmed that, unlike other studied populations, some priest-offenders could self-correct. In 55 percent of the cases, there was only one reported victim (and thus no reported recidivism).[27] Nonetheless, it was also quite clear that the possibility of recidivism could not entirely be eliminated and that Catholics, by and large, did not have confidence in a "therapeutic solution."

A key decision to be made in the *Charter* debate was whether a priest who had committed an act of sexual abuse of a minor should be irrevocably barred from ministry. The AHCSA had previously considered the possibility of post-treatment assignments for priests, based on favorable circumstances, prognosis, and disclosure. Now, however, "return to ministry" was no longer a realistic option, not only from the point of view of public reaction but also because of the monitoring procedures it would require. Not all bishops or AHCSA consultants had come to this conclusion, and to make sure that their positions received consideration, the draft of the *Charter* included an exception to removal from ministry for a priest who was not diagnosed as a pedophile and who had committed only one act of abuse. Many bishops and members of the public reacted negatively to this exception, and it was not included in the final *Charter*.

The bishops' decision to adopt what is popularly known as the "zero tolerance approach" was made to restore Catholics' confidence that they could entrust their children to the care of clerics without fear and to discourage this misconduct in the future as forcefully as possible. "Abuse of a minor" was seen hereafter as disqualifying a person from clerical service. Parents expect that the priests who serve their parishes have never been credibly accused of abuse.

While this step was an essential one toward restoring the trust of the people, the majority of the priests across the country perceived it as embodying a significant shift in the relationship between bishops and priests even in matters that did not involve any kind of misconduct.[28] A change of terminology made the situation worse. The draft language of the *Charter*'s Article V referred to "clerics," but this had been altered to read "priests and deacons" to emphasize that only the Holy See has the authority to discipline bishops. This was widely interpreted as an attempt by the bishops to evade their own responsibility in the crisis and to shift the onus of it entirely to priests.[29]

The Conference staff estimated that in the two years between the start of the crisis in early 2002 and the issuance of the John Jay study in February 2004, approximately 700 priests had been removed from ministry. A survey of dioceses conducted and reported by the *St. Louis Post-Dispatch* in March 2002 revealed that more than 230 priests had been removed in the previous two decades. These data contradicted often-made claims that the bishops' pledges to deal with the problem of sexual abuse of minors amounted to nothing more than public relations efforts.

BEYOND THE *CHARTER*

In addition to the steps called for in the *Charter*, the bishops strengthened their commitment to accountability by commissioning annual data surveys to be conducted by the Center for Applied Research in the Apostolate (CARA). CARA now reports the total number of new allegations of sexual abuse, the status of the clergy against whom allegations were made, the total amount of money expended by all dioceses and men's religious institutes as a result of allegations, as well as the total amount paid for child protection efforts. These surveys illustrate that allegations of current abuse have become rare in recent years.[30] Allegations now being reported, as they have been for more than 15 years, usually pertain to misconduct that occurred decades ago, and the accused are often dead, retired, or already out of ministry.

In 2005 and again in 2011, the bishops voted to extend the *Charter*. The document certainly was never perfect, and meeting its mandates, as was expected, created new questions about dealing with issues not foreseen in 2002. Although media attention often focuses on the few situations in which full compliance is lacking, the fact is that bishops and dioceses have remained faithful to the commitment they made to the Catholic people and one another through the *Charter*. Some have gone beyond the requirements of the *Charter* in dealing with this problem and its tragic effects on victims and the whole church community. All of this is documented in public audits and other reports by the Conference and the dioceses.

Media still write about the sexual abuse crisis in the United States in the present tense due to the aftershocks caused by revelations of past undisclosed crimes and a few new ones. Repercussions also take the form of litigation and legislation in some states "to hold the Church accountable."

However, the evidence exists that abuse of minors by clergy has, for now, been largely wrung out of the Catholic priesthood and that the bishops are more alert to the pain of victims, more sensitive to ways of promoting healing, more vigilant in preventing abuse, and more cooperative with authorities in reporting cases of it than before.

The *Charter* achieved its goal in 2002 of equipping the bishops with the necessary set of standards and tools to address the crisis at hand. But behind these standards and tools is a "spirit of the *Charter*" that requires a permanent commitment to making the protection of children and young people a priority, maintaining a safe environment, and treating sexual abuse of a minor as a "fatal error" that bars the offender from ministry. Actions guided by this spirit, more than words set down on paper, will permit the bishops to restore the trust that was eroded and prove the *Charter* represents a true conversion of mind and heart.

NOTES

1. United States Conference of Catholic Bishops, *Charter for the Protection of Children and Young People* (Washington, DC: Author, 2002).
2. John Jay College of Criminal Justice, *Nature and Scope of the Problem of Clergy Sex Abuse in the Catholic Church in the United States: 1950–2002* (New York: Author, 2004).
3. In-depth studies of the priesthood conducted by sociologist Andrew Greeley and psychologist Eugene Kennedy in the 1970s identified a lack of maturity in many priests and a series of other issues that they labeled and discussed. However, they did not identify this deeply disturbing behavior.
4. During the period covered by this chapter, the Catholic Bishops' Conference in the United States was reorganized. The "twin Conferences" of the National Conference of Catholic Bishops and the U.S. Catholic Conference (NCCB/USCC) became a single entity, the U.S. Conference of Catholic Bishops (USCCB). For the sake of consistency, the phrase *Bishops' Conference* or simply *Conference* is used throughout.
5. Mr. Chopko served for more than 20 years as the chief legal officer of the Bishops' Conference. Father Kiley served for nearly a decade as executive director of the Conference's Secretariat for Priestly Life, and Monsignor Maniscalco served as the Conference's media relations director and then secretary for communications for more than 13 years. All three served as staff to the Ad Hoc Committee on Sexual Abuse (AHCSA), Mr. Chopko and Msgr. Maniscalco from its inception in 1993.
6. Bishops Accountability, *The Problem of Sexual Molestation by Roman Catholic Clergy: Meeting the Problem in a Comprehensive and Responsible manner.* Retrieved January 16, 2011, from www.BishopsAccountability.org.
7. *Ibid.*
8. D. Pilacrcryzk, "Statement on Sexual Abuse of Minors by Clergy and Others in the Church's Employ." *Origins* 22 (1992): 177.
9. National Conference of Catholic Bishops, "On File." *Origins* 22 (1992): 418.
10. National Conference of Catholic Bishops, "Recommendations on Child Sexual Abuse. Think Tank Held in St. Louis." *Origins* 23 (1993): 105.
11. C. Connors, "Brief Overview of Conference Involvement in Assisting Dioceses with Child Molestation Claims." *Origins* 23 (1994): 666.
12. Eparchies are dioceses in the Eastern Catholic tradition.
13. Pope John Paul II. "Vatican—US Bishops Committee to Study Applying Canonical Norms to Clergy Sexual Abuse Cases: Letter to US Bishops." *Origins* 23 (1993): 102.
14. J. Filteau, "US Church Law Changed to Ease Laicization for Sex Abuse." *Catholic News Service* (1994, August 15): B03.
15. National Conference of Catholic Bishops, *Efforts to Combat Clergy Sexual Abuse against Minors: A Chronology* (undated). Retrieved May 3, 2011, at www.usccb.org.

16. United States Conference of Catholic Bishops, *Plan for the Ongoing Formation of Priests* (Washington, DC: Author, 2001).

17. United States Conference of Catholic Bishops, "Bishops Meeting to Address Sexual Abuse of Minors Problem." *Origins* 31 (2002): 681.

18. Pope John Paul II, "Address to Vatican Meeting with US Cardinals and Bishops Conference Officials." *Origins* 31 (2002): 757.

19. *Ibid.*

20. H. Flynn, "Draft Test of US Conference of Catholic Bishops Charter for the Protection of Children and Young People." *Origins* 32 (2002): 65.

21. *Ibid.*

22. United States Conference of Catholic Bishops, "Charter for the Protection of Children and Young People." *Origins* 32 (2002): 102.

23. United States Conference of Catholic Bishops, *Revised Essential Norms Receive Vatican Approval.* December 16, 2002. Retrieved May 3, 2011, from www.usccb.org. United States Conference of Catholic Bishops, "Draft Test of US Conference of Catholic Bishops Charter for the Protection of Children and Young People." *Origins* 32 (2002): 65.

24. *Ibid.*

25. W. Gregory, "Presidential Address, Opening Dallas Meeting of US Bishops." *Origins* 32 (2002): 97.

26. John Jay College of Criminal Justice, *Nature and Scope of the Problem of Clergy Sex Abuse in the Catholic Church in the United States: 1950–2002* (New York: Author, 2004).

27. *Ibid.*

28. A survey conducted by the *Los Angeles Times* found that "only 34% [of priests surveyed] rated the *Charter's* fairness to priests accused of abuse as 'good' or 'excellent,' with 45% calling it 'fair' or 'poor' in that regard." For further explanation, see Larry B. Stammer, "Most Priests Say Bishops Mishandled Abuse Issue," *Los Angeles Times*, Oct. 20, 2002, A1, A31–32.

29. By comparison, religious superiors of accused priests were saying publicly that, while they accepted the *Charter's* mandate with regard to removal from ministry, they felt obliged to retain accused religious priests as members of their religious "families," bound to them by the traditional vows of poverty, chastity, and obedience. This intensified the need for dialogue between diocesan bishops and their priests and with the leadership of religious communities.

30. P. Zapor, "Annual Audit Shows Decline in Sex Abuse Reports." *Catholic News Service* (2010, March 24): 1–3.

Chapter 4

The Failure of the Dallas Charter and Canon Law: A Blessing in Disguise

Terrence A. Carroll

Since through God's mercy we have this ministry, we do not lose heart. Rather, we have renounced secret and shameful ways; we do not use deception, nor do we distort the word of God. On the contrary, by setting forth the truth plainly we commend ourselves to every man's conscience in the sight of God.

2 Corinthians 4:1–2

Since its inception in 2002, the *Charter for the Protection of Children and Young People*, commonly called the *Dallas Charter*, has been critiqued regarding its effectiveness as an adequate response by the U.S. Conference of Catholic Bishops to the clergy abuse scandal in the United States. To many, the failures of the *Charter* and a related document, the *Essential Norms*, have been well documented.[1] This chapter will briefly review how the Church has historically dealt with the issue of clerical sexual abuse and, more particularly, how canon law evolved in the Church's attempts to address this longstanding issue.

Also, we will explore the critical and controversial question of whether the Church today has learned from the clergy abuse scandal in addressing other issues, including the role of women, celibacy, clericalism, and homosexuality. More important, can and will the Church seek the meaningful input of its laity as it looks ahead to its many challenges? The answers to these and other questions will shed light on a complex scandal that continues to unfold and will help us to better understand in which directions the Church can choose to move as a result of the scandal. Not only the legacy of the *Dallas Charter* but also the future of the Catholic Church likely remain at stake.

SEXUAL ABUSE OF MINORS: A CENTURIES-OLD PROBLEM IN THE CATHOLIC CHURCH

History shows that in practically every century since the Church began, the problem of clerical abuse of minors was not just lurking in the shadows but so open at times that extraordinary means had to be taken to quell it. If there is anything new about the sexual abuse of minors by members of the clergy, it is that over the past fifty years a conspiracy of silence has covered it. Rather than stifle the practice, this pall of secrecy has provided an atmosphere where abuse would fester as a systemic infection. In the process, the lives of children, priests, and bishops—and, indeed the credibility of the Catholic Church, have been shattered.

Preface, *Sex, Priests and Secret Codes*, Doyle, Sipe and Wall,
Volt Press (2006)

Even prior to the *Boston Globe* articles in 2002, the American public of all faiths and backgrounds was reacting with shock and outrage at the level of hypocrisy, arrogance, and secrecy displayed by the Church hierarchy over the scandal. A major institution, which had received the trust and loyalty of the great majority of its lay community, appeared to be consciously choosing the protection of its hierarchical structure over the safety of the most vulnerable members of the Church. Perhaps what is even more surprising in light of the fumbling responses to the scandal by the Church is its long-term familiarity with the problem of sexual abuse among the clergy. Historical literature and documentation indicate that such incidents are by no means novel to the Catholic Church.[2]

One of the major documents regarding homosexuality and clergy sexual abuse of minors dates back to the Middle Ages. Father Peter Damian, a monk who went on to become a cardinal and sought to reform the church regarding sexual immorality, issued the *Book of Gomorrah* in 1051. This book called for a strong response to what Father Damian reported as numerous and significant failings on the part of the Church regarding its clergy's problems with homosexuality and sodomy.[3] Damian's book ends with a specific appeal to Pope Leo IX to take decisive action against these clerics. (It is of some note that the Church continues to discuss the sexual abuse of minors and homosexuality in the same light—even to this day.)

Interestingly, Pope Leo's response to Father Damian is alarmingly similar to the Church's response to our modern-day clergy sex abuse scandal. While he publicly praised Father Damian's findings and verified the truth of his findings and recommendations, Pope Leo refrained from adopting Father Damian's strict tone against offenders. Only clerics who offended repeatedly and over a long period of time were excluded, and, despite Father Damian's special focus on the victims of the abuse, Pope Leo emphasized the sinfulness of the clerics and the need to repent.[4] Indeed, Pope Alexander, elected in 1061 after Pope Leo's reign, attempted to suppress Father Damian's work by confiscating the book.[5]

Today, we again see a delayed and inadequate reaction from Rome despite the acknowledgment of the problem of sexual abuse of minors by clergy.

Later, Pope Leo addressed clergy sexual abuse within the development of canon law and the punishable offense of clerical sodomy.[6] The Decree of Gratian in 1140 AD, composed of legal, scriptural, and theological sources, explicitly referenced the sexual abuse of minors, stating that violators would be subject to either banishment or capital punishment, depending on the seriousness of the offense.[7] The Decree, also known as the *Decretum Gratiani*, excerpted a canon from the 1102 Synod of Lyndon, which recommended that clerics found guilty of sodomy be either deposed or excommunicated.[8] These documents, among others, indicate the Church's clear awareness of the problem of clergy sexual abuse centuries prior to the current scandal, which many believe is unparalleled in the history of the Church.

A later example of how the Church's response to clergy abuse mirrors its modern response relates to the Council of Trent, which convened in 25 sessions from 1545 to 1563.[9] The Church responded to the secular pressure of the Reformation Period by reforming a number of canons relating to the deportation of priests by bishops as punishment for "depraved and scandalous" lifestyles.[10] If the bishops could not deport priests, they were to be financially cut off from the church. Additionally, members of religious orders who committed publicly known crimes were subject to serious punishment, and a report detailing the disciplinary action was to be sent to the local bishop.[11] The sexual abuse of minors was not explicitly acknowledged in these reform canons, but in 1566, Pope Pius V issued *Romani Pontifices*, a constitution with legislation against "crimes against nature," which included clerical sodomy.[12] This canon recommended that bishops subject offenders to secular authorities after being first degraded by an ecclesiastical court.[13] Pope Pius also issued *Cum Sicut Nuper* in 1565, condemning solicitation of penitents in the confessional, particularly aimed at the Spanish Catholic Church.[14] Yet it was not until 1622 that Pope Gregory XV extended that legislation to the universal church.[15]

In 1741, Pope Benedict XIV issued the papal constitution *Sacramentum Poenitentiae*, condemning priests who granted absolution to those whom they solicited. While Pope Benedict was essentially restating the previous 1622 law, he felt the need to re-emphasize its points, as that law had been diluted to the point of ineffectuality.[16] Additionally, this restatement of the law added what seems to work as a waiver on any possible statute of limitations, as it states that it does not matter when the solicitation occurred, and the cleric could be prosecuted and punished despite any lengthy elapsed time period.[17] This marked a major turning point for the Church, as it explicitly acknowledged the protection of those victims made especially vulnerable by confession, and its significance is marked by the fact that this document was included as an appendix directly referenced in the first official codification of the Church's laws, the 1919 *Code of Canon Law*.[18]

Interestingly, in contrast to its historical promulgation of Church legislation, the Vatican issued unusually secret legislation in 1922, and again in 1962 (*De Modo Procedendi in Causis Solicitationis*), regarding solicitation and clergy sexual abuse. This document was distributed only to bishops and major religious superiors in the worldwide Catholic Church but was not publicized in the official Vatican legal bulletin.[19] Additionally, the legislation, which discussed a special procedural law for solicitation cases, was accompanied by directions to keep the information in secret diocesan archives, without any comments or publicity.[20] Many canon lawyers and bishops expressed surprise to hear of the document's existence when it was made public in 2003.[21] While it is unclear if the process set forth by the document was ever used in clergy abuse cases in the past, it does demonstrate the Church's tendency to maintain the strictest confidentiality regarding clergy abuse cases, even within its own internal structure.[22]

Despite growing knowledge that pedophilia was not treatable,[23] the Catholic Church in the 1970s followed an American trend and focused on therapy and the use of psychiatric treatment for priests as a response to allegations of clerical sexual abuse of minors. Yet this approach was misguided, in that oftentimes a bishop would send a priest to therapy with the primary goal of receiving a favorable report in order to return the priest to ministry.[24] In spite of having the foresight to send sexually abusive priests to therapy, bishops would fail to heed recommendations and seriously analyze psychologists' evaluations, believing that therapy "treated" the priests accordingly, and reassigning priests to active ministry.[25] Canon law protocols were largely ignored during this period prior to the adoption of the *Dallas Charter*.[26]

These examples of the Church's historical responses to the issue of clerical sexual abuse of minors indicate the institution's deeply entrenched failure to effectively respond when weighed against the choice of avoiding scandal. Indeed, it is not surprising that the problem has now evolved into a worldwide embarrassment and crisis.[27]

THE EVOLUTION OF CANON LAW AND CLERGY SEXUAL ABUSE

Every church, although based on what its members believe to be divine revelation, is also a human institution. As human communities, churches require rules.

James Cordien, *An Introduction to Canon Law*,
Paulist Press (2004), p. 3

As shown above, canon law has proven to be an important indicator of the Church hierarchy's attitudes regarding sexual abuse. However, the church suffers from a historical lack of openness and transparency. For example, according to canon 1719, the findings of an investigation regarding allegations of clergy sexual abuse remain hidden in secret archives.[28] The secret archives, as provided for in this canon, appear unaffected by the recent canon law amendments that have been enacted as a response to the sex abuse scandal.[29]

Canon 1395, §2 specifically provides for punishment of a cleric accused of sexual abuse with a minor:

> If a cleric has otherwise committed an offense against the sixth commandment of the Decalogue with force or threats or publicly or with a minor below the age of sixteen, the cleric is to be punished with just penalties, including dismissal from the clerical state if the case warrants it.

However, there are other canonical provisions that seem to heavily favor the clerical system in place.[30]

Despite recent amendments that have been made to canon law, in order to expedite the punishment process toward priests who sexually abuse minors, the *Dallas Charter* and the *Essential Norms* remain reverent to existing canon law that protects the internal, structural status quo.[31] For example, while canon 9's retroactivity provisions hampered many victims from bringing forth claims of abuse from decades past, a new provision has been issued to extend the statute of limitations for sexual abuse allegations concerning minors, from 10 to 20 years from the victim's 18th birth date.[32] Additionally, canon law has recently been revised to include special faculties, or exceptions, to existing canon law, which allow the doctrinal congregation to waive the statute of limitations on a case-by-case basis.[33] While these may seem like improvements to canon law, the waiver was already being applied in the same manner in sexual abuse cases over the past decade. Also, the secular courts have been moving away from any limits on claims based on a statute of limitations. Regretfully, the new norms amending church law in 2010 do not impose any punishments upon bishops who ignored the abuse by priests within their dioceses, possibly perpetuating the abuse and exacerbating the resulting scandal.[34]

THE *DALLAS CHARTER*

The man of integrity walks securely, but he who takes crooked paths will be found out.

Proverbs 10:9

The *Dallas Charter* has received mixed reviews regarding its effectiveness. Some believe that the *Charter* overreaches in a manner that is not proportional to the issues it seeks to address. Others argue that the *Charter* does not go far enough to create actual change within the Church system to prevent the recurrence of such a scandal. The author believes that experience has shown there are at least two serious issues that have flowed from the establishment of the *Dallas Charter* and its norms.

First, one of the most controversial features of the *Dallas Charter* is its zero-tolerance policy. Article 5 of the *Charter* provides that a cleric shall be removed from ministry for a single act of sexual abuse. Critics state that this policy is simply not proportional, as some situations are only isolated incidents. They argue that a removal from ministry is quite possibly the worst thing that could happen to a priest—it is more complex than an individual losing a job because there is the belief that his vocation is a sacrament, a calling from God.[35] Additionally, these critics argue that a removal from ministry unnecessarily removes Church support and oversight of the individual.

Although this argument is weakened by the question of how much support and oversight were actually provided the offender if such crimes went unnoticed or were ignored when these individuals were indeed under Church supervision, it is certainly debatable whether laicization is appropriate for a single, minor incident that happened many years ago. Yet, as discussed below, the hierarchical clamp on the process prevented any real analysis of the gradations of misconduct, and discounted the wisdom of the laity in deciding a remedy. In effect, in order to save themselves and their positions, the bishops decided, under the guise of zero tolerance, to throw some clergy "under the bus" when their single bad acts would not reasonably justify the same punishment as the serial offenders who preyed on young people.

Further, critics continue to argue that the zero-tolerance policy works on the presumption of guilt and that the automatic removal of the accused from ministry pending an investigation may be wrong if based on an unfounded and frivolous allegation. Although this appears to be a "guilty until proven innocent" theory,[36] here the Church really has no choice. The protection of the faithful community requires that there be a prompt response. The real harm frequently comes in the "middle of the night" removal of a priest with little or no explanation made to the members of the ministry served by the cleric. This is unfair and can unnecessarily damage reputations in those cases where the allegations are unfounded. In their panic to appear responsive, the American bishops most certainly removed persons from the priesthood that most concerned Catholics would find an overreaction, in some cases to events occurring decades ago.

Yet there are many arguments in favor of the zero-tolerance policy.[37] Generally, statistics demonstrate that there are more repeat offenders than there are isolated incidents. Indeed, the belief that these were merely isolated incidents led to the original debate as to how the issue developed and evolved into the massive scandal that it did. Many in the hierarchy refused to acknowledge that this was a systematic pattern exacerbated by the willingness of the Church to give clerics the benefit of the doubt, The zero-tolerance policy likely helped to reduce the number of cases of clergy abuse against minors in the United States.[38] Furthermore, forgiveness of individual offenders can indeed occur without the reinstatement to active ministry work.[39]

A second major issue surrounding the implementation of the *Dallas Charter* relates to the reluctance of many bishops to address the matter of allegations of sexual abuse by order priests.[40] Approximately one-third of the priests in the United States are not "diocesan" but are members of a religious of an order, e.g., Franciscan, Jesuit, and so forth. In some dioceses, as many as half of the allegations of sexual abuse were made against order priests.[41] As order priests, they are more easily re-assigned to different states and countries, than are diocesan priests.[42]

Even though a bishop has the complete discretion to determine who can minister within a diocese, some bishops cite the lack of authority to discipline order priests as a reason to not refer such cases to their respective *Charter* review boards. However, dioceses are frequently made parties to claims against order priests and do contribute toward settlements in many cases. There is no dependable way, however, to track claims against order priests other than through civil litigation or the rare public announcement of allegations provided by the superior of a men's religious communtiy.[43]

This is a serious and shameful error because victims do not differentiate between diocesan and religious order priests. The transparency and accountability that the *Dallas Charter* was to bring to this scandal is vitiated when so many cases are treated differently or in ways that are hidden from the faithful.[44] In some cases, dioceses have been essentially forced by the courts to make this information accessible and public.[45] Notwithstanding these particular cases, information as to the number of allegations, any discipline imposed, and financial settlements in cases involving religious order clerics or brothers should be as readily available to the laity as it is with diocesan priests.

Beyond these two criticisms and despite improvements made to canon law, some argue that the *Dallas Charter* does not adequately address the issue of clergy sexual abuse because the issue is too historically entrenched and overwhelming to be adequately addressed by a single reactionary document.[46] Both proponents and critics agree that the document was a hastily drafted response to the media's pressure for a Church reaction to the allegations.

Critics argue that the Church should not have succumbed to such pressure, while proponents say that the *Charter* was an important initial step that must be clarified and expanded in many areas.

The *Charter* does not provide clear guidance on several matters. For example, the *Charter* is vague as to how to conduct effective investigations of allegations of clergy sexual abuse of a minor. There is confusion as to who is in charge of the investigations and the bishop's role in the investigation once he has received the investigative report. The *Charter* defers to canons 1717 through 1719 regarding the investigative procedures, causing many to fear that it does not go far enough in providing clear change in response to the scandal. The most recent amendments to canon law that allow for a more streamlined process in punishing accused clerics do not radically change canon law inasmuch as consolidate what is already being practiced.[47] Furthermore, the definition of abuse, although modified, refers to the definition of morality, not to the legality or criminality of the sexual abuse of minors.

The efficacy of the *Charter* is largely controversial, as the document is non-binding to the Catholic dioceses in the United States. However, the accompanying *Essential Norms* are binding, yet they must also be interpreted and applied consistent with canon law. The limitations imposed by canon law greatly challenge any meaningful change that could be inspired by these documents.

Although the final verdict on the effectiveness of the role of the *Dallas Charter* and Church law in this scandal has not been rendered, the overwhelming weight of opinion is that the bishops did little to repair the lost trust of the laity. And, in trying to remedy the process to punish sexually abusive clergymen, the Vatican also generated controversy regarding its teaching on other issues, particularly celibacy and the role of women.[48] It remains to be seen whether the trust has been permanently damaged in these other venues as well.

These other issues will now be explored in the context of the aftermath of the clergy abuse scandal.

A TIME AND PLACE FOR HEALING?

The larger problem is the inability of the church leadership to come to terms with the modern world . . . The problem is a long-term one, and in no way is it solved.
                    Hubert Feichtlbauer, quoted by Rachel Donadio and
                    Nicholas Kulish, "Amid Scandals, Questions of Where the
                    Pope's Focus Lies," *New York Times*, Feb. 16, 2009

While the Church continues to face dissension and controversy over a wide range of concerns, the hierarchy must be able to reach a place of healing with the greater lay community. At the same time, it is highly unlikely that a scandal of this type or magnitude will reoccur in the Church's future. The lay Catholic community simply will not allow it.

As traditional as the Church remains, ever-changing social trends and technologies demand that the Church adapt. The Church exists in a time unlike any other, with the open and free flow of information around the globe paired with an omnipresent media. Additionally, while the Church continues to promote from within and exalt those who uphold traditional values, it is a fact that a new generation is being created—a generation more aware of the Church's place in the greater society and a generation that has lived and dealt with the Church through this scandal. Acknowledging the obvious fact that the Catholic Church does not enjoy the powerful and influential position that it once held, especially within the United States, the Church should be careful not to ignore these external changes. Furthermore, the Church is in no position to negotiate out of such reality as the scandal has rendered many dioceses and religious orders bankrupt or nearly bankrupt from the numerous settlements with abuse victims—not to mention having a priesthood that is decimated by a lack of vocations and resignations.

While the publicity from the scandal is incredibly damaging to the Church, it has empowered individuals to end their silent suffering and come forth openly and honestly about their abuse without the overwhelming fear of revictimization. Victims and their support groups now exist in an environment that encourages participation in an open dialogue with the Church as a personal step toward reconciliation. Others, too, who feel alienated from the Church across a wide range of issues are more willing to speak out and seek change.

As a result, the Church faces two options: adapt to the needs of the laity or maintain the status quo in an increasingly irrelevant and narrow Church. This decline will only worsen if the Church chooses to stay the course. This time must be recognized as an opportunity for the Church to adjust its structure to the world within which its members live.

By accepting this external reality, the Church opens itself up to healing the existent divisions within its own community. For example, one of the most negative outcomes of the clergy abuse scandal is the deep mistrust of the hierarchy by members of the laity. Many of these individuals and families have long-standing ties with the Church—including its traditions, the location of parishes within neighborhoods, and its role in education and health care. These relationships are now in jeopardy as a result of the scandal and the revelation of the depth of the cover-up done in the name of clericalism and hierarchy. But by dealing with the wounds of the scandal, the Church can lay the foundation to regain the trust and faith of its larger community in this and a a wider range of problems.

HEALING DIVISIONS WITHIN THE CHURCH

In the name of Christ, I refuse to be anti-gay. I refuse to be anti-feminist. I refuse to be anti-artificial birth control. I refuse to be anti-Democrat. I refuse to be anti-secular humanism. I refuse to be anti-science. I refuse to be anti-life.

Anne Rice, quoted by Mitchell Landsberg, "Anne Rice Discusses Her Decision to Quit Christianity," *LA Times*, Aug. 7, 2010

The clergy abuse scandal and the obviously inept hierarchical response have opened the door for reassessment of many other issues of significance to Catholics. Controversies regarding celibacy, homosexuality, and clericalism challenge the Church to deal with modern-day criticisms. A major issue that continues to haunt the Church relates to the role of women.

At the same time that the Vatican freed bishops from being accountable for criminal activity (by failing to order them to report every instance of abuse and refusing to create sanctions against those who cover up abuse), it saw fit to define new kinds of crimes that have everything to do with gender, but nothing to do with sexual abuse.[49]

While the Church issued new norms in 2010 to amend canon law, it denounced the ordination of women, stating that it was as grave a sin as the sexual abuse of minors. This apparent insistence of the Church to uphold a "spiritually violent" atmosphere against women in its structure is yet another scandal.[50] In the long run, such issues may dwarf the clergy abuse scandal in their significance. They also challenge modern reform groups to determine whether these changes must be made internally within the existing Church structure, or externally, fundamentally rejecting many principles of the Church in order to create effective change.[51] One would hope that the Church responds to the opportunity presented by the clergy abuse scandal by meeting this and numerous other challenges in a positive and healthy manner.

THERE ARE BETTER APPROACHES

It is hard to imagine a more total contradiction of everything Jesus Christ stood for, and it would be difficult to overestimate the pervasive and lasting harm it has done to the church.

Bishop Geoffrey Robinson, *Confronting Power and Sex in the Catholic Church*, Liturgical Press (2008), p. 7

As it critically evaluates its internal structure and policies the Church hierarchy is now faced with the challenge of either moving forward by redefining its leadership role in Catholic society or giving allegiance to the status quo. It will only move forward upon full recognition of its own sins, that is, admitting its fault to the fullest extent and asking for forgiveness from those who have been wronged, including the laity that trusted its leadership. In particular, bishops, who have so far managed to escape personal accountability (civil and criminal), must show courage and humility in leading the Church to find the lessons our Lord would want them to learn from this experience.

I have attempted to outline some of the many missteps and mistakes that have been made in the Church's response to the clergy abuse scandal. Perhaps, with the passage of time, Church authorities can reflect upon their reactions and be open to change. However, unless dialogue with the faithful is part of the renewal, very little will happen. The *sensis fidei* must be the goal, and it cannot happen without the wisdom of the laity as an accepted norm.

REJECTION OF CLERICALISM AND TRUST IN THE LAITY

A huge failure of the Church continues with its hierarchical structure and the privileged treatment of the clergy. Not only did clericalism and protection of its elite clergy contribute to the sexual abuse scandal, they have also been barriers to thoughtful reform as authority figures struggle to justify and maintain their power.[52] While radical changes in canon law would bring greater credibility to the Church, there is another, more reasonable goal: increased trust in its lay community. The laity, including the disaffected and disassociated, remain a community of willing individuals who could bring their wisdom to the Church to help it live its core values of community, love, and justice. To do so, the Church will have to lift its veil of secrecy and let go of its hold on internal power.

Specifically, the Vatican and bishops need to reach out to the laity and request their input, advice, and consent in addressing the multiple issues facing the Church. The Church appears to be moving rather meekly in this direction with the adoption of new norms by the Congregation for the Doctrine of the Faith. Now, the doctrinal congregation has the right to judge members of the ruling class (cardinals, bishops, and papal legates), moving away from the rule that allowed only the pope to deal with cases regarding the allegations of violations of church laws by these powerful clergymen.[53] The new norms also allow laity to serve as judges and lawyers on church tribunals in sex abuse cases, without the previous requirement of a canon law doctorate.[54] However, the hierarchy will have to move far beyond these modest steps if the respect and broad support of the laity are to be regained.

Historically, synods (called by the bishops) have been a source of providing a thoughtful, prayerful, and open process to address Church problems. While perhaps more Protestant than Catholic in origin, synods (or conventions) could bring forth an open and public dialogue among the Church clerics and laity. Synods could create the environment of a more open community of faithful Christians instead of a concentration of authority within the hierarchical structure of clericalism.[55] The laity should not only have input into the agenda for any synod but should also have meaningful roles in reaching consensus. The bishops would need to agree to act on any recommendations.[56]

It is now clear that the Church's preference to hide within its hierarchical structure and protect its clerics at the expense of the Catholic population only exacerbated the clergy abuse issue. Despite the merits of any recommendations by concerned lay and clergy, it remains unclear how the Church will actually respond to its many challenges. If history teaches us anything, it is that the Church is slow to change and eager to maintain its status quo. It remains a simple fact that the Church is on the decline in much of the world, both in its position of moral authority in general society and internally as it scrambles to explain how its own canon law was completely overwhelmed by scandal.

OUR FUTURE CHURCH

The clergy abuse scandal has worsened over this past decade because of the Church's failure to respond to the growing breach of trust between the hierarchy and the laity. The hierarchy's inability to comprehend their clerical bias is a grave error that continues to cause great harm to the Church. It remains the primary reason for so little dialogue on serious issues of faith and morality that go beyond the clergy sexual abuse scandal. The leadership of the Church must find the humility and strength to begin to involve the laity in a serious way in order for true healing to occur as well as for the Church to ultimately survive and thrive in a post–clergy abuse scandal era. The Catholic Church must see itself as bringing harmony to the internal yearning (faith) of its members and the external expression of that yearning (religion). Whatever the faults of the Church have been shown to be, if repeated in the face of new challenges, there will be even more injustice to the People of God.

We are all God's children, no one more important than the other. Catholics who feel anger and a sense of estrangement and betrayal by the hierarchy must accept the imperfection of this human institution. Similarly, the hierarchy must reach out to the laity in ways that invite discussions in good faith, acknowledge their grievous failures and accept the prospect of change her ever, with God's grace, wherever that will lead. Only then will the obvious failures of canon law and its progeny, the *Dallas Charter* and *Essential Norms*, become a blessing in disguise. Let us pray that all Church members find refuge in the Holy Spirit on this journey. There is no other option for this faith community that seeks to reflect the life of Christ.

> *That the Church is sinful is why, finally, each of us can feel at home in it . . . In the end, the Church is the community of the forgiven, but that forgiveness is a condition of change. At last we can complete the Domine, non sum dignus prayer, all of us, together: sed tantum dic verbo et sanabitur anima mea. Say but the word, and my soul will be healed.*
>
> James Carroll, *Practicing Catholic*, Mariner Books (2009), p. 322

NOTES

1. J. L. Allen, "Vatican Set to Issue Changes in Sex Abuse Rules," *The National Catholic Reporter* (2010, July 6). Retrieved on April 29, 2011, at http://ncronline .org/blogs/ncr-today/vatican-set-issue-changes-sex-abuse-rules (hereinafter "Allen article"). N. P. Cafardi, "Something Missing: Church Universal Still Lags Behind," *The National Catholic Reporter* (2010, July 16). Retrieved April 29, 2011, at http:// ncronline.org/news/vatican/something-missing (hereinafter "Cafardi article"). T. P. Doyle, "The Vatican's New Norms," *The National Catholic Reporter* (2010, July 16). Retrieved April 29, 2011, at http://ncronline.org/news/vatican/vaticans -new-norms.
2. T. P. Doyle, A. W. R. Sipe and P. J. Wall, *Sex, Priests, and Secret Codes: The Catholic Church's 2000-Year Paper Trail of Sexual Abuse* (Los Angeles: Volt Press, 2006; hereinafter "Doyle, Sipe and Wall"). T. P. Doyle and S. C. Rubino, *Catholic Clergy Sexual Abuse Meets the Civil Law*, 31 (FDMULJ 549, 2004), 574–584, hereinafter "Doyle and Rubino."
3. Doyle, Sipe and Wall, 20.
4. *Id.*, 21–22.
5. *Id.*
6. Doyle and Rubino, 581–3.
7. *Id.*, 583.
8. *Id.*
9. Doyle, Sipe and Wall, 34–35.
10. Doyle and Rubino, 583–4.
11. *Id.*, 584.
12. Doyle, Sipe and Wall, 36.
13. *Id.*
14. Doyle, Sipe and Wall, 43.
15. *Id.*

16. *Id.*, 44.
17. *Id.*
18. *Id.*, 44–5.
19. *Id.*, 47.
20. *Id.*
21. *Id.*, 50.
22. N. Cafardi, "The Scandal of Secrecy," *Commonweal* (2010, August 13). Retrieved April 29, 2011, at http://www.commonwealmagazine.org/scandal-secrecy.
23. T. D. Lytton, *Holding Bishops Accountable: How Lawsuits Helped the Catholic Church Confront Clergy Sexual Abuse* (Cambridge, MA: Harvard University Press, 2008), 160.
24. Doyle and Rubino, 573.
25. *Id.*, 572–575.
26. Doyle, Sipe and Wall, 62.
27. R. Donadio, "Abuse Loosens Church's Culture of Silence in Italy," *The New York Times* (2010, June 26). Retrieved April 29, 2011, at http://www.nytimes.com/2010/06/27/world/europe/27vatican.html?ref=europe.
28. Canon 1719: "The acts of the investigation, the degrees of the ordinary by which the investigation was opened and closed, and all that preceded it are to be kept in the secret archive of the curia if they are not necessary for the penal process."
29. Allen article. NCR Staff, "PR Win Slips Away from the Vatican, "*The National Catholic Reporter* (2010, August 3). Retrieved April 29, 2011, at http://ncronline.org/news/vatican/pr-win-slips-away-vatican.
30. J. S. Brennan, "The First Amendment Is Not the 8th Sacrament: Exorcizing the Ecclesiastical Abstention Doctrine Defense from Legal and Equitable Claims for Sexual Abuse Based on Negligent Supervision or Hiring of Clergy." *Journal of Practical & Clinical Law* 243 (2002): 250.
31. Allen article.
32. *Id.*
33. *Id.*
34. Cafardi article.
35. Doyle and Rubino, 555–9. G. Grisez, "Sin, Grace, and Zero Tolerance." *First Things: A Monthly Journal of Religion & Public Life* 151 (2005): 27–33, 27–8.
36. *Id.*, 28, 31.
37. *Id.*, 20.
38. *Id.*, 25.
39. Cafardi article.
40. R. Dunklin and B. Egerton, "Orders Have Let Abusers Remain." *Dallas News* (2002, August 8). Retrieved April 29, 2011, at http://www.bishop-accountability.org/news3/2002_08_08_Dunklin_OrdersHave_Kevin_Dunne_1.htm. D. Horn, "Religious-Order Priests' Abuses Overlooked," *The Cincinnati Enquirer* (2004, March 20). Retrieved April 29, 2011, at http://www

.enquirer.com/editions/2004/03/20/loc_loc1abuse.html (hereinafter "Horn article").

41. Seattle Archdiocese Case Review Board Report, June 2004, Retrieved April 29, 2011, at http://www.seattlearch.org/NR/rdonlyres/38A458D3-FF96-4A3C -AAD2-4E01B0CAEB9B/17434/CaseReviewBoardReportRedacted.pdf.

42. Horn article.

43. *Id.* R. Becker, "Religious Brother Facing Sex Charge," *Chicago Tribune* (1998, April 21). Retrieved April 29, 2011, at http://articles.chicagotribune.com/1998 -04-21/news/9804210251_1_sheahan-christian-brothers-chat-room. W. G. Kelly, K. Clark, S. Roggendorf and P. B. Janci, "Of Compelling Interest: The Intersection of Religious Freedom and Civil Liability in the Portland Priest Sex Abuse Cases," *Oregon Law Review* 85 (2006): 481.

44. G. F. Bunting, "L.A. Priest Blamed for Legacy of Pain," *Los Angeles Times* (2002, December 14). Retrieved April 29, 2011, at http://articles.latimes.com/2002/ dec/14/local/me-priest14.

45. *The Portland Archive for the Priest Abuse Documents from the Portland Archdiocese Bankruptcy Case.* Retrieved April 29, 2011, http://www.archpdxpriestfiles .com/.

46. A. Dulles, "Rights of Accused Priests: Toward a Revision of the Dallas Charter and the 'Essential Norms,'" *America* 190, no. 20 (2004, June 21): 19–23. Retrieved April 29, 2011, at http://www.americamagazine.org/content/article.cfm?article _id=3638. K. E. McKenna, "The Dallas Charter and Due Process," *America*, 187, no. 7 (2002, September 16): 7–11. Retrieved April 29, 2011, at http://www .americamagazine.org/content/article.cfm?article_id=2477.

47. Allen article.

48. R. Donadio, "Vatican Revises Abuse Process, But Causes Stir," *The New York Times* (2010, July 15). Retrieved April 29, 2011, at http://www.nytimes.com /2010/07/16/world/europe/16vatican.html?_r=1&scp=1&sq=vatican&st=cse. J. Manson, "New Norms Are Much More Than a PR Disaster," *National Catholic Reporter* (2010, July 23). Retrieved April 29, 2011, at http://ncronline.org/blogs/ young-voices/new-norms-are-much-more-pr-disaster (hereinafter "Manson article").

49. Manson article.

50. *Id.*

51. *Id.*

52. Doyle and Rubino, 597.

53. T. Doyle, "Revisions Skirt the Fundamental Issue," *The National Catholic Reporter* (2010, July 16). Retrieved April 29, 2011, at http://ncronline.org/ news/vatican/vaticans-new-norms.

54. NCR Staff, "PR Win Slips Away from Vatican," *The National Catholic Reporter* (2010, August 3). Retrieved April 29, 2011, at http://ncronline.org/news/ vatican/pr-win-slips-away-vatican.

55. R. B. Kaiser, "A Conversation with Robert Blair Kaiser," (2010). Retrieved April 29, 2011, at http://robertblairkaiser.com/Kinterview.html.

56. Robert Blair Kaiser is a former American priest who now writes extensively about the Catholic Church, particularly regarding reform proposals including the use of synods. He has written a number of novels and true accounts regarding the Catholic Church and has worked as a correspondent for *Time* magazine.

Chapter 5

The Charter Report Card: Have the Bishops Lived up to the Promises Made in Dallas?

Kathleen L. McChesney

The *Dallas Charter* was seen by some observers as a sincere effort on the part of the U.S. Conference of Catholic Bishops (USCCB) to respond appropriately to allegations of abuse; to take measures to prevent future abuse; and to be accountable to the faithful in these matters. Skeptical victims, on the other hand, viewed the *Charter* as a public relations ploy, created by men who had no intention of complying with its mandates and who cared little about fulfilling its goals. As it turns out, both viewpoints are somewhat accurate. Many bishops have taken positive steps to protect children, whereas others have either ignored or misinterpreted aspects of the *Charter* as requiring little or no effort on their part.

If successful implementation of the *Charter* is measured solely by a significant reduction in the number of incidents of sexual abuse of minors that have occurred in recent years, then success has surely been achieved. Since the Center for Applied Research in the Apostolate (CARA) began to annually record the number of new allegations of victims who are under the age of 18, the number of allegations has dropped from a high of 22 in 2004 to 4 in 2007.[1] In 2010, seven new allegations were made by victims under the age of 18.[2]

Although many of the victims of sexual abuse committed by Catholic clergy waited years before making their allegations, there is no indication that there are large numbers of incidents that have occurred in recent years that have not yet been reported. On the other hand, the number of reports of "historical cases," that is, allegations of abuse that occurred in previous years, remains high but is decreasing. In 2004, there were 1,083 such reports made, dropping to 498 in 2010.[3] Most of these incidents took place between 1970 and 1979.[4]

It would be very simple to look at these numbers and assume that the "crisis" of sexual abuse of minors committed by Catholic clergy is a horrible anomaly that should be relegated to a few, albeit ugly, paragraphs in the history of the Church in the United States. The issues that surround this type of abuse are much more complex, however, and the objectives of the *Charter* more enduring. Some say this crisis will not be over until there are no current or past cases to report. Another perspective comes from those who say the crisis will not end until the Church reinvents itself as the charitable, inclusive, caring institution that it claims to be. Whatever constitutes the gold standard for the protection of the young and the vulnerable in faith-based environments, there is no argument that it is the only standard to which Church leaders should aspire.

COMPLIANCE WITH *CHARTER* MANDATES

As described by Maniscalco, Kiley, and Chopko in Chapter 3, the *Charter* was an evolutionary document begun in 1994 under the auspices of the U.S. Bishops' Restoring Trust program. The *Charter* is a collection of four general "promises" to the public: (1) to promote healing and reconciliation with victims/survivors of sexual abuse; (2) to guarantee an effective response to allegations of sexual abuse of minors; (3) to ensure the accountability of our procedures; and (4) to protect the faithful in the future. Each promise includes specific actions that U.S. bishops must take or face the consequences of being the subject of a public report documenting their intransigence.

Once the *Charter* was adopted by the bishops, it became the responsibility of the National Review Board and the Office of Child and Youth Protection to identify or create a method to audit compliance with the *Charter*. Key to this process was selecting an external group whose members could perform this audit with the requisite integrity, objectivity, and maturity to provide a credible, unbiased review of the actions—or inactions—of the bishops throughout the United States.

The Gavin Group, a Boston-based consultancy led by a former FBI executive once responsible for the internal examination of that agency's policies, procedures, and practices, began to conduct compliance audits in 2003. These audits were similar to the accreditation processes used to review educational institutions throughout the country. For example, the auditors conducted in-depth interviews of the diocesan bishop, key members of his staff, and a random number of victims. The auditors also performed extensive evaluations of the diocesan efforts to implement educational programs about sexual abuse and prevention. While not a perfect process, these on-site reviews in all 195 U.S. dioceses provided the initial catalyst for adherence to *Charter* mandates and have become a fair-minded model of what must be done in the foreseeable future to protect children in Catholic Church environments.[5]

THE REPORT CARD

The results of the yearly compliance audits are documented in annual reports prepared and made public by the Secretariat of Child and Youth Protection (formerly the Office of Child and Youth Protection). By and large, most dioceses in recent years have been found to be "fully compliant" with the directed actions contained in the *Charter*.[6] However, that measurement is based primarily on quantitative information provided by the audited dioceses. While these data are valuable and the basis for a reasonable assessment of a bishop's fulfillment of the promises of the *Charter*, they do not provide a complete picture of the diocesan commitment to protecting children. Furthermore, the effectiveness of their efforts is not formally evaluated but determined by the number of allegations of abuse that occurred during the year of the audit.

How, then, have the U.S. bishops done in living up to the four pledges they made to deal with this very human problem of abuse? Not surprisingly, there are inconsistencies among the dioceses in the interpretation of the *Charter*'s words and its validity as a course of action. Thus, the many different approaches to implementing the *Charter*'s directives complicate any type of evaluative process.

The following subjective, nonempirical ratings and discussion represent this author's point of view gleaned from personal experience as the first Executive Director of the USCCB's Office of Child and Youth Protection and interactions with Catholic clergy, laity, and abuse victims and their families. By this observer's standards, the bishops have done some things quite well and some things poorly, if at all. Certainly others, particularly those who were harmed by priests or deacons, may differ with these conclusions.

Promise #1: To Promote Healing and Reconciliation with Victims/Survivors of Sexual Abuse of Minors
Bishops' Grade: B–

Pastoral Outreach

The *Charter* focused first on the need for pastoral outreach to those who had been abused by Catholic clergy, directing each bishop or his representative to offer to meet with victims and their families. Prior to the adoption of the

Charter, some bishops had a policy of personally meeting with these individuals to offer support and compassion. After the adoption of the *Charter*, many bishops who had previously delegated these types of encounters took on the responsibility themselves. Despite confusion about whether to meet with victims who had reported their abuse many years ago, the compliance audits confirmed that offers to meet with victims were being made and, in many cases, meetings were conducted.

Still, there were bishops who declined to meet with victims for a variety of reasons. A common justification for this apparent lack of concern for the abused was that such a meeting would be a *de facto* admission of the guilt of the alleged offender and/or the administrator who knowingly left the predator in ministry. There were also many instances, however, in which a victim declined to meet with anyone representing the Church—especially a member of the clergy.

Meeting with victims and their family members is not easy, even for those most experienced in working with people in psychological distress. Because each case is unique, there are no magic words or one-size-fits-all statements that will guarantee a positive outcome for the victim. However, a bishop who is a gifted pastor and able to empathize with a person who is suffering is more likely to be effective in promoting healing and reconciliation.

Reporting Allegations of Abuse

By 2003, all of the dioceses had established mechanisms to enable men, women, boys, and girls to report allegations of abuse. These processes became fairly sophisticated over time, and some dioceses established a dedicated 24-hour telephone number for immediate response to those who chose to call. All of the dioceses appointed individuals to function as "competent . . . assistance coordinators" to provide for the immediate care of victims. The vague qualification for this position, however, allowed bishops to appoint a member of the clergy to respond to a victim's allegations. Although some members of the clergy assigned to these roles provided extraordinary, compassionate aid to victims, a few victims and their advocates believed that such appointments were further evidence of the bishop's insensitivity to their pain.

The assistance provided by the dioceses and religious institutes has included, among other things, funds for professional counseling, small grants for immediate food and shelter needs, healing masses, and meetings with the victim's family members. Notably, since 2004, more than $52,000,000 has been paid by dioceses and religious institutes to therapists working with and selected by victims.[7]

Lay Review Boards

Importantly, the *Charter* requires participation by laypersons in the assessment of allegations of sexual abuse of minors and the determination of an accused cleric's suitability for ministry. Diocesan review boards were established in all dioceses for these purposes. Great care was given to the selection of the board members, and they now include parents, renowned child welfare professionals, psychologists, educators, and the like. The *Charter* allows these boards to include clergy, even bishops, as members, and many dioceses do. However, there is a real risk that a cleric's presence or demeanor will prevent candid discussion or create an imbalance of power within the board.

The boards, whose responsibilities parallel those set forth for review boards in the canonical document *Essential Norms for Diocesan/Eparchial Policies Dealing with Allegations of Sexual Abuse of Minors by Priests (Norms)* have no substantive authority. The boards are only allowed to recommend actions to the bishop, who makes the ultimate decision about a potential or known offender.

The operating procedures and effectiveness of the diocesan review boards vary for several reasons. The USCCB did not provide guidelines for the conduct or training of the boards; therefore, each bishop was able to establish his board, its policies, and its procedures as he saw fit.[8] For example, some boards meet regularly and provide guidance on all issues related to the *Charter*, whereas others meet only when a case arises that requires their review. The decisions about which cases the boards will review, the information the boards will receive about each matter, and the ultimate disposition of each allegation is made by the bishop.

Some review board members have complained of instances wherein the bishop did not follow the advice of the board or the bishop would not allow the board members to deliberate on matters outside of his presence. Moreover, a comprehensive compliance audit of this aspect of the *Charter* is difficult to conduct in light of privacy concerns for the victim and the alleged offender or the fact that a particular case is in civil or criminal litigation.

Standards of Ministerial Behavior

One of the key lessons learned from the crisis was that many adults did not understand what constitutes inappropriate behavior with children. Because abuse involves touching, as well as other common actions, the physical and verbal boundaries between the adult and child must be clear. All of the dioceses created or refined their existing standards of ministerial behavior for clergy and laypersons who have regular contact with children. There are many instances, however, wherein a child needs the soothing hand of a trusted adult, and most dioceses struggled to create policies that were not so restrictive as to have a chilling effect on providing compassionate care to those in need.

Openness and Transparency

Criticisms about the lack of communication between the dioceses and the faithful resulted in the *Charter* directive that dioceses are to be "open and transparent in communicating with the public about sexual abuse of minors by clergy within the confines of respect for privacy and reputation of the individuals involved." Furthermore, dioceses are directed "to inform parish and other church communities directly affected by ministerial misconduct involving minors."

Nearly 10 years after these words were written, there is still great debate as to the definitions of *open, transparent,* and *directly affected.* Most dioceses posted information on their websites and distributed letters, pamphlets, and other materials describing their actions to prevent abuse, such as educational programs and background investigations. Instructions in English and other languages were provided in bulletins and posted in Church facilities to assist victims in making reports of abuse. Some bishops even implored victims to come forward through their homilies and other messages. Nonetheless, opportunities for the bishops to reach out directly to individual parishes and parishioners to reinforce their commitment to protecting children and to highlight the identities and responsibilities of victim-assistance and safe-environment program leaders were often missed.

Although the types of actions taken thus far reflect a greater openness relative to the issue of abuse than in past decades, a continued complaint of victims is that some bishops withhold the names of clergy who have been credibly accused of abuse. The websites of some dioceses contain the names of these offenders, but most do not. There is still no single source of information about clergy abusers in the United States provided by the Church, leaving the media and the public to rely on the bishopaccountability.org website and other news articles for information. If the offenders have been convicted of certain sex crimes, they are listed as sex offenders on various public registries, but there is no special category for those offenders who are or were Catholic priests.

The lack of transparency regarding the offender's name, location, and offenses remains a great disappointment to victims.

Promise #2: To Guarantee an Effective Response to Allegations of Sexual Abuse of Minors
Bishops' Grade: C+

Dealing with Clergy Offenders

One of the most significant aspects of the *Charter* deals with the removal of priests from ministry. In essence, the *Charter* establishes a zero-tolerance policy for clergy abusers, supported by the *Norms* and canon law, and states that

> When even a single act of sexual abuse by a priest or deacon is admitted or is established after an appropriate process in accord with canon law, the offending priest or deacon will be removed permanently from ecclesiastical ministry, not excluding dismissal from the clerical state, if the case so warrants.[9]

The directions and guidance provided in the *Norms* and the *Charter*, however, are complex and can be difficult to interpret, even for experienced canon lawyers.

The actions of the bishops with regard to the removal of priests have not been as visible as they could be for a number of reasons such as protection of the victim's identity, concern for the offender's reputation if the allegation should be untrue, or the potential for increased litigation. Allegations that resulted in criminal prosecutions or civil suits (especially since 2002) are easily tracked by the interested public, but many cases, though credible, are still confidentially handled by the bishop and the Holy See. Culpable priests in these instances have been allowed to retire, seek voluntary laicization, or commit to a life of prayer and penance. In a few instances, these individuals have disappeared and Church leaders have made little attempt to locate them.

Notifications to Law Enforcement

Prior to 2002, hundreds of boys and girls or their parents had reported allegations of sexual abuse to a parish priest, diocesan official, or attorney—but not to the police. Some dioceses had policies, or at least procedures, in place by 2002 to immediately notify law enforcement and/or child protection officials of allegations received. Teachers and/or clergy in many locations were mandated by state law to report suspected or reported abuse to the proper authorities.

It was not until the passage of the *Charter* in 2002 that the important step of mandatory reporting of new allegations became a universal policy for all dioceses. Based on the information provided by the dioceses, the compliance auditors have reported that all new cases of minors abused since 2003 have been reported to law enforcement. However, the *Charter* does not direct the dioceses to notify law enforcement with regard to adults who make allegations about abuse that is new or occurred in the past. Changes in the statutes of limitations in some states and the diverse perspectives of state and county prosecutors about dealing with cases from the distant past have created some confusion with regard to the best way to comply with the *Charter* on this issue. Most diocesan personnel favor reporting all allegations to law enforcement regardless of when they occurred—truly evidence of a sea change in the thinking of bishops and their staffs. It has finally been recognized by most bishops and their lawyers that placing an allegation in the hands of a professional investigator is, in fact, the best way to objectively examine a case. Furthermore, victims are now advised that they can and should contact civil authorities directly if they so choose.

Promise #3: To Ensure the Accountability of Our Procedures
Bishops' Grade: B

National Review Board

The bishops wisely created the National Review Board as a consultative body to the USCCB and to collaborate with the Bishops' Committee for the Protection of Children and Young People on matters of child and youth protection. The board's first leader, Governor Frank Keating, and its initial members courageously and aggressively pursued their mandates to study the problem of abuse and to commission a national study to determine the nature and scope of the problem as it existed within the Catholic Church in the United States. The board members, all professionals representing various disciplines dealing with the protection of children, provide guidance on policies and best practices in preventing abuse. Most recently, the board has commissioned and overseen the national study conducted by the John Jay College of Criminal Justice to identify the causes and context of clergy sexual abuse in the United States.

National Office for Child and Youth Protection

It is not uncommon for corporations experiencing an unanticipated crisis to establish some type of office or infrastructure to deal with the event and prevent similar events from occurring in the future. By establishing the Office of Child and Youth Protection (now the Secretariat for Child and Youth Protection) the bishops recognized that clergy abuse was a long-term problem that required a coordinated response led by an executive director who could be respectful to the culture of the Church without being intimidated by individual bishops. The office has been headed by two different laywomen since 2002 who serve at the behest of the bishops—but for the support of the victims.

Annual Compliance Audits of Implementing and Maintaining the Standards of the Charter

In collaboration with the National Review Board and the Bishops' Committee for the Protection of Children and Young People, the Secretariat for Child and Youth Protection oversees the annual *Charter* compliance audits of every diocese in the United States and prepares an annual public report of the results. These audits, as described earlier in this chapter, along with data from the *Annual Survey of Allegations and Costs* conducted by the Center for Applied Research in the Apostolate, provide detailed information about every diocesan bishop's efforts to implement and maintain the standards of the *Charter*. However, because the *Charter* called for a more overarching diocesan review rather than a specific look at individual parish participation in implementing the *Charter*'s mandates, the auditors review the actions of only a small number of parishes each year. During a parish review, the auditors identify the specific support that the pastor or his staff provides to victims and their families and the methods he uses to prevent abuse.

The ongoing use of an external compliance review process is one of the *Charter*'s greatest strengths in combating abuse. Although the compliance process is limited by the thoroughness and candor of the bishop and his diocesan staff, such systems provide the additional impetus that is sometimes needed to ensure that the protection of children remains a key diocesan and parish priority. Furthermore, fraternal correction among the bishops is expected when a brother bishop fails to follow a *Charter* directive. The faithful can play a monitoring role as well by reviewing diocesan actions noted in the annual *Charter*-compliance reports, diocesan statements, and website postings and making their concerns known.

Studies of Clergy Sexual Abuse

The study *Nature and Scope of Clergy Sexual Abuse in the Catholic Church in the United States, 1950–2002*, conducted by the John Jay College of Criminal Justice, is an unparalleled work in this topic (see Chapter 2). No other institution in the United States has been subject to such a comprehensive sociological study in which participation was mandatory for the entire pool of possible respondents. Calling for and participating in this research was a very bold step for the bishops, knowing it would create a historical record of the most scandalous events in history of the Church in the United States, become supporting material for future plaintiffs' actions, and shatter the confidence of many Catholics who had hoped that the incidents of abuse were rare and overstated. Regardless of the anger and sadness caused by the information gathered by this study, the new knowledge was staggering in terms of what it can teach educators, parents, and youth leaders about abuse and its prevention. To that end, the bishops have made a significant contribution toward the security of children from all faiths and in all types of environments.

A second report, *The Causes and Context of Clergy Sexual Abuse in the Catholic Church in the United States*, (also conducted by the John Jay College of Criminal Justice) is equally defining and thorough. The findings indicate that the abusive behavior was primarily the result of priest-abusers with such problems as intimacy deficits who exhibited emotional and psycho-sexual maturity levels similar to adolescents. Life stressors, as well as inadequate seminary education on how to live a life of chaste celibacy also contributed to the causes of abuse. Like the first study, this one provides extensive new knowledge about child sexual abuse that will be of immense value to therapists, child-protection professionals, parents and Church leaders.

Promise #4: To Protect the Faithful in the Future
Bishops' Grade: A–

Safe Environment Programs

Of all of the commitments made to the faithful, it is perhaps in the area of protecting the faithful in the future that the bishops have had the most success and exhibited the greatest leadership compared to other youth-serving organizations. The *Charter* directs the dioceses to "provide education and training for children, youth, parents, ministers, educators, volunteers and others about ways to make and maintain a safe environment for children and young people." Notwithstanding the proven capability of the Catholic Church to the United States to provide high-quality education at all levels, instituting specialized abuse-awareness training programs for these diverse groups was a daunting task that required substantial time, personnel, and financial resources. Moreover, some wary parents protested the Church's involvement in delivering instruction in the area of personal conduct and sexual exploitation to their children. Providing young people with the knowledge of the potential dangers that may exist from strangers or even known individuals is a positive step toward reducing the risk of a child becoming a victim of abuse and was a key factor in helping to convince some skeptics of the value of these lessons.

Through a variety of educational programs that comport with Catholic moral principles, more than five million children have been equipped with the skills to help protect themselves from abuse, and more than two million adults have been trained to recognize the unique behaviors of sex offenders and what actions to take if they observe those indicators of abuse. Some communities have required similar training for educators and those who work with youth for many years, and now other churches and youth-serving organizations are beginning to emulate these expansive programs. As of 2010, the Catholic Church in the United States has expended more than $170,000,000 to provide these abuse-awareness and prevention courses to its members.[10]

Background Evaluations

Another key component of the bishops' initiative to protect the faithful in the future is the requirement that dioceses evaluate the backgrounds of priests, deacons, parish and school personnel, and volunteers whose duties include "ongoing, unsupervised contact with minors" and "employ adequate screening and evaluative techniques in deciding the fitness of candidates for ordination."[11] Background evaluations, consisting primarily of criminal history checks, are an effective deterrent for pedophiles, lay or otherwise, who try to obtain assignments working around children. In fact, a manager for a large archdiocese reported that since he began screening applicants 10 years ago, he has rejected more than 300 individuals who had criminal convictions for sexual assault.

Background evaluations were performed for more than two million volunteers and employees, 52,681 clerics, and 6,028 candidates for ordination between 2004 and 2010.[12] The process, while very effective, is particularly challenging when attempting to screen candidates from countries other than the United States. The need for improvements in the methods for conducting evaluations of clergy will be even more important if the number of foreign-born priests increases as expected in the years to come.

Transferring/Relocating Priests

The *Charter* sets forth an institutionalized procedure regarding the reassignment or relocation of clergy from one entity to another, for example, from a religious institute to a diocese or between dioceses. The process requires the man's bishop or major superior to document any information available regarding the man's inappropriate sexual contact with children or the possibility that he may be a danger to young people. The compliance audits help to ensure that these procedures are being followed; however, the process would be more credible if the basic facts about these transfers (i.e., name, locations) were listed on a central, open-source database.

Apostolic Visitation and Priestly Formation

The bishops confirmed their support for an Apostolic Visitation (Visitation) of the U.S. seminaries and religious houses of formation in the *Charter* and participated in this initiative in 2008. Though the Visitation was conducted by clergy, some laypersons were invited to be "visitors" during the on-site reviews so as to provide their professional insights and knowledge from their related respective areas of expertise. The summary report of the Visitation described the seminaries and religious houses of formation as generally healthy but in need of strong leadership (i.e., rectors) and called for greater consistency of educational and formational standards among the institutions. With regard to issues of morality or immorality, which is at the core of these offenses, the report took special note of the "ambiguity vis-à-vis homosexuality" and "laxity of discipline" over students' off-campus activities in some seminaries. Bishops and superiors general have special responsibilities toward their seminarians and the growth and development of new members of the clergy. The results of this Visitation highlight the many complexities of molding men to serve the Church in holy and healthy ways and, more important, reinforce the need for bishops and superiors general to be actively involved in the cleric's formation process.

* * *

After 10 years of expended time and resources, has the *Charter* become a vessel of promises fulfilled, as many had hoped? Or is it merely an empty urn, the result of a lack of compassion for, and understanding of, victims? Was it a sincere effort to deal with the crisis or a complicated attempt to manipulate the public's perception of the Church?

The answers to these questions are both yes and no. Certainly many of the promises made have been accomplished: the establishment of processes to receive allegations and to report them to law enforcement, the removal of offenders from public ministry or the priesthood, the provision of compassionate care for victims and their families, the creation of abuse-prevention programs involving awareness education and background screening, the annual public accounting of allegations received, and the conduct of unprecedented studies into the nature, scope, causes, and context of the issues. Considering the costs to the Catholic Church to achieve these goals and the fact that the Church in the United States is now a leader in child abuse-prevention programs, success but not victory can be modestly claimed.

There are still missing pieces of the puzzle, however, that are so significant that until they are more fully addressed, the Church will continue to be deserving of public criticism. The openness and transparency that was called for in the *Charter* remains illusory; for example, there are data about numbers of victims, allegations, and offenders, but no comprehensive list of abusers and the actions taken against them exists. Much more work needs to be done with regard to seminary recruitment and formation, particularly with regard to the culturalization of foreign-born seminarians and the inconsistent application of the prohibition against married priests.

A primary misunderstanding about the *Charter* from its creation has been that it will provide a "look back" at the culpability of Church leaders (i.e., bishops) in allowing known offenders to continue in ministry after receiving psychological treatment. The reality is that the *Charter* commitment to accountability is a promise the bishops made going forward—an intractable viewpoint that will forever disappoint victims.

Long after "issue fatigue" has fully taken over the hearts and minds of most Catholics, the *Charter* will endure as a strong, effective, and practical guide for preventing and responding to incidents of child sexual abuse. Because sexual abuse can never be totally eliminated, this document must live on indefinitely as a priority in this Church as it seeks to create a more holy world. The bishops who adopted it, and their successors, must remain committed to its principles if the young and the vulnerable are to be safe in the Catholic Church in this and in all future generations.

NOTES

1. United States Conference of Catholic Bishops, *Annual Report on the Implementation of the Charter for the Protection of Children and Young People* (Washington, DC: United States Conference of Catholic Bishops, 2008), 21.
2. United States Conference of Catholic Bishops, *Annual Report on the Implementation of the Charter for the Protection of Children and Young People* (Washington, DC: United States Conference of Catholic Bishops, 2011), 34, 45.
3. *Ibid.*
4. *Ibid.*, 38, 47.

5. The Conference of the Major Superiors of Men agreed to establish abuse-prevention policies consistent with the *Charter for the Protection of Children and Young People*. After a review process, a private firm "accredits" many religious communities in the United States if they are determined to be adhering to the *Charter*'s mandates.

6. The characterization of "all dioceses" in this chapter refers to all dioceses and eparchies in the United States with the exception of Lincoln, Nebraska. The Bishop of Lincoln, Fabian Bruskewitz, allowed the Gavin Group to audit the diocese in 2003 but refused to participate in subsequent audits. Because the *Charter* is silent on this issue, the only consequence of his refusal to be audited was a notation in the OCYP's annual reports.

7. United States Conference of Catholic Bishops (2011), 41, 51.

8. The USCCB's Office of Child and Youth Protection made available the nonbinding *Diocesan Review Board Resource Booklet* (December 2008). Retrieved March 2, 2011, at www.usccb.org.

9. CIC, c. 1395 §2; CCEO, c. 1453 §1 (*Sacramentorum sanctitatis tutela*, article 4 § 1).

10. United States Conference of Catholic Bishops (2011), 41, 51.

11. United States Conference of Catholic Bishops, *Program of Priestly Formation, Fifth Edition* (no. 39) (Washington, DC: United States Conference of Catholic Bishops, 2006).

12. United States Conference of Catholic Bishops (2011), 25.

Chapter 6

Was Archimedes an Insider or an Outsider?

Michael R. Merz

Archimedes is famously quoted as saying, "Give me a lever and a place to stand, and I will move the earth." To move a large physical object, you obviously must stand outside it. But if your goal is to move, to change, a huge, ancient human institution, is your best stance inside or outside? Members of the National Review Board, charged with helping the Catholic Church in America grow out of the child sexual abuse crisis and prevent its recurrence, have debated among themselves and with others about how "inside" or "outside" to be. They have experimented with many variations in stance, trying to make lay contributions more effective. This chapter describes those experiments, compares them with efforts by others to change the "American" Church on this issue, and evaluates the present state of those efforts.

I served as a member of the National Review Board from 2004 to 2009, the last two years as its fifth chair, and continue as a consultant. I had no prior involvement with the issue, either as a judge or a church member, before the crisis broke in 2002. At that time, I was serving on the Cincinnati Archdiocesan Pastoral Council. During a Council meeting discussing the crisis, I decided it was appropriate to reveal my own abuse as a teenager by a parish employee. Then Cincinnati Archbishop Daniel Pilarczyk heard my comments and asked to nominate me when there were vacancies on the National Review Board. Thus I was among the first group of "replacement" members on the Board, joining in October 2004.

Crises in human events are often resolved by adopting documents drafted by a few people in the heat of the crisis, accepted by a larger authoritative group, then projected into the future to keep the crisis from happening again. The American Constitution is like that—and so is the Dallas *Charter for the Protection of Children and Young People (Charter)*.

Like the Constitution, the *Charter* was written in one short period, the spring of 2002. Like the Constitution, it was adopted by a much larger group of people in the midst of strong emotions, in Dallas, Texas, in June 2002. Like the Constitution and any founding document, its implementation has largely been in the hands of those who did not draft it. And, like the Constitution, its implementers debate whether it is the last final word on what is to be done or a starting point, a "living" document that points the way but does not answer all the questions.

The core substantive principles of the *Charter* were not new in 2002. For example, in 1992, the United States Conference of Catholic Bishops' (USCCB) Office of Media Relations repeated recommendations the Conference had been making for some time:

> [W]hen there is even a hint of . . . an incident [of clerical sexual abuse of a child], investigate immediately; remove the priest whenever the evidence warrants it; follow the reporting obligations of the civil law; extend pastoral care to the victim and the victim's family; and seek appropriate treatment for the offender.[1]

But merely as recommendations, these principles had not prevented the crisis of 2002.[2] The bishops had to accept the principles as binding on all of them, and the *Charter* was the mechanism they chose. The central idea was that if all bishops agreed to follow the *Charter* and adopted mechanisms to make sure they did so, the crisis could be properly and credibly handled.[3]

The substantive principles from 1992 are carried over to the *Charter*. Article 1 gives outreach to victims pride of place. Article 2 requires dioceses to have a victim assistance coordinator and a diocesan review board, with a majority of lay members not employed by the diocese, to advise the bishop on both individual cases and diocesan policies. Article 3 corrects a prior omission by prohibiting confidential settlements with victims unless they request it. Article 4 requires each allegation to be reported to public authorities, even when the victim is no longer a minor. Article 5 adopts a new zero-tolerance policy: removal for even one credible allegation, regardless of when it occurred. Articles 6 and 7 require clear policies on appropriate behavior and open communication with parishes where abuse has occurred.

Articles 12 and 13 are the major prevention measures, not foreshadowed by prior national recommendations. Article 12 requires every diocese to provide safe-environment training to children and to those who work with them under Church auspices. Article 13 requires background screening of all Church employees who have contact with children. Article 14 incorporates by reference restrictions on transfers of offending priests.

Structural change comes with Articles 8, 9, and 10. In Article 8, a committee of bishops is commissioned to focus exclusively on this subject. Article 9 creates a national Office of Child and Youth Protection within the USCCB staff. And Article 10 creates the National Review Board to oversee the Office and advise the bishops on child sexual abuse issues. While a bishops' committee on abuse had existed for about a decade, a national staff and a national review board were entirely new entities established by the *Charter*.

The *Charter* gives the Review Board several discrete tasks: review the annual report of audits of diocesan compliance with the *Charter*, oversee the Office of Child and Youth Protection, and complete two studies, one on the nature and scope of the abuse and one on its causes and context. But the Board is also given a broad mandate: it "will offer its advice as it collaborates with the [bishops' committee] on matters of child and youth protection, specifically on policies and best practices."

The *Charter* does not include instructions as to the institutionalization of the board, that is, how many members it will have, the terms of office, or the backgrounds of the members. It does not prescribe a size, a budget, or a meeting schedule.

Bishops' Conference President Wilton Gregory wasted no time in making the fundamental first decisions about the Review Board. He assembled a core group of four prominent lay Catholics: Governor Frank Keating of Oklahoma, Justice Anne Burke of Illinois, attorney Robert Bennett of Washington, DC, and Dr. Michael Bland, a Chicago psychologist who is himself an abuse survivor. Within a month they had recommended and Bishop Gregory had appointed nine colleagues: publisher William Burleigh; canonist and law school dean, Nicholas Cafardi; former state Catholic Conference director, Jane Chiles; university president, Alice Hayes; attorney Pamela Hayes; Justice Petra Maes; psychiatrist Dr. Paul McHugh; former Congressman and White House counsel, Leon Panetta; and businessman and philanthropist, Raymond Siegfried. Although the *Charter* does not require it, all were lay and all were Catholic.

At the Board's first meeting in July 2002, Bishop Gregory advised the Board to promptly hire a director for the Office of Child and Youth Protection to begin the two studies mandated by the *Charter*, and to avoid areas of Church life not related to child protection, stating "It is not a time to redesign the Church." He also said the bishops were pursuing a way to hold one another accountable on the issues of sexual abuse of children, a matter not addressed in the *Charter*.

All of the original Board members were accustomed to exercising power within institutions. They knew that "a crisis is a terrible thing to waste"[4] and sensed the leverage inherent in their commission to deal with this crisis. They moved swiftly to persuade Kathleen McChesney, executive assistant director of the FBI, to leave her position and take the helm of the Office. The Board selected the John Jay College of Criminal Justice to conduct the study on the nature and scope of the sexual abuse crisis and set an ambitious deadline for its work. The Board's Research Committee quickly began extensive interviews to provide its own assessment of causes of the abuse and to make recommendations for policy changes. Its Safe Environment Committee began soliciting best practices to recommend for the training required by the *Charter*. By November 2002, the Board resolved to write to Bishop Gregory about the need for a mechanism for bishop accountability.

As early as the fall and winter of 2002, the Board began to experience some episcopal resistance to its work. Although the *Charter* had been adopted by a nearly unanimous vote, not all the bishops were enthusiastic about the results. A prominent prelate refused to allow any of his priests to say Mass for the Board when they met in his archdiocese—not a policy setback, but demonstrating a decidedly negative tone.

By June 2003, a serious obstacle to the nature and scope study arose from the refusal of the Catholic Conference of California to provide data to John Jay College, asserting a concern for the privacy of the accused. This provoked a strong public response from Governor Keating, undermining his effectiveness as chair and leading to his resignation.

On its first anniversary, the Board publicly reported the progress noted here and the hiring of William Gavin, another former FBI official, to conduct the first series of diocesan audits. Privately, the Board had asked Bishop Gregory to appoint Justice Burke as chair to succeed Keating, but he had balked, asking for three nominees instead of only one. The impasse led to Justice Burke's being interim chair until the end of her term. The Board also supported Director McChesney's plan to expand the Office's staff from three to six, but that did not occur.

In February 2004, the Board released John Jay College's study on the nature and scope of the sexual abuse crisis and its own report on the crisis, *A Report on the Crisis in the Catholic Church in the United States*. The Board's report contained 25 detailed recommendations for further study or action. The recommendations were parceled out to the relevant Bishops' Conference committees for reaction.

The very next month, the USCCB's Administrative Committee, the Conference's board of directors, voted to postpone any action on Board recommendations until after the November general meeting of bishops, including funding the "causes and context" study called for by the *Charter* and performing any additional audits of diocesan compliance with the *Charter*. These were two key commitments made in the *Charter* itself, entirely apart from recommendations for improvement and new best practices. The Board nearly revolted; a mass resignation was averted only by William Burleigh's wise counsel that the key question was, "How best can we position the board so that it endures into the future as a fairly independent group of lay people in a position to oversee the safeguarding of children from clerical [sexual] abuse?"

The Board had submitted a list of nominees for replacement of members who were leaving, but only one of them would eventually be chosen. The Board had strongly identified itself as a lay board, but Bishop Gregory announced in September 2004 his intention to appoint a religious sister[5] to the Board, with the "strong encouragement" of the Administrative Committee. When the Board reacted strongly, the sister in question withdrew her name.

Six members rotated off the board in November 2004. At a joint meeting that month with new members, they passed on their experience, emphasizing how hard they had worked to achieve consensus with one another and remain independent of the bishops. The Board also learned that all of the recommendations in their Report were to receive responses by March 2005; that Dr. McChesney was leaving in December and her replacement would be picked by the Conference General Secretary rather than the Board; and that the Board was supposed to have a voice in the *Charter* revision in 2005.

At their June 2005 meeting, the bishops approved revisions to the *Charter*.[6] While none of the substantive parts of the *Charter* were changed, the amendments to the article 10 reflected tensions with the original Board. New members were not to be appointed without the approval of both the Administrative Committee and their own bishop. The Board was to be governed by the statutes and bylaws of the USCCB and by operating guidelines it was to adopt with the approval of two different committees of bishops. Board members were to be accountable to the Conference president and the conference's executive committee. No mechanism for bishop accountability was added.

The Board had an interim chair again until June 2005, when Bishop William Skylstad, the new Conference president, appointed Dr. Patricia O'Donnell Ewers, former president of Pace University, for a three-year term. Although she had not been among those nominated by the Board, she proved an excellent choice. The Board was frustrated by its exclusion from *Charter* review, its insufficient staffing, and the lack of response to its recommendations.[7] Dr. Ewers helped the Board recognize that a confrontational style would not be effective; that a board founded, formed, funded, and staffed by the Bishops' Conference could not credibly claim to be completely independent; and that a new collaborative style of relating to the bishops was more likely to bear fruit.

When Bishop Gregory Aymond of Austin, Texas, was elected chair of the bishops' Committee for the Protection of Children and Young People, Dr. Ewers set out to build an alliance. The Board planned its winter meeting for Austin and Bishop Aymond hosted a dinner for the Board at his home. Of itself, such a gesture does not prevent or repair a single act of child abuse, but it was a far cry from a different bishop's refusal of the Eucharist to the Board to the Board in January 2003. The Board was immediately able to negotiate with Bishop Aymond several small changes to its proposed operating guidelines, and his informal approval made the required formal approval by the various bishops' committees routine.

In June 2006, the Board and the Bishops' Committee for the Protection of Children formed the first of several task-specific joint working groups with lay and bishop members. This model worked well over the next several years as the groups nominated new Board members, vetted and recommended best practices for safe-environment programs, and ultimately participated in the 2010 *Charter* review. This short-circuited the cumbersome process of having Board recommendations reviewed by a committee of bishops (inevitably months later) and then having the Board react to the committee's comments, causing decisions to be postponed for a long period of time.

Moreover, recommendations that started out with the endorsement of several bishops rarely encountered the resistance that the purely lay recommendations had received. No Board nominee cleared by the joint nominations group was ever rejected by the Conference's Administrative Committee. Although the process is not final as of this writing, no objection has yet surfaced to the joint working group's *Charter* revision suggestions. And, working together, the Bishops' Committee and the NRB persuaded the Conference to release funds to begin the causes and context study, money that Conference officers had withheld pending the raising of all matching funds for the work.

Prior to this new working model, the more traditional process of Conference approval for Board projects was used, causing the delay of several Board projects for a considerable period of time. For example, in early 2004, the Board had begun preparation of a resource document and guide for diocesan review boards. Various drafts were reviewed and rejected by the Conference's Canonical Affairs Committee,[8] usually months after their approval by the Board. Without direct communication, the Board was left speculating about how to gain approval. Finally the Board threatened, confrontationally, to publish the document without episcopal approval. Even with this threat, it took another year to get the document published.[9]

Another important example of a stalled project is the Board's recommendation that the annual *Charter* compliance/audit process be extended from dioceses to parishes. While this would obviously be expensive, it is at the parish level that the *Charter* must be effective to prevent abuse. The Board's recommendation for parish audits, made independently of bishop involvement, met stiff resistance by bishops who believed this went beyond what the *Charter* called for.[10] Nonetheless, some bishops volunteered for parish audits and seem generally pleased with the results. The program remains voluntary.

How should our fellow Catholics evaluate the National Review Board now, almost 10 years into its existence? On the one hand, there has been no backsliding by the Bishops' Conference. Offenders have been and are being permanently removed from ministry—there has been no wavering from the zero-tolerance rule. Almost all children receive safe-environment training, which is repeated with age-appropriate materials as they grow older. Those who minister to children, whether cleric or lay, have their backgrounds checked for any history of abuse. Despite initial resistance, the annual audits have become a part of national church life. The important causes and context study was published in 2011. Institutionally, the Board membership remains all lay, despite several strong efforts to add one or more priests. The Board nominates its own members and chair, sets its own agenda, and has formed strong alliances with a number of bishops.

On the other hand, there is no mechanism for personal accountability of bishops and no bishop (in this country) who has been removed for quietly transferring offending priests to places where they could re-offend. No funds are available for studying whether safe-environment programs have been effective, and it was very difficult for the Board to raise funds for the causes and context study. Most significantly, the Catholic faithful still have little idea what has been done to deal with the crisis.[11]

The National Review Board is, of course, not the only group trying to bring about change in the Church on the issue of clerical sexual abuse. Voice of the Faithful is a lay group formed in the Boston area in 2002 in the heat of the crisis. At its first general meeting that summer, more than 4,000 people gathered to discuss what had happened and what should be done. In the years since, their highly educated and articulate leadership—usually of the Vatican II generation—has ceaselessly advocated in support of victims and for more lay involvement in Church governance (including on issues other than child abuse) and more episcopal accountability. While they are, in my judgment, loyal Catholics, they have been outsiders to the official structures, often forbidden to meet in church facilities.[12] They have struggled to maintain a staff structure and communicate broadly by using only voluntary donations. But they are in the same position as other Catholic reform groups: pleading from the outside for change to those inside who believe that change is unnecessary, inopportune, or should be ever more "restorationist," that is, in the opposite direction from lay involvement.

More effective change agents have been the victims' advocacy groups, most notably Survivors Network of those Abused by Priests (SNAP). By very productive alliances with the plaintiffs' bar and the press, they have brought about important changes in the way the Church deals with accusations of abuse. Their litigators have obtained massive discovery of priest personnel files for offenders, vigorously cross-examined leading prelates, and obtained monetary settlements that have led to divestment of important church properties (e.g., the archbishop's residence in Boston and the archdiocesan offices in Los Angeles).[13] In some states, they have obtained the repeal of statutes of limitations, important to their cause because most of the reported abuse occurred in the 1960s and 1970s. All told, American dioceses have paid more than $2 billion in settlements since 1984, leading to the bankruptcy of several dioceses.

The victims' groups are, of course, defiantly independent of the Church. They are not, however, independent of the plaintiffs' bar. Although SNAP has steadfastly refused to open its books, it admits to receiving large donations from leading plaintiffs' attorneys.[14]

These changes effected by victims groups are not within the Church but imposed on it by the legal mechanisms of civil society. Changes in behavior dictated by settlement agreements negotiated by attorneys, even if desirable in themselves, are not the sort of lay participation in governance many lay Catholics have in mind. Even substantively, the changes may not be the most desirable for the Church: no bishop has lost his miter as part of a settlement, but a great deal of money that would have been available for charitable work or to support inner-city parishes has gone instead to victims of aberrant priests[15] and their lawyers.

Why did bishops so strongly resist the recommendations from the Board they created by nearly unanimous vote in Dallas? Why did the Board have to become less independent and more collaborative to achieve the modest results to its credit? I believe the answer lies in the culture of clericalism. I adopt here the idea of clergy given by George Wilson: clergies are professional groups who become distinct from others as "part of the differentiating process of organizational development in any society."[16] Development of clergies—distinct professional groups—helps modern societies operate in much more complex ways than simple societies because they specialize in particular kinds of knowledge.

But clergies develop cultures that separate them from others—special languages, titles, or forms of dress—ideas or practices not necessarily related to their social contribution but that provide bonding within the group and barriers to outsiders. Having specialized knowledge they can apply at critical leverage points enables clergies to amass power—power they are tempted to use for group aggrandizement rather than for the common good.

Viewed in this way, clericalism is a common phenomenon in contemporary society and a necessary adaptation to complexity. But the cultures that clericalism can create can also blind insiders to outsiders. Priests are told they are ontologically changed by their ordination;[17] and bishops are invested with many symbols that demonstrate that they are above and apart from others.[18] Why should they listen to advice from the merely baptized?

My own conclusion is that bishops can lose the fear and develop the trust that enables collaboration across clericalist boundaries. It is hard work because bishops are, by necessity, managers of large organizations and readily acquire the habit of command. And command is easier than collaboration. Conversely, it is easy for outsiders to make demands for change, but the hierarchy of the Roman Catholic Church has proven its ability to reject demands over a very long time. Rather than bloodying our heads by making demands, let us offer collaboration. And let us protect institutions like the National Review Board that offer venues for that collaboration.

NOTES

1. USCCB Office of Media Relations, *Policy on Priests and Sexual Abuse of Children* (Washington, DC: Author, 1992). Quoted in N. Cafardi, *Before Dallas: The U.S. Bishops' Response to the Clerical Sexual Abuse of Children* (Mahwah, NJ: Paulist Press, 2008). Nicholas Cafardi, Dean Emeritus of the Duquesne Law School, was an original member of the National Review Board and its third chair (2004–2005). The book is an excellent review of what happened on this subject before 2002.

2. In point of fact, the vast bulk of the abuse that was revealed in 2002 and later years happened in the 1960s and 1970s. See John Jay College, *The Nature and Scope of Sexual Abuse of Minors by Catholic Priests and Deacons: 1950–2002* (Washington, DC: USCCB, 2004). Why it occurred then, why it declined precipitately after 1980, and why so much of the reporting did not occur until 2002 and later is the subject of John Jay College, *The Causes and Context of the Sexual Abuse Crisis in the Catholic Church* (Washington, DC: USCCB, 2011).

3. The U.S. Conference of Catholic Bishops does not have power to legislate for the Catholic Church in America (except for some minor liturgical matters). The Charter is, therefore, like a contract, a mutual commitment. It is accompanied

by a set of implementing Essential Norms that became law for the American Church after Vatican approval.

4. Quotation often attributed to former White House Chief of Staff Rahm Emmanuel.

5. Religious sisters are, of course, not clerics, but they are generally perceived by the public as Church insiders.

6. The promised involvement of the Board in considering revisions never happened. The Board never saw the final text of the proposed revisions until after they had been adopted.

7. To the detailed recommendations the Board published in February 2004, which were supposed to be responded to by March 2005, only one response was received: a four-page rejection from the Canonical Affairs Committee.

8. Now known as the Canonical Affairs and Church Governance Committee.

9. It has since received very good reviews from the Diocesan Review Boards.

10. Bishops who protest going beyond or improving on the *Charter* complain of "charter creep." One is reminded of those who insist that the Constitution can only mean and be used to accomplish what the framers expressly intended.

11. A formal survey in 2007 by the Center for Applied Research in the Apostolate at Georgetown found most American lay Catholics had little or no idea about audits, background checks, or safe-environment training.

12. When the author accepted an invitation to speak to one local chapter, he was scolded by the bishop for not seeking permission first!

13. The definitive description of how these alliances have been formed and worked is T. Lytton, *Holding Bishops Accountable: How Lawsuits Helped the Catholic Church Confront Clergy Sexual Abuse* (London: Cambridge University Press, 2008).

14. David Clohessy, SNAP's national director, acknowledged in the December 19, 2004, *Beaufort Gazette* that several of the highest-profile attorneys had contributed the largest nonsurvivor donations SNAP had received (p. A4).

15. The wave of abuse committed in the 1960s and 1970s is attributable to about 4 percent of the men who were priests during the period.

16. G. B. Wilson, *Clericalism: The Death of Priesthood* (Collegeville, MN: Liturgical Press, 2008), 10. Wilson notes that clergies do not have to be "ordained" in the theological sense. But admission to the bar serves precisely the same sociological function as ordination.

17. On the origins of this idea, see D. L. Toups, *Reclaiming Our Priestly Character* (Omaha, NE: Institute of Priestly Formation, 2008).

18. A priest friend of my wife was close to another priest who was named bishop. He said to him, "You realize you'll never hear another honest opinion or eat another bad meal."

Part III

CHURCH CULTURE

Chapter 7

Changing the Culture

Bishop Geoffrey J. Robinson

In his recent Pastoral Letter to "the Catholics of Ireland,"[1] Pope Benedict gave his understanding of factors that have contributed to the scandal of abuse. All must agree with some of the things he mentions, such as poor selection processes, inadequate formation, "a tendency in society to favour the clergy," and a misplaced concern for the reputation of the Church. But I have two serious reservations when he speaks of the secularization of society, the consequent loss of sacramental and devotional practices, and false interpretations of the Second Vatican Council.

The first reservation is that he appears to think of abuse as a modern phenomenon caused by recent negative elements in secular society,[2] with the implication that, if we overcome these elements, abuse will disappear.[3] The second is that he still speaks of abuse as primarily a sexual sin against God rather than a crime against an innocent minor, and so presents the traditional remedies of prayer and penance to prevent sin and confession and a purpose of amendment in order to overcome it. As a serious analysis of the situation, providing a plan of action for the future, I find the document alarmingly inadequate.

There are some causal factors that are common to all offenders and others that are particular to each individual offender. In between these two, there are unhealthy factors within given societies or organizations that can foster a culture in which abuse will more easily occur or can compound the problem by contributing to a poor response. Abuse is most likely to occur when the three elements of unhealthy psychology, unhealthy ideas, and unhealthy living environment come together,[4] and a poor response is most likely whenever anything within the culture causes the good of people to be subjected to the good of the institution.

I suggest that the major fault of this section of the papal document is that it fails to look at any teaching, law, practice, or attitude of the Church itself as in any way contributing. It fails to see that there might be elements of the "Catholic culture" that have contributed either to abuse or to the poor response to abuse. In this chapter, I shall suggest 12 elements in that culture that deserve serious consideration.

THE ANGRY GOD

In any religion, everything, without exception, depends on the kind of God that is being worshipped. It is the single most important fact about any religious system, for every aspect of the system will flow from it. And there has been a long history of the angry god in the Catholic Church, with the Inquisition being merely the most glaring example.

This created a church in which, despite the talk of love, practice was based too much on fear rather than love, and authorities always had the support of the angry god for their words and actions.

Spirituality was too often seen in the negative terms of self-denial, self-abasement, and rejection of the "world," and the Christian life was too often seen as consisting overwhelmingly in right behavior before a judgmental God. A constricting guilt played too large a part. These are unhealthy ideas that have contributed to unhealthy actions.

Much of the Church's reaction to abuse has been that of a body used to the power that comes from an angry God and defending that power. Indeed, together with the unhealthy element of the angry God, we must place the other unhealthy element of the Church Triumphant, for the two have walked together and fed off each other. Both have subjected the individual to the institution.

THE MALE CHURCH

In relation to abuse itself, the sexual abuse of minors is a male problem. Yes, some women have also offended, but overwhelmingly, offenses have been by men. In relation to the response to abuse, the temptation to subject all other matters to the overriding importance of one's own good name and honor, with the consequent hiding of anything that would bring shame, is also a largely a male concern, with a long history behind it in many so-called "honor-shame" cultures.

Sexual abuse has arisen in a church in which all power is in the hands of men, where all the dogmas, teachings, laws, customs, and even attitudes are those of men. All authority is in the hands of men, and all the imagery is masculine, for, after all the talk, God is still fundamentally seen as male. Indeed, even men's ways of being human beings have been seen as normative for all human beings. Women have had no voice in articulating the Church's doctrine, morals, or law. Banned from the pulpit and the altar, their wisdom has not been permitted to interpret the gospel nor their spirituality to lead the Church in prayer.[5]

It is surely reasonable to assume that, if women had been given far greater importance and a much stronger voice, the Church would not have seen the same level of abuse and would have responded far better.

A CULTURE OF CELIBACY

The predominant culture has not just been male, but celibate male, for all power has been in the hands of celibate males. In the atmosphere created by this fact, celibacy was the ideal, and the only concession made was that, in the words of Paul, "it is better to marry than to burn" (1Cor. 7:9), so that marriage was seen to involve an element of failure to strive for perfection.

This compounded the problem of male dominance, for, unlike other societies, women were not even present beside the men who made the decisions.

I am not suggesting that the preference for celibacy is the sole or even predominant cause of abuse, but I believe it has made a significant contribution, both directly and indirectly. It has certainly been the major contributor to the other massive problem the Church has not yet begun to face: the sexual abuse of adult females.

Actually, celibacy itself is not the problem, but obligatory celibacy is. A celibacy that is freely embraced out of a passionate love for God and people is not unhealthy. But a celibacy that, some time after ordination or final profession, becomes unwanted, unaccepted, and unassimilated is both unhealthy and dangerous, for it is a celibacy without love. It then contributes to unhealthy psychology (e.g., depression), ideas (e.g., misogyny), and living environment (e.g., loneliness).

The preparation for a life of celibacy in the seminaries and novitiates was negative ("Don't do this, avoid that"), and there was little assistance in building healthy friendships, especially with women. The only answer given to the problems this creates was that God would provide all the love and friendship one might need. And yet it is not enough for authorities to say that priests and religious freely took on the obligation of celibacy, that divine love is abundant, and that all that is needed is that they pray harder. This undervaluing of the importance of human love and friendship contains serious dangers.

Given sufficient motivation, some young persons might be prepared to embrace a life without genital sex, but no young person in his or her right mind should ever embrace a life without love. Sadly, many priests and religious are living their lives without an adequate sense of loving and being loved. This can lead not only to one or another form of abuse but also to such things as alcoholism, misogyny, and the seeking of power.

Properly understood, celibacy is a gift, and it must be seriously questioned whether it is possible to institutionalize a free gift of God in the way the Catholic Church has by the law of celibacy. If obligatory celibacy is to continue, it is essential that authorities should know far more about the lived reality of celibacy in the lives of priests and religious.

Concerning the response to abuse, it seems obvious that celibate males will not respond to the abuse of children with the instinctive fierceness and passion of people who have their own children, so celibacy has also contributed to the poor response.

MORAL IMMATURITY

Before a judgmental God, the all-important consideration is that we avoid wrong actions. But if human beings are to grow, two things are necessary: right actions and taking personal responsibility for those actions.[6] Yes, right actions are necessary, for we will not grow by lying, stealing, or committing murder. It is equally necessary, however, that we take personal responsibility for our own actions. If a 40-year-old man is still in all things doing what his parents tell him to do and never thinking for himself, his growth has been most seriously impaired.

A one-sided insistence on doing the right thing (and obeying the Church in deciding what is the right thing to do), to the detriment of actually thinking for oneself and taking responsibility for one's own actions, produces immature human beings. It, too, is based on fear rather than love.

Moral immaturity does not prepare people to cope with the many and varied temptations that will come to them over the course of a lifetime and must be added to the list of factors contributing to the unhealthy climate in which abuse can arise. And the same immaturity has not helped authorities to respond to abuse.

ORTHODOXY AND ORTHOPRAXIS

Far too often, orthodoxy (right beliefs) has been put before orthopraxis (right actions). If a priest is loyal to all papal teachings, his moral "mistakes" can easily be forgiven. But if he is not loyal to even one teaching, no amount of good actions will redeem him. A pedophile priest can be forgiven, but not someone who is unsound on contraception or the ordination of women.[7] This, too, has been part of the unhealthy culture. It reflects the unhealthy idea that faith is intellectual assent to propositions rather than a response of my whole being to God's love.

SEX AND THE ANGRY GOD

For centuries, the Church has taught that every sexual sin is a mortal sin.[8] According to that teaching, even deliberately deriving pleasure from thinking about sex, no matter how briefly, is a mortal sin. The teaching may not be proclaimed aloud today as much as before, but it was proclaimed by many popes,[9] it has never been retracted, and it has affected countless people.

The teaching fostered belief in an incredibly angry God, for this God would condemn a person to an eternity in hell for a single unrepented moment of deliberate sexual desire. Indeed, it is the teaching on sexual morality more than anything else that has kept the idea of the angry God alive and strong within the Church. Belief in so horrendously angry a god specifically in the field of sex has been a most significant contribution to the unhealthy culture I am seeking to describe.

Furthermore, this teaching placed the emphasis on the sexual sin against God rather than the offense against the abused minor. Pedophilia was, therefore, to be dealt with in exactly the same manner as any other sexual sin: confession, total forgiveness, and restoration to one's former state, and this was a significant part of the motivation for the practice of moving priests around from one parish to another.

The problem is overcome only when, in forgiving a past wrong, we also see the necessity to take all precautions to prevent future wrong, and we will do this only when we place the emphasis not on a sexual offense against God but on an action that is deeply offensive to God precisely because of the harm caused to innocent children. I do not believe that God is upset by sexual desires or acts in and of themselves alone, but God is very upset by harm caused to people.

If the Church moved away from a sexual morality based on the artificial concepts of natural and unnatural[10] toward a morality based on persons and relationships, we would finally be basing sexual morality on the gospels rather than on a theory that has little reference to the gospels.[11] We would all have a healthier basis for our understanding of sexuality and for living our lives as sexual beings.

THE MYSTIQUE OF THE PRIESTHOOD

Every high priest chosen from among human beings is put in charge of things pertaining to God on their behalf . . .

Hebrews 5:1

The Greek text says only that one human being exactly like all the others is chosen for the task of priesthood,[12] but the Latin translation that was used from the time of St. Jerome until just a few years ago said *assumptus*, "taken up," and from this developed a mystique of the priesthood (and, to a lesser extent, of religious life) as "taken up" above other human beings. Countless Catholic people have experienced this attitude in priests. It is exactly the kind of unhealthy idea that can contribute to abuse, and sexuality is only one of the ways in which it can make priests or religious think that they are special, unlike other human beings, and not subject to the restrictions that bind others.[13]

The privileges of this mystique will always be attractive to many inadequate personalities. It also gives priests and religious privileged access to minors and a powerful spiritual authority over them, making it so much easier to abuse.

It is never easy to change an ethos or mystique, but this one must change, for it denies the essential humanity of the priest or religious and so establishes a series of false relationships at the heart of the community. Priests and religious are ordinary human beings. This ought to be a most obvious statement, but authorities, priests, religious, and Catholic people all have much work to do in this field. I find that, wherever there are priests or religious trying to climb down from their pedestals, there are always not only church authorities but also many Catholic people insisting that they climb right back up again. There is a most dangerous insistence that priests and religious must be perfect or, since they can't achieve that, at least appear to be perfect. An extraordinary number of people believe the naïve idea that "Priests and religious are celibate, so they can't really have sexual desires and feelings the way the rest of us do."

PROFESSIONALISM

Over several decades, there has been a strong move toward greater professionalism in most fields of human activity, but priests and religious have limped a long way behind. Their attitude has been one symptom of the idea of being above other human beings and so not needing the assistance and controls that others do. In the light of all that has happened, there is a crying need that priests and religious should rapidly catch up with the wider society in this field of being truly professional in all they do.

Among the elements that need serious and immediate consideration are:

+ Better selection processes of candidates, with a selection panel wider than just clerics and with full use of a psychological assessment.
+ A training that places as much emphasis on human development as on religious and priestly development, for you simply cannot have a good priest who is not first a good human being.[14]
+ A proper professional appraisal every five years, with the community participating in commenting on all aspects of the work of the priest or religious, including any signs of harmful or dangerous activity.
+ A spiritual director.
+ A supervisor with whom priests or religious can discuss their work and how they have dealt with problematic situations.
+ In-service training, with promotion or even renewal of an appointment (e.g., as parish priest) dependent on regular attendance.
+ A code of conduct that sets out expected and acceptable modes of conduct in various circumstances.
+ A form of dress that serves to identify the priest or religious but is not antiquated and does not serve to stress their "otherness" from ordinary people, such as a distinctive tie.
+ Attention to living conditions such that a healthy emotional life is facilitated.

A further consideration needs to be added. It is not healthy that any group of people should believe that they have a job for life no matter what they do. The Code of Canon Law makes provision for the removal of a parish priest when his ministry "has for some reason become harmful or at least ineffective, even though this occurs without any serious fault on his part."[15] In the same way, there needs to be provision for the removal from priesthood or religious life altogether of the person who, even without fault, has shown a radical unsuitability for that life. Indeed, there can be serious scandal in keeping such a person within the priesthood or religious life. Yes, there would need to be stringent safeguards to prevent injustice, but the good of the people must come first.

A POPE WHO CAN'T ADMIT MISTAKES

Infallibility, in practice, extends beyond dogmas to much more pedestrian levels such as laws and even policies. Whether it be a solemn dogma or an ordinary teaching or merely an ancient law or practice, it would be extraordinarily difficult for a pope of today to state that all his predecessors had been wrong.

If we look back over the issues already raised in this chapter, it would be difficult for a pope of today to admit that the Church's most basic presentation of God had contained too much anger, that women have been and still are denied their proper place in the Church, that the dominant culture is celibate, that there has been too much emphasis on obedience and too little on responsibility, that what people believe has been given preference over what they do, that the entire teaching on sexual morality needs revisiting, that the Church has fostered a mystique of the priesthood that is unhealthy, and that there has been too little professionalism.

The pope would have great difficulty in putting celibacy on the table for discussion or even in admitting that the papacy had handled the entire issue of abuse in anything less than an exemplary manner. At all costs, papal authority must be preserved, so anything that a line of popes has insisted on, whether proclaimed infallibly or not, will be defended. Everything will be sacrificed to this all-important consideration. If we are looking at the causes of the poor response to abuse, this one must be given a very high place.

LOYALTY TO A SILENT POPE

Before ordination as a bishop, every candidate is required to take an oath of loyalty to the pope—not God, not the Church, but the pope. Every bishop is meant to be "a pope's man," and bishops take this oath seriously.

If, when accusations of abuse first arose, the pope had made a public statement telling bishops to respond fearlessly and openly, always putting victims before the good name of the Church, I believe it would have had a powerful effect.

Accusations of abuse first came to public notice in the early 1980s, and for the following 20 years, the pope was Pope John Paul II. Sadly, it must be said that he responded poorly.[16] For 20 crucial years, loyalty was loyalty to a largely silent pope, so silence and concealment became the response of bishops.

Needless to say, I cannot guarantee that every bishop would have followed the pope if he had spoken out. What I believe I can state with conviction is that the powerful loyalty to the pope of all bishops would have worked in favor of victims, whereas his silence meant that their loyalty worked against victims.

With authority goes responsibility. Pope John Paul many times claimed the authority, and he must accept the responsibility. The most basic task of a pope is surely to be the "rock" that holds the Church together, and by his silence in a crisis, the pope failed in this most basic task. I felt that the demand was being made that I give my "submission of mind and will" to the silence as well as to the words of a pope, and in the matter of abuse, I could not do this.

A CULTURE OF SECRECY

Within Italy, there is a powerful culture of *bella figura*,[17] that is, of always presenting a good external appearance to the world. It goes back to Roman times and is very deeply entrenched. Those imbued with that culture would have serious difficulties in ignoring it and speaking openly about faults.

For many centuries, secrecy has been an important part of the culture of the Vatican. Wrong actions can easily be pardoned, and the unpardonable sin is that of making those wrong actions public. I speak here from personal experience, for a bishop guilty of the sexual abuse of an adult female was actually promoted while I was rebuked for criticizing the Vatican's handling of the matter.

The Acts of the Apostles show that Peter, the first pope, was not above criticism and had to answer to the Church for his actions (11:1–18). Today, on the contrary, the pope is held to be above criticism, is not answerable to the Church, and must be protected and defended in every way possible.[18]

This culture of obsessive secrecy has been a powerful factor in the mishandling of abuse. It is a sad fact that, if the entire church has been slow to respond properly to abuse, the slowest part of all has been its central bureaucracy. In being so defensive, blaming the media regarding the fairness of the way the Church has been treated as the central issue, protesting that the Church is better than other organizations that have got off lightly, defending the pope at all costs, and dissociating the Church from wrongdoers within it, various members of that bureaucracy have shown that they have missed what truly matters.

THE SENSE OF THE FAITHFUL

The Second Vatican Council spoke of the *sensus fidei* or *sensus fidelium*,[19] that instinctive sensitivity and power of discernment that the members of the Church collectively possess in matters of faith and morals.

It is surely simple fact that the People of God as a whole would never have got us into the mess we are in, for their *sensus fidei* would have insisted on a far more rigorous and, dare I say it, Christian response. It is their children who have been abused and it is they who have had their faith weakened or destroyed. They have even, in one way or another, had to pay for the mess. The pope and the bishops have lost credibility, and it is only the People of God who can restore it to them. If the Church is to move forward, these painful lessons must be learned, for this is an issue on which to leave out the People of God has been positively suicidal.

It will be seen that most of the factors I have mentioned largely find their origin in the first, the angry god. A beautiful paragraph about God's love in a papal document will not be enough, and it will take immense effort to eradicate the angry god from all aspects of the Church. Ultimately, the Church cannot think itself out of the angry god, for the change can come only from the lived experience of God's love.

There is still a long way to go before we fully understand all the causal factors involved in regressive pedophilia in priests and religious. We must not wait for convincing scientific proof that the particular factors I have mentioned have, in fact, contributed to either abuse or the poor response but, because they are unhealthy, remove them now. If there were a concerted attack on these factors, for example, through a council, the Church would at long last be seen to be truly confronting abuse.

NOTES

1. Pope Benedict XVI, "Pastoral Letter to the Catholics of Ireland," March 19, 2010.
2. "In recent decades, however, the Church in your country has had to confront new and serious challenges to the faith arising from the rapid transformation and secularisation of Irish society. Fast-paced social change has occurred, often adversely affecting people's traditional adherence to Catholic teaching and values. All too often, the sacramental and devotional practices . . . were neglected. Significant too was the tendency during this period . . . to adopt ways of thinking and assessing secular realities without sufficient reference to the gospel . . . Only by examining carefully the many elements that gave rise to the present crisis can a clear-sighted diagnosis of its causes be undertaken and effective remedies be found." *Loc. cit.*, no. 4.
3. The Year of the Priest (2009–2010) did not have the effect that many hoped for precisely because it, too, seemed to be based on the idea that, if priests returned to the traditional practices of piety, all problems of the priesthood would be solved.
4. D. Ranson, "The Climate of Sexual Abuse," *The Farrow* 53 (2002, July/August): 387–397.
5. See E. A. Johnson, *The Quest for the Living God* (New York: Continuum, 2007), chapter 5, "God Acting Womanish."

6. "The right to the exercise of freedom, especially in moral and religious matters, is an inalienable requirement of the dignity of the human person." *Catechism of the Catholic Church*, no. 1738. See *ibid.*, no. 1731 and *Gaudium et Spes*, no. 17.

7. The recent case of Sister Margaret Mary McBride is a good example of this, for she was treated far more swiftly and harshly than the worst pedophile. My information concerning the case comes from an article in *The Tablet*, June 5, 2010, pp. 4–5.

8. See Noldin-Schmitt, *Summa Theologiae Moralis*, Feliciani Rauch, Innsbruck, 1960 Vol. I, Supplement *De Castitate*, p. 17, no. 2. The technical term constantly repeated was *mortale ex toto genere suo*. The sin of taking pleasure from thinking about sex was called *delectatio morosa*.

9. For example, Clement VII (1592–1605) and Paul V (1605–1621) said that those who denied this teaching should be denounced to the Inquisition.

10. "Such teaching . . . is founded on the unbreakable connection, which God established and which men and women may not break of their own initiative, between the two meanings of the conjugal act: the unitive meaning and the procreative meaning." Pope Paul VI, encyclical letter *Humanae Vitae*, July 26, 1968, no. 12. A conjugal act that contained both of these meanings was seen as natural; one that did not was seen as unnatural.

11. For a fuller explanation of this point, see Chapters 9 and 10 of my book *Confronting Power and Sex in the Catholic Church* (Melbourne: John Garratt Publishing, 2007).

12. The Greek verb *lambano* means simply "to take" and does not imply "to take up."

13. Since the time of Constantine, the priesthood became "a distinct professional unit, ultimately synonymous with 'officialdom'. . . . In the Middle Ages this was to develop into a definition of ministerial priesthood in terms of the conferring of power. Yet, as Yves Congar explains, the defect of this approach is that it translates into a linear scheme: Christ makes the hierarchy and the hierarchy makes the Church as a community of faithful. Such a scheme, even if it contains part of the truth . . . places the ministerial priesthood before and outside the community." David Ranson, "Priesthood, Ordained and Lay," *Australasian Catholic Record*, Vol. 87:2 (April 2010), p. 152.

14. As a bishop, I received many complaints about priests, some justified, some not. I could not help noticing that overwhelmingly, they were complaints about human failures (e.g., rudeness) rather than priestly failures. All of the best priests I have known have first been good human beings.

15. Can. 1740.

16. I do not make this statement lightly, but no other statement is possible. The extreme examples were his mishandling of the two cases of Cardinal Groer and Maciel Macial Delgollado.

17. *Bella figura* literally means "beautiful figure or image," while *brutta figura* means "ugly figure or image," and the two phrases are much in use in Italy.

18. The latest symptom of this is the statement from the Vatican Press Office (June 28, 2010), "It must be reiterated that, in the Church, when accusations are made against a cardinal, competency falls exclusively to the Pope." The words of cardinals reflect on the popes who appointed them, so no one else may be allowed to criticize them.
19. *Lumen Gentium*, no. 12.

Chapter 8

Vicissitudes of Response to Pastoral Malfeasance: A Sociological View of Church Polity

Anson Shupe

Polity, or governance structure, makes a critical difference in how elites and laity of a church or religious group respond to and experience ministerial scandals. This is a proposition first advanced in 1995,[1] and now, with the hindsight of 15 years and a much larger array of incidents of clergy malfeasance across many religions, it seems even better supported. In this chapter, I want to explain the critical, if ironic, role played by a particular type of church political organization—the hierarchical—in initially facilitating but ultimately discouraging further pastoral misbehavior. My focus is on the modern Roman Catholic Church during its two waves of priestly scandals, the first wave starting in the early 1980s and then the second wave coming again to awareness in 2002. These dates are, of course, somewhat arbitrary since it has been aptly chronicled that the scandals and problems with clergy sexuality have a hoary history in the clerical wing of that ecclesiastical organization.[2]

A TYPOLOGY OF CHURCH POLITIES

The sociology of religion recognizes three forms of polity in religious organizations. (The name of each is lowercase, hence generic, and not referring to specific denominations.) These are admittedly purely conceptual or ideal types, but they are nevertheless useful as models in analyzing real church governance.[3]

The first, *episcopal*, type emphasizes an ecclesiastical hierarchy made up of ranked clergy in an established "apostolic succession" or other historical linkage of legitimizing. There exists a clear chain of command consisting of such officers as popes or presidents, ordained bishops, priesthoods and orders, elders, and other personnel in descending order of authority. Power, in other words, flows top-downward. Examples would include the Roman Catholic Church and Orthodox churches as well as the Church of Jesus Christ of Latter-day Saints. The secular political equivalent would be a monarchy or oligarchy in which power is most centralized. The episcopal type can be pictured as a pyramid.

The second, *presbyterian*, type emphasizes political control through the hands of a presbytery or similar body of elected representatives often termed *elders* or *delegates* that constitutes a less strict or centralized hierarchy. Laity holds some indirect control over elites through their elected representatives. Examples would include Protestant denominations such as the Presbyterian Church (USA), the United Methodist Church, or the Assemblies of God. The secular political analog would be the republic. The presbyterian type can be pictured as the base of a pyramid, with slanted sides, minus the apex.

The third, *congregational*, type places ultimate authority in decentralized lay church governance through more egalitarian member control. The local congregation, in other words, is autonomous of any outside supervision. Such local congregational oversight includes the supervision of doctrine, hiring and firing of clergy and staff, expulsion of members, and all budgetary management. This is not to say that a founder or presiding pastor cannot run the church as a personal fiefdom due to lax lay oversight or personal charisma. Examples of the congregational type include numerous Protestant Independent Baptist/Bible/charismatic/fundamentalist congregations as well as the various "parachurches" run as private/personal enterprises by televangelists. The important point is that congregational-type churches are effectively independent of any denominational supervision or control. The secular political equivalent would be the ideal of small-town democracy. The congregational type can be pictured as a rather flat rectangle.

I emphasize the caveat that "internal" hierarchies of authority may exist or develop within any of the three types. Certainly each will, in any event, see boards of elders or presbyters, deacons, and so forth. But the critical discriminating question, "To whom if anyone outside the local congregation is the local pastor accountable?" actually then creates a dichotomy: episcopal-presbyterian, or what here I term *hierarchical*; and *congregational*. The answer to the above question in the hierarchical case is often multilayered; the answer to the question in the congregational case is simple: no one. Thus, a Catholic priest who preaches a homily advocating an easing of the Vatican's or bishop's stance on elective abortion may expect to hear from his bishop at the very least. A United Methodist minister who advocates stricter restrictions on ministry for women may likewise expect a summons from the district superintendent or, ultimately, the region's bishop. Not so with a pastor in a congregational-style church wherein the laity can vote with their feet to leave if unhappy or start a campaign to oust him if they choose, and perhaps not successfully in the latter case. And the cases of ministers espousing "rogue" beliefs and practices in the congregational instance can become a good deal more extreme, for in fact there is no outside agency to define what is "rogue."

RESPONSES TO SCANDALS IN HIERARCHICAL AND CONGREGATIONAL CHURCHES

Hierarchical churches have already passed through the institutionalization process that German sociologist Max Weber termed "the routinization of charisma" and the "prophetic-to-priestly" transition.[4] They are no longer small in size with charismatic maverick leaders and beliefs that are considered "deviant" or unconventional by larger society. Hierarchical churches are established bureaucracies, well accepted and integrated into the larger cultural environment.

These traits both inhibit quick redress when leadership scandal is first uncovered but eventually lead to more permanent "fixes," both proactive and reactive, of the group's ability to cope with clergy malfeasance. Factors that encourage initial response inertia (such as denial and dismissal of harm, subterfuge and cover-up, "neutralization" of critics, and so forth) include:

+ The insulation and impersonal bureaucratic "distance" of policy-making and decision-making elites from rank-and-file laity.
+ The ubiquitous "circle-the-wagons" protective "we–they" mindset of like-minded professionals versus the clientele population they serve (whether police, doctors, professors, or pastors).
+ The well-established church tradition that prompts a defensiveness toward thoroughly investigating or prosecuting any particular case of malfeasance that is regarded as an anomaly (i.e., the result of only "a few bad apples in the barrel").
+ The "company man" worldview that is more concerned with the public image of the bureaucracy both in terms of the general public and believers personally unaffected by the malfeasance.
+ The lack of meaningful bureaucratic precedent for dealing with wayward functionaries when it is discovered that the misbehavior of clergy is more widespread than episodic.

Yet, as the events of 2002 and the remedial efforts of the Catholic bishops demonstrate, a hierarchical church is capable of recognizing clergy malfeasance (even if the pressure comes from overwhelming outside publicity as well as embarrassing victim movements within its laity). Moreover, because a chain of command within the church organization exists, steps for correcting leadership policy can become more readily adopted and implemented.

To be sure, initial corrective steps are not always totally or even partially successful, much less enthusiastically accepted by all levels of elites even in less hierarchical polities. For example, two particularly dysfunctional attempts by separate hierarchical-presbyterian Protestant denominations to address abuse scandals can be found in Marie Fortune's *Is Nothing Sacred?* and Ronald R. Stockton's *Descent and Order*.[5] Fortune's Protestant church's denominational affiliation was left vague; Stockton's was openly identified as Presbyterian. In both cases, the clergy whom plaintiffs claimed had been sexually harassing and physically abusive both had histories of questionable behavior and rather specific accusations made against them. (In the Fortune study, an armchair social psychologist might even suggest the pastor was a serial sociopathic liar with inclinations toward serious physical abuse and rape.) In both cases, the local church boards and denominational officials displayed a mixture of disbelief, profound embarrassment, a lack of organizational precedent for defining (much less investigating and adjudicating cases of) ministerial misconduct, and a downright failure of administrative nerve to confront the issues of victims' pain and anger. Moreover, in both case studies, the congregational boards and many congregants in the church ended up labeling the plaintiffs as troublemakers and blaming these victims for the scandals. In Fortune's study, the abusive pastor successfully bargained his way out for an ostensibly "graceful exit" by volunteering to leave for the price of a favorable future referral (as he had done before in prior church appointments).

The process of addressing lay accusations of pastoral abuse went much the same in Stockton's study. Reviewing the Stockton analysis of the Presbyterian church investigative fiasco, Roman Catholic priest and noted sociologist of religion Andrew M. Greeley noted: "I am grateful to Professor Stockton for revealing that another denomination can mess up an abuse case as badly as my own, and perhaps even worse."[6]

Elsewhere I have also noted that many Roman Catholic bishops seemed hesitant (to put it mildly) and uncertain as to how to enforce the new zero-tolerance policy adopted at their Dallas conclave in 2002.[7] But the important thing is that policies created with or without a great deal of ballyhoo generate new definitions of fiduciary violations and standards of accountability. These, in turn, reinforce the ultimate legal repercussions that can result due to lax fiduciary oversight by elites.

Thus, hierarchies, once mobilized near the top, tend to mobilize ranks and offices underneath. Congregational groups, on the other hand, often prove inept at containing or meaningfully dealing with leadership scandals because they are sociologically the opposite of hierarchies. Not only may they lack policy precedent, but their leadership is also much closer to the less institutionalized prophetic style, encapsulated in one or a few charismatic individuals, than to the priestly mode. Congregational-style religious groups tend to lack traditions; in some cases, they have virtually made up beliefs and practices. And there is no outside voice to act as a check on excesses, immoral or illegal, that a "rogue" prophetic leader may have created whole-cloth out of personal inspiration or even pathology.

In *Rogue Clerics* and previous works, I have cited a number of cases in which congregational-style leaders imposed a host of sometimes bizarre, even dangerous, destructive rituals and practices on congregants, including the examples of the Branch Davidians at Waco, Texas, and the Peoples Temple at Jonestown, Guyana.[8] One particularly sensational example of a congregational-style church that virtually imploded due to the eccentricities of its maverick pastor was the Community Chapel of Seattle, Washington, in 1975. There, a charismatic self-appointed preacher without benefit of formal theological training or ordination eventually created a megachurch that started with Bible studies in his home and grew into a 44-acre campus that housed a large center chapel with more than 3,000 members, a kindergarten-through-high school Christian academy, a Bible College, and a total worth of around $10 million. The pastor gradually introduced what he termed "moves of God" to the congregants, including prohibitions against facial hair on men, singing hymns that were not directly written by church members, and celebrating traditional holidays such as Christmas and Easter. He also went beyond conventional Pentecostal-style tongue-speaking to encourage "spiritual dancing" between the sexes that entailed physical touching and stroking as well as creating "spiritual connections" between married and single persons and among already-married spouses (but not with their own spouses). Displays of eroticism among adults and teens became rampant in the main chapel during services, spouses began meeting other persons' spouses for "spiritual connection" trysts, and divorces began to mount following outright acts of adultery. It was found, after the entire church collapsed into a tiny remnant amid great media publicity, that the libidinous pastor himself had been conducting "spiritual connections" with more than 30 women in the congregation.

The obvious point is that this Seattle independent church had no norma-tive history, no outside standards for what was biblical or even spiritual, and actually no authority above the pastor to rein in his excesses. Hierarchical churches may attempt through their elites to "neutralize" scandalous practices and incidents, but the latter cannot become "normalized" as they can be in congregational churches.

The modern response of the Roman Catholic Church in North America to the discovery of priest sexual abuse has followed the path of hierarchical phases or waves that I traced above: first, a bureaucratic inertia displayed in prelates' reluctance to even admit or address the progressively emerging aware-ness of sexual malfeasance within the ranks of its celibate priesthood; second, a fairly rapidly achieved commitment throughout elite ranks to acknowledge and then do more than pay lip service to a new policy of zero-tolerance for sex-ual deviants. This sequence can be seen in the perception of modern sexual abuse scandals as evolving in two historical waves.

WAVE I: 1984–1998

The attempts of parents to inform bishops of predatory serial pedophile priests, of some Catholic clergy to cry for honest recognition of the problem, and of the mass media to report sporadically on scandals as if these were isolated and unrelated and only regional or local, is now fairly well known to long-time observers and critics of the abuse phenomenon. Of media coverage during the first wave in particular, it has been written concerning the Roman Catholic institution and its hoary history that this ecclesiastical legacy simply proved overwhelming for many editors and journalists. Hence, they were unprepared to interpret the rash of scandals as anything more than episodic . . . a larger, systematic cover-up, both in this country elsewhere, by church oligarchs was unthinkable.[9]

In addition, an important 1985 internal report by two priests and an attor-ney forthrightly warning of the endemic levels of the priest sexual abuse prob-lem in the Catholic Church and its far-reaching economic consequences in potential lawsuits (not to mention horrendous publicity and damage to the faith of many laypersons) was ineffectively received.[10] As I've noted before, "The Doyle-Mouton-Peterson report of 1985 purchased little attention from Roman Catholic ecclesiastical elites who basically dismissed its unpleasant importance . . . the periodically emerging local scandals involving local way-ward clerics were largely assumed to be grotesque anomalies."[11]

Television news magazines, novels, and movies dealt with the topic, but as a sensational phenomenon, it was not perceived by the media or by most Catholics (except victims and their advocates) as a national or international problem. Meanwhile, the prelates continued to contain and neutralize the "problem" (which seemed to have been defined by them as one of victim complaints rather than one of priestly behavior). A few archbishops more than subtly suggested that alleged victim greed, rather than outrage, was behind the large financial settlement claims, some apologists suggested the whole thing was really a hysteria or scare involving only a few hundred priests,[12] and Pope John Paul II, in 1993 at a much-publicized World Youth Day rally in Denver, Colorado blamed it all on decadent North American culture (as if Europe never has had this problem).

Meanwhile, the hierarchy responded to victims with *emotional normative tactics* (appealing for silence and forgiveness on the basis of Church loyalty, concern for the Church's reputation in a largely Protestant—therefore "hostile"—culture, and so forth), *remunerative settlements* in the form of millions—and later tens and then hundreds of millions—of dollars, often accompanied by sealed court records and promises of silence, and *pressure* or even threats of legal action against lay victims to obtain silence. Overall, the "problem" addressed by the hierarchy elites was primarily one of "corrective face-work," that is, of containing news of sexual scandals and preserving public relations when containment was impossible. Despite sending deviant priests off to various institutes and retreats for rehabilitation (which was generally ineffective) and encouraging penitent prayer (also questionable for definite results), direct intervention that recognized the problem as systemic was clearly secondary to nonexistent.

There were exceptions to this reaction of denial (such as the Doyle/ Mouton/Peterson report), but these emerged largely outside the formal hierarchy. For example, in a series of early books, journalists as well as victims and therapists with a Roman Catholic orientation did attempt to warn that the priest abuse problem was serious and systemic.[13] They called the problem to the attention of other professionals, but there is minimal evidence that they had much of a policy impact on the Roman Catholic hierarchy except to annoy the latter.

WAVE II: 2002–PRESENT

Historians and sociologists of collective behavior generally refer to the "spark" that "lit the sitting powder keg" in any revolution, rebellion, social movement, or riot as a "precipitating event," or, as I choose to call it, a "cultural tipping point." In other words, some incident or, in this case, some scandal is so egregious, so pronounced, so undeniable that it cannot be ignored or passed off as an anomaly. This was what happened with Martin Luther nailing his 95 theses of complaint against the Roman Catholic Church to the castle door at Wittenberg in 1591 and with 42-year-old Black woman Rosa Parks being arrested for refusing to yield her seat on a public bus to a white man in 1955 segregated Montgomery, Alabama. So it was also with the 2002 Boston priest pedophilia scandal.

The Boston archdiocese was the fourth largest in the United States, and as the scandal unfolded, Boston's Cardinal Bernard Law ended up testifying in court or to attorneys as a deponent numerous times. Hundreds of victims came forward and more than 118 lawsuits were brought against the Cardinal, the archdiocese, and priests. The archdiocese had to sell more than $200 million in Church properties as its legal costs reached $1 billion to settle more than 500 claims. In time, Cardinal Law essentially fled the United States, ostensibly to fill some relatively minor Vatican post. The Reverend Sean O'Malley, the new permanent Boston Archbishop, had previously taken a firm hand in settling the Father James Porter (and others) sexual abuse scandals during the previous decade during the first wave of scandals. As he sought to restore the color of integrity to his mission, O'Malley found himself inheriting hundreds more new claims by alleged victims.

Boston was merely a precipitating event for much more extensive media coverage (i.e., the *National Catholic Reporter*, the *Boston Globe*, among many other outlets) that soon spread nationwide. As I (and others who had been following the priest crisis in the Roman Catholic Church) tried to explain to historically myopic journalists from around the country seeking comments on the scandal, it did *not* all start in Boston. Rather, the Boston mess was one in a continuing and unfolding pattern of similar situations of heinous fiduciary violations involving the Church. While media focus seemed to rest uniquely on the Catholic ecclesiastical institution, journalists had to be reminded that a host of other specialized journalists, ex-members of churches, therapists, and a relatively few social scientists had reported similar incidents in Protestant and non–Western religions in the United States and in Canada, Europe, Africa, and Asia for years.

This "tipping point" scandal confronted the Catholic hierarchy with a crisis of public relations and lay nervousness that, in turn, prompted the roughly 200 Catholic bishops of dioceses to deal with it by seeking a national anti-abuse policy at the much-publicized 2002 United States Conference of Catholic Bishops' annual conclave in Dallas, Texas. Well attended also by victims' advocacy groups such as The Linkup, SNAP (Survivors Network of Those Abused by Priests), Survivors First, and the newly formed Internet-based Voice of the Faithful (among others), the bishops *en masse* for the first time had to listen directly to victims' stories, angry recriminations, calls for accountability and even proclamations for structural change in the hierarchy.

The Conference created the *Charter for the Protection of Children and Young People*, calling for better screening of candidates for the priesthood, more ready prosecution of alleged deviants, more timely redress of victims' complaints, establishment of investigative boards and so forth. A zero-tolerance policy for sexual abuse was trumpeted. Former law enforcement professionals were put in charge of an Office for Child and Youth Protection. At the same time, there were charges from victims' groups of these measures really being only half-hearted attempts at window-dressing solutions. A National Review Board to oversee Church policies was set up, but its independence was questioned, particularly since it was organized through the Bishops Conference headquarters in Washington, DC, and the Board was not able to investigate directly individual allegations. Moreover, individual bishops, understandably conflicted and little experienced at containing scandals other than by normative persuasion, quiet financial settlements, or referring cases to church attorneys, alternately began blaming victims again. Or they blamed the larger American Protestant culture for being "litigation happy" and contaminating Catholics with secular commercial values, or they complained of vague guidelines for reporting abuse, or they reinforced their professional insular attitudinal stereotype by asserting that "Christ like" compassion for abusive priests should be paramount. The bishops' immediate confusion and problems of adjusting to a new standard of accountability were evident in media coverage.[14]

But a start had been made. The bishops made a more definitive, and, it could be argued, more meaningful move in 2004 by commissioning the respected John Jay College of Criminal Justice in New York to determine, using voluntarily produced diocesan data, the characteristics of perpetrators and victims, estimates of prevalence and incidence, and estimated formal costs of victim lawsuit settlements against the Church. Such data were admittedly limited and likely to reflect underestimates due to the voluntary report process by dioceses and the understandable reservations of bishops to report moral failings of an illegal nature under their respective fiduciary watches. Nevertheless, it was a remarkable beginning toward assessing the problem given the history of bishopric evasion, denial, and neutralization of a widespread problem. (Predictably, Catholic apologists and critics alike made very different sense of the data collected.)

This sort of meaningful proactive and reactive activity is likely to continue momentum for several salient reasons:

First, only a truly insensitive or arrogant prelate would disregard the recent history of priest scandals and the consequences of ignoring it. Catholic prelates and priests are now on notice. So are entrepreneurial attorneys. There are now a number of law firms around the United States specializing in handling clergy malfeasance cases. These cases have lucrative settlements for the firms, making clergy malfeasance a growth industry in the legal profession.

Second, even if bishops reluctantly or inconsistently follow a zero-tolerance policy of policing their fellow elites, many more laity than before are now empowered to seek redress. The intense media coverage and the publicized anti-abuse policies have created a precedent of discovery in the legal sense, and victims need no longer wonder (as Frank Fitzpatrick, Jeanne Miller, and other primary or secondary victims had to do during Wave I) if they are unique or alone. Wave II scandals, much more than Wave I scandals, finally brought the abuse out of the sacristy, or closet. Wave II victims, with their staggering collective lawsuit settlements, have served as role models for the possible and the probable future victims.

Third, journalists, always inclined toward scandal, found a rich trove of news in the Boston scandals. The possibility of an enormous continent wide and international-scope sexual scandal by purportedly celibate pastors in the world's largest Christian denomination is no longer unthinkable. The media are on the alert. That is undoubtedly why print and televised media so quickly picked up and disseminated the spring 2010 priest sex abuse "scandals" (or, really, outbreaks of media awareness; the abuses in question had really happened years prior) in Ireland, the United States, Germany, Scandinavian countries, and literally in the Vatican itself. But more than just the accusations of clerical abuse, the official Vatican reaction itself became news. In particular, the familiar "old-boys-circle-the-wagons" defensiveness was paraded out for exposure and criticism, and much-quoted Vatican pronouncements on the abuse issue portrayed a culture of aloofness, as illustrated by:

+ The failure of Pope Benedict XVI to deal directly with the topic in his Easter Vigil homily.
+ Senior prelate spokespersons who tried unsuccessfully to dismiss the spreading wave of accusations as merely "petty gossip," to portray it all lamely as a "vile smear operation orchestrated by anti–Vatican media aimed at weakening the papacy and its moral authority."
+ Efforts by senior spokespersons to compare the media revelations of scandal after scandal within such a short period of time, by a stupidly insensitive analogy, to the Jewish Holocaust.[15]

So likewise on alert is a new generation of academics and young entrepreneurial social scientists, including graduate students, seeking criminological topics for doctoral theses and academic publications leading to tenure and promotion. In addition, there is now a dialogue, formal or otherwise, underway between lawyers who specialize in clerical abuse litigation and academics who have their own theoretical and conceptual interests in "bad pastors" as a current example highly relevant to the subdisciplines of criminology and elite deviance.

CONCLUSION

The hierarchical response of the Roman Catholic Church to further revelations of priestly sexual abuse of congregants after 2002 has not gone smoothly. After all, one cannot reasonably expect traditions of elite privilege and insulation to be undone by Catholic bishops in one policy or in less than a series of accumulating policies. And no one outside the hierarchy seriously expects the watchdog victims' advocacy groups to ease up on their vigilance. Why should they? Clergy malfeasance is likely not going away anymore than other forms of human deviance. That wariness is a legacy of these advocates having been for so long deliberately mislead by hierarchical agents with a litany of denials, misrepresentations of the bishops' concerns for laity, and outright lies. The recent reactions of top Catholic prelates in the Vatican (and elsewhere internationally) to 2010 scandals displayed what could easily be interpreted as lack of sympathy for victims and more concern for face saving and have only reinforced victim anger and resentment as well as the suspicion that true acknowledgement of the Roman Catholic Church's "criminogenically" inherent sexual abuse problem will only be thoroughly addressed by "the geriatric solution," that is, when the current cohort of aged prelates passes on and is replaced by a more savvy generation.

The May, 2011 John Jay College of Criminal Justice report[16] on sexual abuse by Catholic priests illustrates all these points. The report in large part chose to emphasize the cultural milieus of the 1960s and 1970s as heavily responsible for the Church leaders being overwhelmed and unprepared to deal with drug use, promiscuity, and so forth (on which individual priest abuses are blamed) rather than the administrative role of the bishops and upper hierarchs as serving (in criminological terms) as *accessories after the fact* facilitating cover-ups of abuses, discouraging reporting to civil authorities (by various normative, remunerative, and coercive means.), and simply stone-walling victims. Critics (myself included) charged that having the diocesan leaders provide the victimization data was akin to having a fox himself (or his confederates) provide data on how many chickens he had devoured in the henhouse. That is simply bad social science victimization accounting. The dangers of minimalization (from leaders who have engaged in such biased reported for decades) are obvious.

Yet the report did signal (1) the Church's eventual acknowledgement of its serious internal problem; (2) at least its continued, if limited, willingness to submit to some outside scrutiny; and (3) an imperfect movement towards correction, if not real internal reform.

Nevertheless, my central point is that the post–2002 bishops' responses, with all their flaws, are something only a hierarchical religious group is capable of instituting. Congregational churches are often the fiefdoms of individual charismatic leaders or, at best, at the mercy of lay discernment in fiduciary matters, but they are not generally given to wise self-examination. Hierarchical groups, whether prodded by internal issues or outside pressures, are capable of doing *just that* more decisively.

NOTES

1. A. Shupe, *In the Name of All That's Holy: A Theory of Clergy Malfeasance* (Westport, CT: Praeger, 1995).
2. T. P. Doyle, A. W. R. Sipe and P. J. Wall, *Sex, Priests, and Secret Codes* (Los Angeles: Volt Press, 2006).
3. See J. Wilson, *Religion in American Society: The Effective Presence* (Englewood Cliffs, NJ: Prentice-Hall, 1978), 159–165; and D. Moberg, *The Church as a Social Institution: The Sociology of American Religion* (Englewood Cliffs, NJ: Prentice-Hall, 1962), 61–62.
4. M. Weber, *The Theory of Social and Economic Organization*, trans. by A. M. Henderson and T. Parsons (Glencoe, IL: The Free Press, 1964); and M. Weber, *The Sociology of Religion*, trans. by E. Fischoff (Boston: Beacon, 1964).
5. M. Fortune, *Is Nothing Sacred?* (San Francisco: Harper Collins, 1989); and R. R. Stockton, *Descent and Order: Conflict, Christianity and Polity in a Presbyterian Congregation* (Westport, CT: Praeger, 2000).
6. A. M. Greeley, "Incidence and Impact of Childhood Sexual Abuse." In *Bad Pastors: Clergy Misconduct in Modern America*, edited by A. Shupe, W. A. Stacy and S. E. Darnell, p. 247 (New York: New York University Press, 2000). In Shupe 2008, cited in endnote 7, I mention a number of pastoral abuse cases in other religious groups, including Buddhist sects in the United States.
7. A. Shupe, *Rogue Clerics: The Social Problem of Clergy Deviance* (New Brunswick, NJ: Transaction, 2008), 125–130.
8. *Ibid.*, 6–7, 18, 20–6, 91, 111–12, 154–58; and Shupe 1995, *op cit.*, 61–63, 104–108. See also J. R. Hall, *Gone from the Promised Land: Jonestown in American Cultural History* (New Brunswick, NJ: Transaction, 1989); S. A. Wright (Ed.), *Armageddon in Waco* (Chicago: University of Chicago Press, 1995); M. Ecols, *Brother Tony's Boys* (Buffalo, NY: Prometheus Books, 1996).
9. Shupe 2008, 159.

10. M., Peterson, T. P., Doyle and F. R. Mouton, *The Problem of Sexual Molestation by Roman Catholic Clergy: Meeting the Problem in a Comprehensive and Responsible Manner*. Unpublished paper delivered to the American Catholic Bishops, 1985. See also www.survivornetwork.org and/or www.thelinkup.com.

11. Shupe 2008, 125.

12. P. Jenkins, *Pedophiles and Priests: Anatomy of a Contemporary Crisis* (New York: Oxford University Press, 1996), 166–167.

13. See, for example, Stiles, H. (aka Miller, J.). (1987). *Assault on Innocence*. Albuquerque, NM: B+K Publications; Sipe, A. W. R. (1990). *A Secret World: Sexuality and the Search for Celibacy*. New York: Brunner/Mazel; Berry, J. (1992). *Lead Us Not into Temptation: Catholic Priests and the Sexual Abuse of Children*. New York: Doubleday; Burkett, E. & Bruni, F. (1993). *A Gospel of Shame: Children, Sexual Abuse, and the Catholic Church*. New York: Viking Press.

14. See Shupe, A. (2008). *Ibid*, pp. 125–130 for a review of media reports in the conference's aftermath.

15. Out of the many media releases, two brief but comprehensive (and typical) Associated Press articles were written by journalist Frances D'Emilio: "Abuse-Scandal Reaction Likened to Holocaust." (April 3). and "Top Cardinal defends Pope." (April 5).

16. John Jay College of Criminal Justice (2011). *The Causes and Context of Sexual Abuse of Minors by Catholic Priests in the United States*, 1950–2010. New York: Author.

Chapter 9

Scandal versus Culture: Mother Church and the Rape of Her Children

A. W. Richard Sipe

The church is my mother. Sometimes she acts like a whore, but she is still my mother.

Dorothy Day

A familial mythopoetic construct permeates the teaching and experience of the Roman Catholic Church. We are all brothers and sisters under one God the Father. Jesus is our brother; he is the bridegroom of the Church—our Holy Mother. Clergy are meant to be spiritual *fathers* who instruct, forgive, and heal as visible representatives of God's word. They are also agents of Mother Church, who protects her children.

Medieval spirituality was infused with the metaphor of a maternal divinity— God as Mother and Jesus as Mother—each the solicitous divine parent. The phrase *Deus Pater Materque* (God, Father, and Mother) is forever memorialized in mosaic in some medieval churches (Torcello, 1006 CE). Julian of Norwich eloquently articulated "a [maternal] divinity whose chief characteristics are protecting, nurturing and sustaining."[1] The current crisis in the Church is the betrayal of the expectations of maternal protection and nurture from Mother Church. Saint Peter Damian (1149 CE) called sexual violation of *spiritual children* by priests "incest" and implored Pope Leo IX to impose zero tolerance for priests who sodomized children.[2]

The Roman Catholic Church in the United States has vibrated with shockwaves in reaction to the widespread knowledge of the existence and extent of priests' and bishops' sexual involvement with young people. When the *Boston Globe* printed its first articles of a "relentless, no-stone-unturned investigation" into clergy sexual abuse on January 6, 2002, a seismic shift of unimaginable magnitude reverberated around the world. Bishop Gregory Aymond labeled that moment as "a time of terror ... [for what] was within our family."[3] The revelations provided the tipping point against deep-seated expectations for purity, protection, and guidance from the Catholic Church and her clergy. The aftershocks resound worldwide in what can be characterized as the biggest religious challenge to Rome and the Vatican since the Protestant Reformation.

The perspective I contribute on this cataclysm is behavioral—harvested from clinical interaction with clerical victims and abusers alike during my participation inside and out of the clerical system. That experience formed the core of a 25-year ethnological report of the celibate/sexual behavior of clergy, including sex with minors.[4] Since that time, I have had an opportunity to review hundreds of thousands of legal document pages that record testimony about Catholic clergy sexual abuse in the United States.

We can measure what the Church has learned about clerical sexual behavior by examining five issues that are foundational to understanding the area of Roman Catholic clergy abuse: *secrecy, scandal, crisis, mandated celibacy,* and *clerical culture.*

SECRECY

The explosive public exposure of sex abuse of minors by U.S. Catholic clergy that precipitated the bishops' Dallas meeting in 2002 breached the secret lives of priests and bishops and the secret operational structure of the Church as never before in the United States.

Blind obedience to the pope is demanded of all prelates, and its implications are best exemplified in the vow cardinals take, "*never to reveal to anyone what is confided to me in secret nor to divulge what could cause damage or dishonor to the Holy Church.*"[5] Secrets (not truth) confirm power. Secrecy is a major tool of clerical control and an operational imperative. The emphasis on secrecy as an essential element of administrative control has led to the production of an ever-more-fragile house of clerical cards and the escalation of a culture of untruth. The credibility of bishops and clergy, especially in sexual matters, has been cracked to its foundations in America (and Ireland); and as of 2010, European countries are rocking with revelations similar to those familiar to Americans.

The whole of human sexuality is suffused with an air of secrecy (despite flagrant displays in secular culture); exposure is doubly troublesome for Catholic clergy. According to church teaching, all sexual activity outside marriage is considered sinful; serious sins must be submitted to a priest in confession to be kept secret by him. Sexual behavior is customarily exercised in private; acts labeled sin (or perverse) are ordinarily hidden; some behavior is relegated to a "secret life." Bishops and priests propagate an expectation that they are perfectly celibate and chaste; therefore, any sex, for them, is secret sin. A public relations spokesperson for the Bishops' Conference proclaimed on national television that stories about celibate violations were exaggerated, testifying, "I am convinced that 99 and 44/100 percent of priests keep their celibacy." However, the weight of factual documentation forever crushed the presumption of universal clerical sexual purity. A "scarlet bond" of priestly brotherhood binds the sexual activity of bishops and priests in a circle of secrecy. Violations, even pedophilia, were a "family matter" to be kept secret within the clerical circle.

Investigations of clergy abuse conducted in Ireland during the past decade (*Ryan Report*, May 2009) and (*Murphy Report*, November 2009) have led to conclusions similar to grand jury investigations in the United States, namely: *the Church mobilized its forces to maintain secrecy, avoid scandal, and preserve material assets and image rather than protect children.*[6]

Documents made public prove beyond any reasonable doubt that some bishops and priests are sexually active even with minor boys and girls, and superiors cover up these crimes. Once the well-guarded secret accounts of clergy sex were ruptured, they indeed became like Humpty Dumpty. Cardinals, bishops, and even the pope cannot render substantiated reports again secret. Proof that they knew and covered for the abusers is documented.

Sex abuse of minors is only one aspect of a secret world of the Church and clergy. Once visited, the clerical secret world can never again revert to a *terra incognita*. Therein rests the scandal of truth.

SCANDAL

Canon law and instructions to the faithful are clear. Do not give scandal—that is: do not say or do anything that could damage the *image* or *reputation* of priests or the Church—or give the enemies of the Church ammunition for attacks. There is no question that the Roman Catholic Church in the United States, Ireland, and mainland Europe is embroiled in a major scandal that predictably hinders the pastoral work and efficacy of priests and bishops. They are compromised; in many quarters, they are held up to derision and suspicion. Records of individual and corporate immorality are now so broadly disseminated that no revision of history will be able to reverse or neutralize the judgment of priests who believe with Fr. D'Arcy "that part of the human structure of the church is rotten to the core."[7]

In 2008, the *Pew Forum on Religion and Public Life* reported, "Approximately one-third of the survey respondents who say they were raised Catholic no longer describe themselves as Catholic. This means that roughly 10% of all Americans are former Catholics." Although the connection between the proportion of men and women who were raised Catholic yet no longer identify themselves as Catholic and the revelations of the scandalous behaviors of priests and bishops is pregnant for research, no causal relationship has yet been proven.

But the scandal of abusive clerics achieved such notoriety in the past decade that secular culture is redolent with allusions, references, and jokes about priests and children as if violation of minors, especially boys, is "a given" in clerical society. Some of the shocking details of abusive behavior slowly became explicit in legal procedures. Accurate and provocative words like *raped* and *sodomized* became common in press accounts of priests' behavior.

Public relations were preeminent to counter revelations. Rome learned its importance as the abuse scandal touched home. The Vatican dismissed the scandal as "the petty gossip of dominant opinion" shortly before June 11, 2010, when Pope Benedict XVI insistently begged forgiveness "from God and from the persons involved, while [we promise] to do everything possible to ensure that such abuse will never occur again." Later, the Pope reflected, "The greatest persecution of the church does not come from enemies on the outside, but is born from sin within the church." Apologies and promises lack meaning while American bishops (or the pope) maintain a preoccupation with secrecy and scandal control without any discernable change.

The Catholic Church writhes in an uncontrollable and irreversible scandal that includes the ever-expanding knowledge that priests and bishops once presumed celibate in fact have steady lovers or anonymous sexual encounters, father children, help partners procure abortions, or become addicted to pornography. Another dimension to the sexual scandal is the significant proportion of clergy who are homosexual—many active—at the same time the Vatican condemns gayness as "intrinsically disordered." The scandal has monumental consequences. The Catholic Church is in crisis.

CRISIS

The dangers posed by a crisis demand action. Great turning points in history can be traced to the decisions made in response to crisis. The Roman Catholic Church is enmeshed in an as-yet-unaddressed crisis of epic proportions and historic dimensions. The public exposure of the surprising extent of clergy sex abuse of minors (6 to 9% in the United States documented) and the collusion of bishops to cover up crime are currently deterrents to clergy abuse. The bishops' reactions in Dallas to the scandal—from oversight and preventive education to public relations—are helpful but limited by damage control and fall short of any real reform. The problem exposed in the scandal is systemic. The crisis dimensions of the scandal are immense by any historical standard and have, so far, outstripped the capacity of any hierarchy to address them adequately.

Since the Dallas meeting, the awareness of clergy abuse has escaped beyond American attention and borders. The Danish physician John-Erik Stig Hansen said, "Sexual abuse by Catholic priests is a global problem inherent in the way the hierarchy of the Catholic church [sic] functions. This is not new." What is new are the questions raised, the intensity and urgency of their presentation, plus the potential of radical danger to established power systems that decisive change would effect.

The clerical scandal pinpoints the centrality of the crisis: human sexuality. The pope, bishops, and priests now do not have sufficient credibility in areas of life and behavior to intervene effectively. Church teaching about abortion, sex before marriage, after divorce and remarriage, contraception, homosexual relationships, masturbation, or the use of condoms to avoid HIV exposure is largely effete.

The larger challenges of the crisis are not limited to behaviors but impinge on the structure of ministry—dangerous questions about power. Why is priestly ministry limited to men? Why can't women be lawfully ordained? Does the all-male power structure generate and perpetuate misogyny and homosexuality? Is mandatory celibacy necessary or even desirable for diocesan clergy? Should clerical celibacy be perpetual? Is blind obedience to the pope moral? Is the phenomenon of "creeping" infallibility inconsistent with tradition and destructive to the Christian mission?

The Roman Catholic Church is in a crisis mode because unsolved issues are vibrant and prominent in the minds of many thoughtful Catholics and crucial to the continued membership of some. No protestations of sorrow or apologies or amends for the harm inflicted by abusive priests and the neglect of bishops to protect the vulnerable will solve the basic problems exposed by the scandal of abuse. The system—clerical culture—is the arena in which decisive battles will be won or lost. The battle lines are drawn as they have been in every reformation era of the Church. Crisis questions exposed by the sex abuse scandal are grounded in a clerical culture that some view as inadequate and corrupt. Irish priest Brian D'Arcy portends the true arc of crisis when he writes,

> A combination of bad theology, the dysfunctional abuse of power and a warped view of sexuality, have contributed to . . . "the systemic failure" to protect the

most innocent and the most vulnerable children. I believe that the evil clerical culture which pervades our institution right up to the Vatican bureaucracy itself needs to be dismantled.

MANDATED CELIBACY

Religiously motivated clerical celibacy can be generative. It embodies the maternal elements of Christian ministry—to protect, nurture, and support the faithful, especially "the little ones" that Jesus called to himself. The violation of this commitment is central to the crisis. The rape of Mother Church's children merits, in Jesus's words, a millstone and drowning—a reaction distinct from the tolerance and cover-up practiced by the American and world's bishops.

Celibate practice and achievement are vital to the Roman Catholic priesthood. It is the one obligation designed to ensure that clergy *adhere to Christ with an undivided heart and can dedicate themselves more freely to the service of God and humankind* (canon 277). Some lapses of celibate practice (sin) can be humanly expectable and even, to a degree, tolerable. Reformations ensue when clerical sexual violations reach a magnitude sufficient to destabilize the essential equilibrium between the faith community and the hierarchy/clergy. Violations have reached a degree that has mortally wounded Roman Catholic ministry.

Sociologist Anson Shupe has written insightfully about the Roman Catholic expectation of clerical celibacy as *le don—(the gift)*—the core of the social exchange between the hierarchy/clergy and the members of the faith community.[8] Celibacy is the basic social contract between the Catholic Church and her members. Medieval historian Mayke de Jong hits close to the mark in the statement that it was from sexual purity that the priesthood was believed to derive its power. Of course, the power is in *celibacy practiced*, not merely pledged. Public confidence in the practice of clerical celibacy has currently deteriorated.

Celibacy conveys clerical power because it is anchored in the awe-inspiring presumption of dedication and selfless sacrifice embodied in the prospect of foregoing all sexual pleasure in order to serve others. The litany of canonized saints—predominantly vowed celibates—sets a standard of perfection and provides examples of heroic service.

Seemingly impenetrable bulwarks protect mandated celibacy as a requirement for ordination to the priesthood. Millennia-old tradition and centuries-old church law reinforce the claim of validity. Despite lack of scriptural backup and in the face of solid theological dissent, recent popes have said that even they do not have the authority to revise the requirement.

Concern for the protection and preservation of church property—a practical if seemingly mundane reality—staunchly reinforces the celibacy law. This preoccupation is not merely of recent origin.[9] Control of clerics' bodies has been coupled with questions about control of inheritance and ecclesiastical property.[10] Of the five duties listed for pastors in 1500 CE, the first four had to do with the protection of property.

The requirement of a promise of nonmarriage and perfect and perpetual chastity prior to priestly ordination—whatever of its undeniable spiritual reality when practiced—is one means of organizational control and power.

Throughout the centuries, the profusion of regulations and penalties concerning priests' sexual behaviors shows how assiduously the Church wanted to control clerical activity, to avoid anything that could compromise the priest's power over the laity, keep him subservient to authority and financially dependent.[11] Several Irish priests named their conundrum: "One disturbing aspect [of the crisis] for me is what I call a 'convenient silence.' Why were we so silent? Why didn't we speak up?"[12]

CLERICAL CULTURE

Roman Catholic clergy live, breathe, and have their being in a culture that is distinct from secular social groups. Priests and bishops seem like ordinary men, but they operate in a unique reality. Roman Catholic clerical culture is male dependent and male dominated. It is a *homosocial* society in doctrine and operation. There is no other culture that equals it in this regard. Its theological structure is exclusively male: God the father, son Jesus Christ, and Holy Spirit are male realities.[13] All ecclesial power and authority are grounded and mediated exclusively by men—pope, cardinals, bishops, and priests. They are automatically granted status and respect, even if not assent, in secular society. Despite the fact that nuns (and women) have formed the shock troops and standard bearers of the Church, their role as "authorities" is strictly limited. Priesthood is denied women.

Clerical culture is a visible and powerful social and spiritual force that justly merits credit and respect. It also provides great theater. Some external trappings set clergy apart. They render a sense of spiritual security and unyielding tradition, especially when dressed in the rainbow range of colorful flowing Mass vestments. Bishops are impressive performing ancient rituals accompanied by plainchant or operatic polyphony. Billowing incense and ballet-like choreographed movement executed in magnificent sacred spaces convey an otherworldly reality. Baptisms, weddings, and funerals are memorialized in towns and villages and made memorable via these men and ritual services.

Roman Catholic clerical culture seems open, apparent, and accessible. It is not.[14] Prompted by the crisis, informed religion writers are beginning to explore the geography of clerical culture.[15] Its inner terrain is neither obvious nor easily traversed.[16] The finer workings of the clerical culture are not fully accessible from the outside. Clerical culture has been intricately constructed and finely honed over a period of centuries. Indoctrination and inculcation into clerical culture are processes that take time to absorb and understand. They include the adjustment to the interaction of an all-male society, in an obedience-dominated, authoritarian "total institution,"[17] established by God, where lifelong employment and support are guaranteed and a single orthodoxy is acceptable, where secrecy is equated with loyalty and is woven into the fiber of operational interactions, and where external appearances—*bella figura*—take precedence over truth and honesty. All the time, members profess perfect chastity.

The investigation of sexual abuse and the resignation of unparalleled numbers of ordained men from the priesthood has led to greater reflection and investigation of the uniqueness of the clerical culture.[18] Irish Jesuit Derek Smyth (2010) spoke from his heart of knowledge about the clerical system when he said,

> For clerical culture, new structures are not sufficient, as there appears to be an *innate abuse system* within this culture. Even though it may now be forced to address the issue of sexual abuse, *abuse* may rear its ugly face in other forms.[19]

Clerical culture is *psychopathogenic*. That means that the elements that constitute the operation of the celibate culture favor, select, produce, and promote men who tend to be what were formerly termed *sociopaths*. Nothing has exposed this core of the culture more clearly than the abuse of minors and the involvement of the most exalted members of the hierarchy who cover up for crimes.

The stated goals of the Church are holy, dedicated to truth and service. Claims that clerical culture rewards untruth appear counterintuitive. Operationally, the culture's shared values and practices function to preserve it regardless of the means used to retain control and image. The clergy sexual abuse crisis has underscored the American bishops' maneuvers, fair or foul, to avoid scandal, maintain secrecy, and preserve financial assets. Those are the conclusions of grand jury reports (New York, Massachusetts, Philadelphia, etc.) and *The 2004 National Review Board's Report on the Crisis of the Catholic Church in the United States.*

The dichotomy between the Church's stated goals and values and its operational methods and practices produces and encourages clerical hypocrisy. Sociopaths (psychopaths) are not men who fail to know right from wrong; they are men who know what is right but don't care.[20] The advertised altruistic agenda of clerical life makes it an exquisite cover for sociopaths and men vulnerable to narcissism. Work with clerical abusers reveals a profusion of "altruism in the service of narcissism." Every clinician who has treated large numbers of priest-abusers gives witness to the conclusion that narcissism is a significant personality component of priest-predators.

More broadly, clerical culture produces in many men an *acquired situational narcissism*, characterized by a sense of entitlement, superiority, lack of empathy, impaired moral judgment, and self-centeredness. Identification with and incorporation into a powerful and godly institution can confer a sense of grandiosity and moral justification for one's personal behavior. These qualities favor a man's promotion within the clerical system.

The dynamic between the two sets of opposing values encompasses clergy from the ordinary parish priest to cardinals. A study commissioned by the American bishops[21] indicated that two-thirds of Catholic clergy are psychosexually underdeveloped. They claim eight percent of priests are mal-developed; certainly this includes a number who abuse minors. The shared attitudes, values, goals, and practices that have been exposed in the *sex abuse crisis*—so named by the bishops in 2002—characterizes the institution of the Church just as much as its stated values and goals do. Jesuit Cardinal Carlo Maria Martini (2008) describes the operation of clerical culture:

Unfortunately there are priests that aim at becoming bishops, and they succeed. There are bishops who don't speak out because they know they will not be promoted to a higher see, or that it will block their candidacy to the cardinalate. This type of careerism is one of the greatest ills in the Church today. It stops priests and bishops from speaking the truth and induces them into doing and saying only what pleases their superiors—something that is a great disservice to the Pope.[22]

It is important to understand clerical culture because *culture trumps reason every time.*

CONCLUSION

No one in June 2002 could possibly imagine the worldwide scope or dimensions that questions about abuse by Roman Catholic clergy would assume by

2010. The head of the U.S. Bishops' Conference, Wilton Gregory, proclaimed triumphantly in 2004, "the problem is history."

My reflections focus on five fundamental issues that impinge on the Catholic Church and underlie its processes of learning about and preventing clergy sex abuse.

Secrecy was and remains foundational to the operation of the Catholic clerical world. Reviewing several thousand legal procedures over the past 10 years demonstrates to me how assiduously—and violently—American cardinals and bishops fight to keep incriminating and embarrassing documents secret.

Within a decade, the fulminating *scandal* fed by revelation upon revelation of Catholic bishops and priests abusing boys and girls and superiors covering up their crimes spread like a string of Chinese firecrackers from Boston's Back Bay to the Vatican and Pope, from Dallas to Dublin and bishops' conferences around the world. Sex abuse by priests is no longer a secret but a scandal, properly so defined: *a widely publicized allegation or set of allegations that damages the reputation of an institution, individual, or creed.* Clergy abuse of the vulnerable is the biggest scandal the Catholic Church in America has ever faced and most probably equals the twelfth- and sixteenth-century scandals in Europe. For example: tapes recorded during an April 2010 meeting between a victim, his bishop-abuser, and a cardinal (Danneels of Belgium), reveal the prelate urging the victim not to tell anyone that the bishop sexually abused him. The European press claimed the tapes provided some of the most damaging documents to emerge in the scandal rocking the Roman Catholic Church.

Again in 2010, another cardinal, Dario Castrillon Hoyos of Colombia, used the familial argument to defend keeping priest abuse secret saying, "it [reporting priest abusers to the police] would have been like testifying against a family member at trial." He also claimed in a radio interview reported by the Associated Press "that Pope Benedict XVI, formerly Cardinal Joseph Ratzinger, was involved in a 2001 decision to praise a French bishop for shielding a priest who was convicted of raping minors."

Not long after February 27, 2004, when the *Report on the Crisis in the Catholic Church in the United States* was published and made public along with the John Jay Report, Illinois Supreme Court Justice Anne M. Burke, who served as interim chair of the National Review Board, said that the bishops did not want change, but only "business as usual." She spoke in 2010 about the problem of "untruth" she sees in the Church and the bishops.

The scandal of sex abuse by Catholic clergy has been a public relations nightmare—gargantuan and impossible. No spin makes gruesome facts go away. Many priests and bishops have violated in criminal ways their responsibilities as representatives of Mother Church. Scandal, of course, is not the real problem no matter how distressing; *the crisis of betrayal* of Mother Church's children is the crux of the scandal. However, the question remains: what has the Church learned about *truth* and *transparency* in the past decade?

There is wide-based agreement that the Catholic Church is in a *crisis* mode. The crisis has to do with human sexuality—specifically, bishops and priests who present themselves as celibate and chaste while they violate minors and the vulnerable under the cloak of their religion. The denial, rationalization, lies, and cover-up of clerical crime by Church authority is in evidence and provides an ongoing scandal and crisis.

There are repeated calls for the abrogation of the requirement of *celibacy* for ordination to the priesthood. Whatever the merits of the arguments, they will not solve the problems of clerical sexual malfeasance. Bishops and priests exist in, maintain, and assiduously preserve a *clerical culture within which secret sexual activity by clergy is tolerated*.

Celibacy and chastity are taught in an educational mode and structure established for diocesan clergy at the Council of Trent. That tradition is dependent on a monastic-like schedule (*horarium*) and a system of sacramental confession and spiritual directors. It is no longer effective. Despite rules and screening procedures, a significant number of clerical candidates are sexually active with one another or with priests—sometimes faculty. Celibate observance of religious-order clerics has not proved better. But sexual activity in the clerical culture is not introduced from the bottom up—from candidates for ordination—but from men established in the culture—priests, spiritual directors, rectors, superiors, even bishops. Homosexuality is a predominant operational orientation in clerical culture from Rome to Los Angeles.[23]

Culture always trumps reason. Is it possible to revise clerical culture? History, theology, and human nature all conspire in favor of reforming dysfunctional systems. Theologically, clerical culture is mutable, no matter how firmly grounded in custom and tradition. Jesuit Bernard Lonergan (1967), wrestling with the possibility of "transition of organization and structural forms in the Church," said, among other things:

> there is in the historicity, which results from human nature, an exigence for changing form, structures, methods; and it is on this level and through this medium of changing meaning that divine revelation has entered the world and that the Church's witness is given to it.[24]

Literary critic Lionel Trilling (1965) talks about the power of forces that change culture. Somewhere in the mind, "there is a hard, irreducible, stubborn core of biological urgency, and biological necessity, and biological *reason*, that culture cannot reach and that reserves the right, which sooner or later it will exercise, to judge culture and resist and revise it."[25] There is hope.

Prevention of sexual abuse by priests and bishops presents a daunting agenda. A revision of clerical culture is required to deal effectively with clergy sexual violations of every stripe. The burden transcends the capacities and limits of law and psychiatry and rests squarely on the very core of religion and spiritual transformation—in theologian Bernard Haering's words, on *"absolute sincerity and transparency."* Prevention will not occur without discussion of the realities of sexuality, celibacy, and the development of explicit and honest norms for sexual responsibility and accountability for human behavior on every level of the Church. The darkness of secrecy breeds betrayal, abuse, and violent assault. Revelations over the last decade have proven that. A Mother Church that sustains, nourishes, and protects her children demands light, accountability, openness, and truth. That is the task unveiled over the past 10 years. It is vital that the Church respond. Any church that cannot tell the truth about itself runs the risk of having nothing significant to be heard.

NOTES

1. T. L. Long, *Julian of Norwich's Christ as Mother and Medieval Constructions of Gender*. Paper presented at the Madison Conference on English Studies, James Madison University, March 18, 1995. Also Cf. C. W. Bynum, *Jesus as Mother: Studies in the Spirituality of the High Middle Ages* (Berkeley, CA: University of California Press, 1984).

2. P. Damian, *Letter 31. Vol. 2,* trans by O. Blum (Washington, DC: Catholic University of America Press, 1990).

3. G. Aymond, "Six Major Lessons Learned from the Sex Abuse Crisis." *Woodstock Report* (June 2007). "First: June 2002 was a time of terror . . . it was within our family." Secondly, "errors that Church leaders made." Thirdly, "experienced the sin, the infidelity, the brokenness of individual clergy and of the Church Leadership." The final three points are more academic. Currently he serves New Orleans as archbishop.

4. A. W. R. Sipe, *A Secret World: Sexuality and the Search for Celibacy* (New York: Brunner/Mazel, 1990); A. W. R. Sipe, *Sex, Priests, and Power: The Anatomy of a Crisis* (New York: Brunner/Mazel, 1996).

5. English translation 1988; also Zenit.org, 2003.

6. Grand Jury Reports: (2002) Suffolk County, NY; (2003) Massachusetts; (2005) Philadelphia.

7. B. D'Arcy, *New Catholic Times* (2010, February 1), 1–2.

8. A. Shupe, *The Spoils of the Kingdom: Clergy Misconduct and Religious Community* (Chicago: University of Illinois, 2007).

9. S. Laeuchli, *Power and Sexuality: Emergence of Canon Law at the Council of Elvira* (Philadelphia, PA: Temple University Press, 1972).

10. R. Trexler, *Synodal Law in Florence and Fiesole, 1306–1518* (Biblioteca Apostolica Vaticana: Citta Del Vaticano, 1971).

11. T. P. Doyle, A. W. R. Sipe and P. J. Wall, *Sex, Priests and Secret Codes: The Catholic Church's 2000-year Paper Trail of Sexual Abuse* (Los Angeles: Volt Press, 2006).

12. D. Smyth, *The Irish Times* (2010, February 9), 1.

13. Although Holy Ghost/Spirit is predominantly a masculine reality, some minor mystical/historical reflections on the Spirit as a female principle exist.

14. C. Kluckhohn and A. Kroeber, *Culture: A Critical Review of Concepts and Definitions* (Cambridge, MA: Harvard, 1952). This critical thinker and anthropologist compiled a list of 164 definitions of *culture*.

15. T. C. Fox, "Cardinal Bernardin, Clerical Culture, Nuns and Homosexuals." *National Catholic Reporter* (2009, August 10.), 1.

16. M. L. Papesh, *Clerical Culture: Contradiction and Transformation* (Collegeville, MN: Liturgical Press, 2004).

17. I. Goffman, *Asylums: Essays in the Social Situation of Mental Patients and Other Inmates* [prisons and monasteries are included] (New York: Doubleday, 1961).

18. M. Murphy-Gill, "Is clerical culture to blame?" *U.S. Catholic* (2010, March 25). Washington, DC.

19. D. Smyth, *The Irish Times* (2010, February 9), 1.

20. M. Cima, F. Tonnaer and M. D. Hauser, "Psychopaths Know Right from Wrong but Don't Care." *Social Cognitive and Affective Neuroscience* 5 (1, 2010): 59–67.

21. E. Kennedy and V. Heckler, *The Catholic Priest in the United States: Psychological Investigation* (Collegeville, MN: Liturgical Press, 1972).

22. M. Martini, *The TABLET* (2008, June, 14), 1.

23. I. Milinari, *Shroud of Silence: An Account of Sex in the Vatican by Five Staff Members*, translated from the original Italian that was banned in Italy and published in Canada in 2006 (Crispina, 2004). Cardinal William Levada told students at the North American College in Rome that they should keep their sexual orientation secret. In 2009, Cardinal Roger told his priests to handle priest sex abuse as a "family matter."

24. B. J. F. Lonergan, "A second collection." In *The Transition from a Classicist Worldview to Historical-mindedness*, edited by W. Ryan and B. Tyrrell, 1–9 (Philadelphia: Westminster Press, 1974).

25. L. Trilling, *Beyond Culture* (New York: Harcourt, 1965).

Chapter 10

Church Governance in Light of the Sex Abuse Scandal: The Need for Financial Accountability, Transparency, and Sound Internal Financial Controls

Charles Zech

One of the by-products of the clergy sexual abuse scandal and its handling by the U.S. Catholic bishops was a new awareness of the U.S. Catholic Church's governance structure. This has occurred on at least two dimensions.

The first dimension was the recognition that the "corporation sole" model of diocesan organizational structure not only did not reflect canon law's inter-pretation of the relationship between a diocese and its parishes, it also failed to protect parish assets (and the assets of other diocesan entities) in the event of a lawsuit filed against a diocese, such as those resulting from the scandal.

The corporation sole model dates from the early nineteenth century. In those states operating under this model, all parishes, missions, and schools within the diocese were part of one civil structure—a corporate sole, a legal entity consisting of a single incorporated office occupied by the diocesan ordi-nary. On the other hand, under canon, law parishes have always been viewed as separate juridical persons, distinct in form and operation from the diocese. Thus, there was a conflict over the extent to which the assets of parishes, schools, and so forth could be included in any settlements awarded by the courts to abuse victims. The courts, naturally, applied civil law rather than canon law and considered parish assets as belonging to the diocese and subject to financial settlements.

To reconcile the differences between civil law (corporation sole) and canon law, many dioceses have reconfigured their organizational structure. Most have moved toward a "nonprofit parish corporation" model in which each par-ish is separately incorporated apart from the diocese. Among other things, this structure requires that each parish have its own governing board. A typical arrangement has been to establish a five-member board in each parish, consisting of three clerics (usually the pastor, serving as board president; the diocesan ordinary, and another high-ranking diocesan cleric, such as the Vicar General) and two lay members of the parish. In most cases, the pastor carries the other two clergy members' proxy on any vote. While this is a significant legal change, there should be no substantial change in the normal operation and administration of any parish. The pastor continues to administer the parish. The parish remains in communion with and accountable to the diocesan ordinary.

The second and, likely, a more noticeable and longer-term change in governance has resulted from a new awareness among the laity that the Church at all levels has not been financially accountable and transparent and that the Church lacked sound internal financial controls. Many felt that if there been more open financial processes in place sooner, that the settlements made with early victims Church to the fact that something was amiss. This timely warning might have averted some of the later abuses. The fact that the scandal has been followed by a series of embarrassing revelations of significant embezzlements against parishes and other Catholic Church institutions only serves to emphasize the point.

Just as confidence in the Church's moral authority has been eroded by the scandal, so too has confidence in its financial structure and governance been damaged. This chapter examines this particular governance issue. It includes an analysis of reports on the findings of a variety of national surveys, some taken at the height of the scandal, that examined parishioners' attitudes toward the Church's financial accountability and transparency. Other surveys were directed at dioceses and parishes to determine the reality of their efforts to be transparent and accountable and to implement sound internal financial controls. The chapter also includes specific Church governance policies that need to be enacted to regain the confidence that was lost.

WHAT THE CHURCH SAYS IT DOES
ABOUT FINANCIAL MANAGEMENT

On paper, the Catholic Church takes its responsibility toward sound financial management and reporting very seriously. Systems to support sound financial practices are in place.

First, this issue is addressed in canon law. Canon 1284 of the Code of Canon Law requires Church administrators to carry out their duties with "the prudence of a good householder," while canon 1287 requires Church administrators "to render an account to the faithful concerning the goods offered by the faithful to the Church, according to norms to be determined by particular law."

Canon 492 is even more specific, as it requires each diocese to have a finance council of at least three members, each appointed for a five-year term. They, along with the diocesan Chief Financial Officer, are required to prepare an annual diocesan budget, examine the annual report on income and expenses, provide advice on investments, and approve the sale of property at or above the amount established by the United States Conference of Catholic Bishops (USCCB), along with other duties. Canon 537 requires each parish to have its own parish finance council, which is to "aid the pastor in the administration of parish goods." However, to the extent that members of the diocesan finance council are appointed by the diocesan ordinary and members of the parish finance council are appointed by the pastor, the degree of their independence may be called into question. They might be perceived as merely "rubber-stamp" bodies for the bishop or pastor.

Finally, canon 212 specifies the duty and right of the faithful to participate in the inner life of the Church, to make their needs and desires known to their bishop, and to express their opinions on matters that pertain to the good of the Church.

To their credit, the USCCB has taken the issue of financial transparency and accountability seriously. In 1995, the National Conference of Catholic Bishops (as it was then known) approved the document *Diocesan Internal Controls: A Framework*.[1] Later in 2002, the USCCB updated this document and issued *Diocesan Financial Issues*.[2] Both of these documents set standards for diocesan financial management and presented a series of recommendations. However, as in all other USCCB documents, the recommendations are not mandates. Individual diocesan ordinaries are free to implement all, some, or none of them.

In 2007, the USCCB's Ad Hoc Committee on Diocesan Audits recommended that "dioceses hire internal audit staff that report directly to an independent accounting/auditing committee and the diocesan bishop or his delegate. The internal audit staff should routinely visit parishes to assess financial management, internal controls and adherence to diocesan policy and directives." Again, this is only a recommendation that cannot be enforced.

Finally, revelations of clergy child sexual abuse in 2002 and settlement payments to victims by the Church prompted Pope John Paul II, in his apostolic exhortation delivered to a group of U.S. bishops in 2004, to state:

> The Synod of Bishops acknowledged the need today for each Bishop to develop "a pastoral style which is ever more open to collaboration with all" (*Pastores*

Gregis, 44), grounded in a clear understanding of the relationship between the ministerial priesthood and the common priesthood of the baptized (cf. *Lumen Gentium*, 10). While the Bishop himself remains responsible for the authoritative decisions which he is called to make in the exercise of his pastoral governance, ecclesial communion also "presupposes the participation of every category of the faithful, inasmuch as they share responsibility for the good of the particular Church which they themselves form" (*Pastores Gregis*, loc. cit.). Within a sound ecclesiology of communion and a commitment to creating better structures of participation, consultation and shared responsibility should not be misunderstood as a concession to a secular "democratic" model of governance, but as an intrinsic requirement of the exercise of episcopal authority and a necessary means of strengthening that authority.[3]

Later that year, in a message to the president of the Pontifical Council for Justice and Peace, John Paul II stated that "financial support . . . places an obligation on the receiver to demonstrate transparency and accountability in the use made of such assistance."

The Catholic Church is generally viewed as a hierarchical, highly centralized organization under the authority of the pope and bishops. This may be true when it comes to Church doctrine, but it is clearly not the case from an administrative perspective. In fact, administratively, the Church is quite decentralized with each diocese and each parish within the diocese enjoying a moderate to considerable degree of autonomy. Parishes generally have reporting requirements to the diocese, but these vary in the degree of oversight from diocese to diocese. Dioceses have virtually no external or regulatory oversight of their parishes' financial statements. While corporations are required to provide quarterly financial statements to the SEC and to hold quarterly conference calls with outside analysts, the Church is subject to almost no recurring external financial oversight. Some dioceses voluntarily post their audited annual financial statements on their websites. Some provide parishioners with an annual financial report, delivering a highly summarized view of the diocese's financial condition. But since they are not required by law to be transparent and accountable in their finances, many dioceses do neither. Most U.S. not-for-profit organizations are required to file IRS form 990, that includes the basic financial statements and sources of funding (donations, grants, etc.). Churches, including the Catholic Church, are excluded from this basic level of public reporting.

While some Church leaders take their responsibility to be transparent and accountable in their finances seriously (the gold standard is the Boston Archdiocese under Cardinal Sean O'Malley), others ignore this basic governance issue. The Archdiocese of Philadelphia, for example, until recently, had not publicly released any financial statements since 2003, in spite of a well-publicized grand jury investigation of cover-up attempts with respect to the clergy abuse scandal and in spite of embarking on a $200 million capital campaign in 2008. Cardinal Egan of the Archdiocese of New York was notorious in his reluctance to release any financial data. When asked about the fact that the Archdiocese had refused to release financial reports to parishioners, he arrogantly replied that his only transparency responsibility was to the members of his diocesan finance council, whom he had handpicked. "I am transparent to the best possible people," he said. "So when you say, 'We don't know,' well, my 'we' knows."[4]

PARISHIONERS' VIEWS OF CHURCH GOVERNANCE, ACCOUNTABILITY, AND TRANSPARENCY

During the height of the clergy sexual abuse scandal, two organizations, Foundations and Donors Interested in Catholic Activities (FADICA) and Villanova University's Center for the Study of Church Management, teamed up to conduct a series of national surveys of U.S. Catholic attitudes toward the Church's financial transparency and accountability.[5] Among the findings were:

+ An overwhelming majority of regular Mass-attending Catholics, in fact two-thirds, agreed that the Church should be more accountable on Church financial issues.
+ Only 41 percent of regular Mass-attending Catholics rated the Church as above average in its competence in the handling of money.
+ In light of the millions of dollars that Catholic parishes contributed to aid victims of natural disasters like the tsunami in Southeast Asia and Hurricane Katrina, only 37 percent of regular Mass-attending Catholics rated the Church's performance in keeping donors informed about how the funds were used as above average.
+ More than three-fifths of regular Mass-attending Catholics agreed that there should be annual independent audits of church finances. When asked specifically about auditing parish and diocesan finances and releasing the results publicly, 63 percent agreed that independent audits should be done at the parish level and 67 percent agreed that they should be performed at the diocesan level.
+ The proportion of regular Mass-attending Catholics who agreed that their parish should hold an annual open forum where the parish's financial planning and fundraising methods can be aired was 80 percent.
+ Only 46 percent of the sample of regular Mass-attending Catholics agreed that they have an adequate understanding of how their contributions to the Catholic Church are used.

+ Only 44 percent of regular Mass-attending Catholics agreed that the Church makes good use of the managerial and financial expertise of its parishioners.
+ "High-donor" parishioners (those who contributed more than $5,000 annually to the Church) showed significantly stronger opinions on the Church's financial accountability. While 39 percent of all parishioners in the survey felt that the bishops were financially accountable, only 27 percent of the high donors agreed with this notion.
+ With regard to the Church's emergency relief appeals, 37 percent of the typical parish donors rated the Church above average in keeping them informed, whereas only 12 percent of the high donors gave the Church an above average rating.

EMBEZZLEMENTS

While U.S. Catholics were still recovering from the revelations surrounding the clergy sexual abuse scandal and all of its implications, they were hit with another bombshell: a series of disclosures of high-profile embezzlements from the Church involving both lay and clergy.

Many of these embezzlements were the result of poor or nonexistent financial transparency and accountability and inadequate internal financial control, all of which are Church governance issues.

In 2008, Professors Robert West and Charles Zech of Villanova's Center for the Study of Church Management released their findings of a national survey of Catholic diocesan chief financial officers.[6] The most startling of these was that 85 percent of the dioceses had experienced one or more embezzlements in the recent past. Among their other findings that speak to the issue of inadequate church governance when it comes to church finances were:

+ Only 55 percent of the dioceses had conflict-of-interest guidelines for the members of their diocesan finance councils.
+ In spite of the directive found in canon 492, only 75 percent of the diocesan finance councils were involved in preparing the diocesan budget.
+ Thirty-six percent of the CFOs ranked the greatest financial risk by their diocese as potential litigation associated with the clergy abuse scandal. Significantly, this was followed closely by concerns over parish finances and controls (34%).
+ The frequency with which internal parish audits are performed ranged from annually (3% of the dioceses) to "seldom or never" (21%), with a median of every four years. The modal response was that audits are conducted when there is a change in key personnel (i.e., pastor or bookkeeper).

+ Of those dioceses that have diocesan high schools, these schools are audited annually in 63 percent of the dioceses, while 17 percent of the dioceses report that they never audit their high schools.
+ Only 39 percent of the dioceses reported have a formal written fraud policy (i.e., a response plan when a possible theft is reported to the diocese).

Based on these findings, West and Zech recommend the following financial environment control policies:

+ Implementation in every Catholic diocese of the policies prescribed in the USCCB handbook *Diocesan Financial Issues*.
+ The establishment of fraud policies in every diocese.
+ Annual internal audits of parishes supplemented by external audits conducted at least every three years.
+ Public disclosure of the names and professions of every member of the Diocesan Finance Council, along with their conflict-of-interest guidelines.
+ At a minimum, quarterly meetings of the diocesan finance council (or one of its subcommittees) to monitor diocesan office, parish, and school financial reports.
+ At least annual (and preferably more frequent) submission of financial data by all parishes and high schools to diocesan offices.
+ Establishment of a uniform budgeting process and standardized software for all diocesan entities.
+ Establishment of communication channels for church workers to report suspected irregularities or fraudulent activities while protecting their anonymity.

PARISH-LEVEL FINANCIAL GOVERNANCE ISSUES

In 2010, a team of researchers from Villanova's Center for the Study of Church Management and Georgetown's Center for Applied Research in the Apostolate (CARA) published the first comprehensive statistical analysis of parish pastoral councils and parish finance councils.[7] Their findings were based on a national sample of more than 600 parishes. Many of the questions directed to the parish finance councils covered issues of transparency and accountability, as well as the adequacy of internal financial controls, at the parish level.

Parish-Level Financial Transparency and Accountability

The process of financial transparency and accountability should include not just keeping parishioners informed of financial outcomes but also giving them a consultative voice in making parish financial decisions. We know that canon law requires each parish to have a finance council. In fact, 93 percent of the parishes in the sample had a finance council in place. How transparent and accountable were these parishes in their finances?

The first issue is the extent to which parishioners have input in the *parish budgetary process*, that is, before final decisions on the parish's spending are made. Since the budget presumably reflects the parish's priorities, sound parish governance gives parishioners input into its development through consultative processes. Some parishes make a genuine effort to keep parishioners informed and solicit their input into the budgetary process. Nine percent of the parishes in the sample held open budget meetings, with parishioners invited to attend. Others presented details of the preliminary budget in the parish's Sunday bulletin or mailed copies of the preliminary budget to each parishioner's home. But in 60 percent of the parishes in the sample, a typical parishioner had no knowledge of and no input into the preliminary budget.

How about the final budget? Here, the record was much better, with 99 percent of the parishes distributing copies of the final budget to parishioners. This was typically done through an insert in the Sunday bulletin or through a direct mailing to parishioners' homes. But too often, these budget reports are highly summarized, banal documents that offer no insights into the parish's priorities or financial condition and, therefore, fail to provide adequate financial transparency and accountability necessary for good parish governance.

Parish Internal Financial Controls

The other element of good financial governance at the parish level is the implementation of sound internal financial control policies that eliminate opportunities for fraud and ensure parishioners that their contributions are safe. The key element here is the segmentation of duties, that is, having different individuals involved in the various stages of parish financial transactions to serve as a system of checks and balances.

For example, parishes should require that more than one person be authorized to sign checks in large amounts. Likewise, the same individual should not be involved in counting the collection, depositing the funds in the bank, writing checks, and reconciling the parish checkbook. Scenarios such as this are, unfortunately, not unknown and provide no controls and too many opportunities for abuse. While the Zech and colleagues study found few cases of this extreme violation of good internal financial controls, there were some troubling findings.

Specifically, that study found that in two-thirds of the parishes, only one person was authorized to sign checks—no matter how large the amount. This was compounded by the fact that:

+ In 5 percent of the parishes, the same person had sole responsibility for both writing checks and reconciling bank statements.
+ In about one-sixth of the parishes, the same person was solely responsible for depositing the Sunday collection and for reconciling bank statements.
+ In nearly one-third of the parishes, only one person deposited noncollection revenues and reconciled the bank statements.
+ Forty percent of the parishes gave one person the sole authority to both approve routine disbursements and reconcile bank statements.
+ Five percent of the parishes gave the responsibility to a single individual for both approving nonbudgeted expenditures and reconciling bank statements.

All of these arrangements violate sound internal financial control practices and reflect poorly on parish governance.

A similar issue lies with counting the collection. Parishes should avoid the practice of having the same individuals (or worse, a single individual) count the Sunday collection every week. But the Zech and colleagues study found that in about 5 percent of the parishes, only one individual counted the Sunday collection. About 40 percent of the parishes employed the same crew of counters week after week, with an average of about 5 members. Nearly half of these failed to include any staff members among the counters. Both of these approaches are fraught with danger.

Among the recommendations issued by Zech and colleagues were that parish finance councils:

+ Employ a guidelines manual.
+ Involve parishioners in the budgetary process.
+ Take responsibility for ensuring that proper internal financial controls, including the segmentation of duties, are in place in the parish.
+ Review financial reports frequently.
+ Communicate frequently with the parish at large.
+ Work with the parish pastoral council to set long-range parish financial and physical plant goals.

CONCLUSION

When one thinks of modifications in Church governance, one might think of large, sweeping changes such as the way we select our bishops or appoint our pastors. Issues like these are important and need to be debated on their own merits. This chapter is concerned with more modest governance changes: requiring Church leaders at all levels to become better stewards of the Church's resources (and parishioners' contributions) by becoming more transparent and accountable in Church finances and ensuring their safety by implementing sound internal financial controls.

Why is this important? Studies have shown that Catholics are among the lowest givers to their church of any U.S. religion. It has been suggested that one reason is that Catholic parishes are typically far less transparent and accountable in their finances than are Protestant congregations. Lower contributions mean a diminished ability to carry out God's work on earth.

Some of the specific actions that would improve Church financial governance at the diocesan level include:

+ Public disclosure on the diocesan website of the names and professions of all diocesan finance council members, along with the diocese's conflict-of-interest statement for diocesan finance council members.
+ Submission of financial data by all parishes and high schools at least annually, and preferably more frequently.
+ Establishment of fraud policies in every diocese.
+ Establishment of communication channels for Church workers to report suspected irregularities or fraudulent activities while protecting their anonymity.
+ Establishment of a uniform budgeting process and standardized software for all diocesan entities.
+ Posting a reader-friendly annual financial statement, as well as an approved budget and strategic plan for the coming year, on the diocesan website.

Some of the specific actions that would improve Church financial governance at the parish level include:

+ Establishment of policies that involve parishioners in the budgetary process, including providing the opportunity for consultation on the preliminary budget.
+ Implementation of sound internal financial controls, including the segmentation of duties.
+ Frequent communication and cooperation between the parish finance council and the parish pastoral council to set long-range parish financial and physical plant goals.
+ Annual internal audits of parishes supplemented by external audits conducted at least every three years and the posting of the results in their entirety on the parish website.
+ Posting a reader-friendly annual financial statement, as well as the approved budget for the coming year, on the parish website and frequently posting

parish financial reports such as the parish balance sheet and a comparison of actual to budgeted figures.

We have seen that, by and large, appropriate guidelines and instructions are in place, through canon law and documents and recommendations issued by the USCCB, to address Church financial governance issues. However, actions associated with the guidelines and instructions need to be implemented. Too often, diocesan ordinaries and pastors feel no external pressure to exercise good financial governance. Parishioners need to make their voices heard through formal processes such as diocesan pastoral councils, parish pastoral councils, and diocesan synods. Until Church leaders recognize that parishioners are insistent on good financial governance, too many of them are likely to give issues such as transparency, accountability, and internal financial controls no more than lip service.

NOTES

1. United States Conference of Catholic, *Diocesan Internal Controls: A Framework* (Washington, DC: Author, 1995).
2. United States Conference of Catholic Bishops, *Diocesan Financial Issues* (Washington, DC: Author, 2002).
3. "Pope's Address to Bishops of Pennsylvania and New Jersey" (2004). Retrieved on July 7, 2010, from http://www.zenit.org/article-11001?l=english.
4. M. Powell, "At 75, a Battle-Tested but Unwavering Cardinal," *New York Times*, April 23, 2007, p. A1
5. *2005 Donor Attitude Survey*, unpublished report issued by Foundations and Donors Interested in Catholic Activities in association with Villanova University Center for the Study of Church Management.
6. R. West and C. Zech, "Internal Financial Controls in the U.S. Catholic Church," *Journal of Forensic Accounting* 9, no. 1 (2008), 129–55.
7. C. Zech, M. L. Gautier, R. J. Miller and M. Bendyna, *Best practices of Catholic Pastoral and Finance Councils* (Huntington, IN: Our Sunday Visitor Press, 2010).

Part IV

REFLECTIONS FROM THE FAITHFUL, THE VICTIMS, AND THE CLERGY

Chapter 11

Response of the Faithful:
Ten Years of Crisis

James E. Post

History is not simply about learning facts. History is a form of memory, and memory is a foundation stone of self-identity. A people who do not know their history, do not know themselves.

Archbishop Charles Chaput

Hope has two beautiful daughters. Their names are anger and courage; anger at the way things are, and courage to see that they do not remain the way they are.

St. Augustine of Hippo

Keep the Faith. Change the Church.

Voice of the Faithful

American Catholics have lived through one of the most tumultuous decades of the Church's 500-year history in North America. The long-term consequences are not fully understood, but clergy sexual abuse has seared the conscience and affected the self-identity of a generation of Catholics. As Archbishop Charles Chaput wrote in describing Christianity's impact on the evolution of European history and culture, "History is a form of memory, and memory is a foundation stone of self-identity. . . . A people who do not know their history, do not know themselves." These words aptly describe the impact of clergy sexual abuse on the faith, practice, and self-identity of Catholics today.

Self-identity has been a critical element of the laity's response to the clergy sexual abuse crisis. A seminal gathering of Catholics took place in early

February 2002. There is no plaque to commemorate that meeting, nor a picture to show the serious faces of the attendees. But there is the vivid memory of a few dozen congregants gathered in the pews of St. John the Evangelist Roman Catholic Church in Wellesley, Massachusetts. What began as a listening session of concerned Catholics discussing the awful facts of clergy sexual abuse became the seed of a larger, consequential movement of lay Catholics that no one anticipated at the time.[1] The parishioners focused on events that collided with their very belief system as Catholics. The criminal trial of Fr. John Geoghan, a diocesan priest accused of sexually abusing more than 130 children in parishes across the Archdiocese of Boston over the course of several decades, revealed shocking facts, including the news that the archbishop of Boston, Cardinal Bernard F. Law, knew of the allegations and failed to remove Fr. Geoghan from active ministry. The *Boston Globe* claimed that Cardinal Law moved Geoghan from parish to parish in an effort to keep him out of court. At each new stop, more unsuspecting children were abused.

The shock and anger generated by these disclosures led to a course of action that has also shocked many Catholics. The people of St. John the Evangelist decided to do *something* to help the Church address this moral crisis and shocking tragedy. Although much was uncertain in February 2002, a few things were clear:

1. Victims of sexual abuse needed help.
2. Priests were involved, but it wasn't obvious who was and who wasn't.
3. The administrative systems of the archdiocese failed to track perpetrators and remove them from ministry.
4. Corrective action was needed to prevent predators from abusing more children.

Ten years later, these premises still hold.

Attendees spoke of their shock and anger, pain and despair. I recall making two observations. First, the situation reminded me of Enron, which had filed for bankruptcy amid scandal a few weeks earlier. We needed to heed Justice Brandeis's famous words: "sunlight is the best disinfectant." The truth will hurt, but we must know it in order to fix the problems. Second, perhaps this was our time to make a difference. The litany of the saints reminds us of women and men who took on the tough issues of their time. Perhaps this was the moment to show our resolve. Ten years later, I believe both things remain true. There has been much disclosure, and many women and men have demonstrated courage in challenging church leaders to make meaningful reforms. But the job is not finished. We need both more sunlight and more committed activists to reform the Church. Scandal continues to stain the moral fabric of the Church, and the need for the laity to engage in repairing the damage is unabated.

The contours of that first conversation shaped what became a highly motivated group of lay Catholics who were determined to make a difference in the way their church—our Church—behaved. We knew this was a fundamental moral issue and that the credibility meltdown we were witnessing required a lay response as well as a response from the ordained. Intuitively, we understood this problem was too big to be left to bishops and clergy alone to solve.

Because St. John the Evangelist was a community of teachers, social workers, lawyers, physicians, administrators, and other professionals, there was no reluctance to analyze, strategize, and formulate action plans. Fixing broken organizations was something that many members had done throughout their professional lives. We were confident of our ability to help the Church and convinced that this issue really mattered.

We were also a *Catholic* community. In our midst were men and women who participated in every form of ministry—Eucharistic ministers, religious education teachers, lectors, social outreach, parish council members, finance council members, and so on.[2] We were mostly pew Catholics, but the group included members who were well educated in scripture, Church teaching, and Catholic social thought. Many were graduates of Catholic colleges and universities; several held advanced (M.Div. and Ph.D.) degrees in religious studies and possessed knowledge of the Church that would help us form a spiritual framework for our work and build the intellectual foundation on which ideas of institutional accountability and responsibility would stand.

The formation of Voice of the Faithful (VOTF) was truly a grassroots phenomenon.[3] Thousands of Catholics from communities across the Northeast came to the weekly meetings held at St. John in the spring of 2002. They were one part revival, one part political rally, and one part group therapy. Each meeting began with prayers that affirmed we were Catholics on a faith-based mission. The politics were practical: how can change be achieved? And the meetings were definitely energizing—empowering—leading more and more laity to believe that they could be a force to fix a broken institution. In July 2002, shortly after the *Dallas Charter* was adopted, and less than six months after the initial meeting, Voice of the Faithful drew more than 4,000 people to its "first international conference." Attendees discussed the *Dallas Charter*, but few believed it was sufficient to repair the extensive damage done to their Church. More was needed, and the crowd's commitment was enthusiastic. Time and events would test the strength of that resolve.

DALLAS AND BEYOND

The June 2002 meeting in Dallas brought bishops, administrators, experts, survivors, and thought leaders to address a scandal that was widespread and growing. Bold steps were needed. One was the adoption of a zero-tolerance policy that activists found promising at the time. It was an idea the media could easily grasp and communicate. Second, the *Charter for the Protection of Children and Young People* represented a new approach to dealing with allegations of clergy sexual abuse. As other authors in this book discuss, the administrative and institutional changes required by the Charter constituted a new way of doing things in Catholic dioceses around the nation.

Two models of change emerged after the Dallas meeting. One model focused on enlightened Church leadership to drive change through a bureaucratic system shaped by centuries of tradition and canon law. Bishops had the primary responsibility for change management by aggressively implementing new policies, procedures, and administrative practices. Audits were to be vital tools in this effort, serving as a methodology to collect data, organize reports, and serve as a basis for specific action plans. Data on clergy sexual abuse had been rarely, if ever, collected in diocesan reports or integrated into a national report. This model called for audits to be published, bringing transparency to Church affairs that was appropriate in a post–Enron environment.

The second change model proceeded from the belief that what mattered most were the outcomes: justice for survivors, protection of children from predators, and restoration of moral values. This approach assumed that the entire Catholic community—lay and ordained—shared responsibility to address each failure and rectify each injustice. This model appealed to Vatican II Catholics who have been taught that all Catholics bear the responsibility for the well-being of the Church.

Ten years after Dallas, these two models of change continue to frame the way the Catholic laity responds to clergy sexual abuse. Whether the issue involves individual settlements, funding for class-action agreements, extending the statute of limitations, or establishment of "look back" provisions, there continues to be a fundamental tension between a leadership-centric model and an outcomes-centric model of change.

The turbulence since Dallas also highlights the tension lay Catholics have felt about all manner of change in a Church that has been buffeted by a series of public issues that cast doubt on the ability of Church leaders to navigate safe passage:

+ Continued disclosure of cases of abuse (e.g., Philadelphia grand Jury report; Chicago in re: Fr. McNamara; John Jay "Causes and Context" study faults culture and bishops).

+ Church closings over parishioner objections and the establishment of parishes "in vigil" in Boston, Cleveland, Toledo, and other dioceses.
+ Diocesan bankruptcies in Spokane, WA; Portland, OR; Tucson, AZ;
  Davenport, IO; San Diego, CA; Wilmington, DE; and Milwaukee, WI, as
  well as the disclosure of financial crises, various frauds, and embezzlements
  across the nation.
+ Health reform debate that produced polarizing legislative battles in Congress
  and divided Catholic support for reform proposals.
+ Catholic "culture wars" that continue to produce sharp debate between tradi-
  tionalist and liberal factions on a variety of issues.
+ Hans Kung's "An Open Letter to Bishops: Church in Worst Credibility
  Crisis Since Reformation," *Irish Times*, April 16, 2010.
+ European clergy sexual abuse scandals exploded in Ireland, Germany,
  Belgium, Italy, and the Netherlands, confirming that clergy sexual abuse is
  a worldwide phenomenon in the Catholic Church.

UNDERSTANDING THE LAITY

Sexual abuse of children struck deep emotional chords among Catholic
parents and grandparents and attacks the psychological bond of love, sacrifice,
and protectiveness between children and adults. The laity also had a psychological bond with the Church, an institution that has been viewed as a place
of safety, protection, and innocence. The story of the Good Shepherd highlights Christ's message of love and protection of the innocent. It has been
impossible for most lay Catholics to reconcile their commitment to the
Church with the knowledge that a priest, pastor, or bishop covered up sexual
abuse rather than safeguard children. Stories of diocesan staffs and lawyers
pressuring victims and their families to remain silent "for the good the church"
have exacerbated this pain and made a compelling case for change.

The Church's need for a "thoroughgoing transformation" was posited by
Peter Steinfels in his book, *A People Adrift*, published in 2003.[4] The opening
sentence reads, "Today the Roman Catholic Church in the United States is on
the verge of either an irreversible decline or a thoroughgoing transformation."
While not specifically addressing the clergy sexual abuse crisis of 2002,
Steinfels referred to earlier incidents of sexual abuse as precursors to what
happened in 2002. Since then, Steinfels's thesis has often framed discussions
among Catholics of the need for and possibility of transformative change in
the Church. There has unquestionably been a deep thirst for change among
lay Catholics and many clergy.

Against this background, the Catholic laity has responded in many different
ways. Indeed, all Catholic adults must search their consciences to discover the

proper course of action given their knowledge, familiarity, and proximity to events. At one end of the continuum are those who have steadfastly refused to believe that their Church and its ministers could have been involved in child abuse. This group, which before 2002 comprised a majority of American Catholics, has diminished ever since. At the other extreme are those who have left the Church entirely. This group is significant, although precise estimates of its size are elusive. In many dioceses, practicing Catholics, as measured by those who actively participate in the sacramental life of the Church, now represent less than 20 percent of registered Catholics. The continued decline in the number of baptisms and weddings in diocese after diocese points to a serious decline in the population of practicing Catholics. The sexual abuse crisis seems to have exacerbated the trends: disengaged Catholics may be the greatest threat to the long-term viability of Catholic civic life in the United States, as in Europe.

Between the poles of denial and disengagement stand the majority of America's 60 million Catholics. They know the Church has been damaged by scandal but remain unsure what to do about it, if anything at all. Attitude separates these Catholics, for there is a fault line among them that separates optimism and hope from pessimism and despair. A decade after the *Dallas Charter*, large numbers of Catholics stand on both sides of the line. Historian James O'Toole has written that the crisis, while profoundly troubling to lay Catholics, has resulted in neither a massive drifting away nor an organized drive to reduce donations or otherwise signal deep dissatisfaction with the local parish and diocesan structure.[5] However, that assessment misses some of the subtle fissures produced by the crisis. Ross Douthat defined one of the polar views in a sharply titled essay in *The Atlantic* (July/August 2010), "*The Catholic Church is Finished.*" According to Douthat,

> People have been driven away by the revelations: . . . for millions in Europe and America, Catholicism is probably permanently associated with sexual scandal, rather than the gospel of Jesus Christ. And, as in many previous dark chapters in the Church's history, the leaders entrusted with that gospel have nobody to blame but themselves.[6]

Charles P. Pierce, a *Boston Globe* columnist, surveyed the state of the Church in 2010 in a lengthy essay titled "Keeping My Faith: What I Believe."[7] Pierce discussed his experience as a modern, middle-aged Catholic and surveyed the larger landscape. The closings of parishes and the all-out legal warfare that has characterized parishioners' efforts to preserve churches that once served thriving Catholic communities are signs of an institution at war with itself. What Catholics long for today, he opines, is a Church that allows seeds of democracy to grow, acknowledging the intelligence and ability of the laity who struggle with their faith as intensely as they confront issues in the secular world. Pierce sums it up in a few colorful words:

> I like my faith in purple—the purple neither of mourning nor of majesty, but the purple of twilight and of morning, the purple of thoughtful pensive times. When I think about my faith, I think about it in those kinds of purples. They suffuse it and they color its edges, too, because that is where my faith is nowadays. *It is a place in me, not a structure outside of myself.* Gold and white are too triumphant, and black is too stark and final, and I don't feel stark and final about it yet. It is a place of purple where days end and begin again. (Emphasis added)

There is no purple for people like Kerry Robinson. Today, Robinson serves as the Executive Director of the National Leadership Roundtable on Church Management (NLRCM), established in 2004. An active Catholic since childhood, she described her reaction to the scandal in 2002 in these terms: "How dare this happen! How dare they compromise the lives and ministries of good, inspiring, selfless people!" For Robinson, the choice was to walk away or be part of the solution. She chose the latter. In her current role, Robinson has worked with Catholic leaders from business and civic life to bring "best practices" to the administrative work of parishes and dioceses. The Roundtable created the "Standards of Excellence" based on best practices in Church management and shared them with bishops and others looking to improve local operations. Robinson's point of view is captured in this passage of her 2010 commencement speech to graduates of Jesuit School of Theology of Santa Clara University:

> These are relentlessly challenging times for the church; to pretend otherwise would be naïve. It is not always easy to be Catholic, let alone to have committed to lives of leadership and service in the church. . . . The best advice I can offer in times of anguish when the institutional church fails to live up to its potential or manifests ignoble qualities comes from my teacher and spiritual director, Sister Margaret Farley: "Always remember what it is you love most about the church, and membership in it. Name it. Claim it. And be radically grateful for it."[8]

Douthat, Pierce, and Robinson form the continuum on which thousands of Catholic laity struggle to define their own Catholic identities. Some have dropped out, may never return, and critique the Church's failings. A few may be as steadfast as Robinson, seeing the good that occurs every day in the name of the Church. Most seem to fall into the great center that Pierce has defined as "purple." Having lost faith in the institution and its leaders, faith has become a "place in me, not a structure outside of me," as Pierce writes. Each of us must grapple with the meaning of the crisis and define our identity and interpretation of how faith can be practiced in a Church that has been so badly stained.

WE REMAIN A PEOPLE OF HOPE

American Catholics have been victims of the clergy sexual abuse crisis. The institution has abused the laity in many ways, yet they—we—have persevered. Despite the darkness of the scandal, we remain a people of hope.

Optimists may be accused of unwarranted trust in an institution that failed to meet minimal expectations of moral behavior. Pessimists may be accused of being cynical and not trusting an institution that is still filled with people who labor each day to bring justice and light to the world. Between those extremes lies the great center, the millions who possess what Gutierrez, Howard-Grenville, and Scully (2010) call a "split identity," seeking reform of the Church they love despite the scandals and leadership failures.[9] This, it seems, is the Christian dilemma: How to keep the faith while working to change the Church? Love of the Church is not unconditional in the way a parent loves a child. But we also understand that we cannot—should not—try to impose conditions on the divine. Thus, we struggle.

Many "cradle Catholics" pray that the institution will find the leadership to accept the community's call to correct the wrongs, reclaim its moral compass, and chart the course for "true north." Those who are converts to the faith have a different challenge. As one VOTF member and leader said, "I chose to join the Catholic Church. I cannot walk away without believing that I made a mistake. And I know that I did not make a mistake."

Optimism rests on such faith. St. Augustine wrote that hope has two beautiful daughters: anger and courage. Anger moved thousands to protest clergy sexual abuse and its cover-up. Courage flowed from the victims who spoke out and from the laity who listened and acted. It sent a signal about the Catholic laity in the twenty-first century. It will not be silent in the face of moral failures and it will not accept institutional abuse.

Ten years after the *Dallas Charter*, what is the status of the social movement provoked by the crisis? What legacy remains in the Church from this generation of activist Catholics? What is the outlook for enduring change in the administrative systems and reputation of the Church?

There are no simple answers to these questions. This lay reform movement is less than 10 years old. Church closings and continued revelations of abuse allegations still stoke anger and upset. But the movement is not widespread and amounts to only a small fraction of the American Catholic population. Still, numbers do not tell the whole story.

First, the survivor community has increased in size and confidence. The Survivors Network of those Abused by Priests (SNAP) has grown and continues to be a vigorous voice of the survivor community. Second, lay Catholics who formed VOTF and other organizations remain committed to justice for survivors and view the next decade as one of an expanded reform effort. Third, a new generation of bishops has replaced many of those who led dioceses a decade ago and failed in dealing with abuse allegations. Much has changed since 2002.

American bishops have learned from the clergy sexual abuse crisis. Bishop Blaise Cupich, chair of the United States Bishops' Committee for the Protection of Children and Young People, identified 12 specific lessons about the issue including two that stand out: (1) The injury to victims is deeper than nonvictims can imagine. Sexual abuse of minors is crushing precisely because it comes at a stage in their lives when they are vulnerable, tender with enthusiasm, hopeful for the future, and eager for friendships based on trust and loyalty, and (2) Despite the justified anger felt by victims toward the Church, bishops need to reach out to them as pastors. Meetings with victims can be challenging for all involved, but they also can be a moment of grace and insight.[10]

Canonists have also drawn lessons from the study of pre- and post–Dallas canon law and procedure. For example, Nicholas Cafardi offered nine succinct lessons that begin with this: A bishop "cannot shirk his duty to investigate canonical crimes."[11]

"Lessons learned" enable an institution to traverse the continuum between continuity and change. Thomas J. Reese, S.J., has written[12] that

> The church must be committed to the task of continuous critical renewal. This is a dynamic process of deliberate self-constitution in which the church holds itself to its ideals and interacts with the world by responding to the needs of the times.

But, Reese adds,

> [In] the history of the church, innovation has rarely come from the hierarchy. It has come from saints, scholars, religious orders, or it has been imposed from the

outside. Historically, it is the hierarchy which ultimately legitimizes innovations by accepting them into the institution.

He concludes, "History will inevitably force change on the church, but it will take longer than many may want."[13]

Meanwhile, the self-identity of American Catholics—who we are—is being molded and shaped every day by the work done to realize the goals first expressed in 2002: justice for every survivor and protection of every child and young person from sexual abuse. We continue to keep the faith and change the Church. One cannot be accomplished without the other.

NOTES

1. See W. D'Antonio and A. Pogorelc, *Voices of the Faithful: Loyal Catholics Striving for Change* (New York: Crossroads Publishing Co., 2007).
2. *Ibid.*
3. See T. C. Bruce, *Faithful Revolution: How Voice of the Faithful Changing the Church* (New York: Oxford University Press, 2011), chapter 1. See also J. E. Muller and C. Kenney, *Keep the Faith, Change the Church: The Battle by Catholics for the Soul of Their Church* (New York: Rodale Press/St. Martin's Press, 2004).
4. P. Steinfels, *A People Adrift* (New York: Simon and Schuster, 2003), chapter 1.
5. J. M. O'Toole, *The Faithful: A History of Catholics in America* (Cambridge, MA: Belknap Press and Harvard University Press, 2008), chapter 6.
6. R. Douthat, "The Catholic Church Is Finished." *The Atlantic*, July/August 2010. Accessed March 2, 2011, at www.theatlantic.com.
7. C. P. Pierce, "Keeping My Faith: What I Believe," *Boston Globe Magazine*, July 11, 2010, pp. 16–21.
8. K. A. Robinson, *Fear Giving Way to Joy*, Speech to graduates of the Jesuit School of Theology of Santa Clara University, Berkeley, CA, May 22, 2010. Reprinted and accessed on August 16, 2010, at www.FaithandLeadership.com, Duke Divinity School.
9. B., Gutierrez, J. Howard-Grenville and M. A. Scully, "The Faithful Rise Up: Split Identification and an Unlikely Change Effort." *Academy of Management Journal* 53, no. 4 (2010): 673–699.
10. B. Cupich, "Twelve Things the Bishops Have Learned from the Clergy Sex Abuse Scandal." *America*, May 10, 2010, pp. 20–24.
11. N. P. Cafardi, *Before Dallas: The U.S. Bishops' Response to Clergy Sexual Abuse of Children* (New York/Mahwah, NJ: Paulist Press, 2008), 146.
12. T. J. Reese, "The Impact of the Sexual Abuse Crisis." In *Governance, Accountability and the Future of the Catholic Church*, edited by F. Oakley and B. Russett, pp. 143–152 (New York: Continuum, 2004).
13. *Ibid.*, 151.

Chapter 12

The Policy Seeks Silence but the Church Needs Prevention

Barbara Blaine

INITIAL EXPECTATIONS

The world expected more. Ten years ago, the spotlight of the world was glaring at the bishops in the United States. The expectation was simple . . . change. The expectation was for enablers to stop covering up for predators, for priests who abuse children to be removed from duty, and for victims to be treated with compassion.

Ten years ago, many were concerned that Church officials cared more about protecting predators than protecting children. Many were concerned that the predators still posed a risk to other children. Many were concerned that the bishops who ignored or concealed the predators were not disciplined; thus, it was unlikely their behavior would change. These concerns expressed in 2002 have proven to be well founded and ongoing.

Ten years ago, the beginning of the truth was exposed. Many priests abused children, not just a few. The abuse happened in every state, not just in remote places. Bishops covered up the crimes and rarely, if ever, reported the incidents to police. Additional children were abused as a result. While news reports announced these truths, most people were hesitant to believe it could be true. Survivors had already known it for years.

REALITY NOW

The most significant development during this decade has come from outside the Church. In fact, it calls into question all the purported "fixes" made by Church officials. In the United States, reports from at least eight different grand juries or state attorneys general regarding their investigations became public during this decade. They make clear that the crisis is ongoing, not merely in the past.

The reports of the investigations, each conducted independently, are remarkably similar and appalling. Each of them uncovered atrocious policies by high-ranking Church officials that allowed established predators to transfer to new positions of prestige and leadership within the Church while parents or parishioners received no warning. Moreover, these reports emphasized the callous nature of such plans in their design to protect the public image and financial interests of the responsible bishops. None found evidence of Church officials having a priority or concern for the protection or safety of children.

Three of the eight reports are presented by attorneys general of the states of New Hampshire, Massachusetts, and Maine. Five are the result of grand jury investigations. They are from Westchester County into allegations from the Archdiocese of New York, Suffolk County into allegations from the Diocese of Rockville Center, New York, and three from Philadelphia investigating the Archdiocese of Philadelphia.

While reports from Philadelphia and Boston are discussed here, similar findings are made in the other reports as well. Ordinary citizens make up a grand jury. These are not individuals with any grudge or agenda, and they take their duty seriously. Jurors pledge to follow their duties of diligence, secrecy, impartiality, honesty, and discretion.

FIRST GRAND JURY REPORT FROM
PHILADELPHIA, PENNSYLVANIA

The first report was the last made public. It was signed and delivered to the court on September 25, 2003, but was kept under seal until September 15, 2005, and only made public on March 29, 2011.

The jurors originally assumed the extent of abuse in the Archdiocese of Philadelphia "was limited to a small number of isolated incidents that occurred decades ago,"[1] but they discovered 120 priests were accused of abusing children in the past 35 years.

They questioned the practices of Archdiocesan officials using "church-sponsored" treatment facilities for the accused where the archdiocese believed "it could influence the evaluation."[2] The Archdiocese sought mental health evaluations "not primarily to diagnose and treat priests . . . [but rather] to provide justification for returning accused priests to ministry."[3]

The Grand Jury determined:

> Based upon all of the evidence, we find that Archdiocesan officials . . . were aware that a significant number of priests presented a danger to children. We find that despite those identified risks, these Archdiocesan managers continued and/or established policies that made the protection of the Church from "scandal" more important than the protection of children from sexual predators. . . . We find that Archdiocesan managers as a whole acted not to prevent the sexual abuse of children by priests but to prevent the discovery that such abuse had occurred.[4]

They made this finding as their term was expiring. With their investigation incomplete, they recommended that "the newly formed Grand Jury should continue the investigation."[5] The Judge agreed and then sealed their report until the following grand jury concluded its investigation. It was unsealed in 2005 as the second grand jury report was made public. No notice was taken of this first report until 2011.

SECOND GRAND JURY REPORT FROM PHILADELPHIA, PENNSYLVANIA

On September 17, 2005, the second grand jury concluded its investigation and issued a 423-page report detailing its findings. The report determined that at least 65 priests had abused hundreds of children. Jurors were clear that the Archdiocesan officials engaged in a concerted effort of concealing and covering up the crimes of priests rather than assisting victims or stopping it from happening to other children. The report said Archdiocesan officials

> . . . could have removed the child molesters from ministry, and stopped the sexual abuse of minors by Archdiocesan clerics. Instead, they consistently chose to conceal the abuse rather than to end it. They chose to protect themselves from scandal and liability rather than protect children from the priests' crimes.[6]

The jurors explained how the Church policy and practices insured more children would be hurt and that the policy regarding reporting crimes to civil authorities was simple; they should not report to the police.[7] They concluded that Church officials ". . . did not merely fail to protect children from terrible danger. They greatly increased the danger and harm to the Archdiocesan children."[8]

THIRD GRAND JURY REPORT FROM
PHILADELPHIA, PENNSYLVANIA

Nearing the end of the first decade since the adoption of the *Charter for the Protection of Children and Young People in February 2011*, a third grand jury report in Philadelphia was released. The results are shocking.

Not only have Church officials refused to make the recommended reforms from the 2005 grand jury report, they have, in fact, continued to recklessly care more about the predators and guarding their secrets than protecting the children. The grand jurors determined that thousands of children remain at risk while the archdiocese allows up to ". . . 37 priests to remain in ministry despite reports that they have engaged in improper behavior with minors."[9] The grand jury said, "We were shocked, therefore to learn how many priests accused of sexually abusing children have still not been removed from ministry."[10]

Also, the grand jury determined the assistance to victims is inadequate and is designed, at least in part, to protect the predators and the archdiocese. They said,

> . . . the evidence presented before us indicates that the Archdiocese continues to engage in practices that mislead victims, that violate their trust, that hinder prosecution of their abusers, and that leave large numbers of credibly accused priests in ministry.[11]

They determined that while appearing to assist victims, archdiocesan officials use information victims disclose to both assist predators and refute the victims they pretend to help. The grand jurors said,

> It would be disingenuous for church officials to suggest there is not conflict between the interests of the victims they claim to assist and their own interest in avoiding criminal liability for priests and civil liability for the Archdiocese.[12]

They give many examples of how the archdiocese misleads victims who put their trust in Church officials and naively assume Church officials' interest is in assisting them.

Church officials even go so far as to trick victims into signing releases of information to obtain records they might use against the victims and then attempt to cover up their misdeeds. The grand jurors saw through their scheme. Regarding obtaining mental health records about a victim, they found,

> The release request was designed, in other words, not only to secure Mark's medical records, but also to release the Archdiocese from liability it might face if it were accused of tricking Mark into signing the release.[13]

The Archdiocese representatives gave the abuse victim the false impression they were advocates for his interests.[14]

One other significant change from previous reports is that this was accompanied by indictments, and of not only predators but also of a high-ranking Church official. The jurors believed that Msgr. William Lynn "put literally thousands of children at risk of sexual abuse by placing them in the care of known child molesters."[15] They also determined that he "showed no interest at all in defending the Archdiocese's children. On the contrary, he consistently endangered them."[16]

Especially troubling about the assessment of the Victims Assistance Ministry is that most dioceses in the United States follow identical policies. Following the *Charter for the Protection of Children and Young People*, the policy now appears to assist in protecting dioceses and predators rather than in healing the wounded victims.

REPORT BY ATTORNEY GENERAL REGARDING THE ARCHDIOCESE OF BOSTON

Early in this decade in Massachusetts, where survivors consider themselves to be at "ground zero" of the sex abuse scandal, the attorney general conducted an investigation into abuse within the Archdiocese of Boston and issued his results in July 2003. It "revealed a dark side to the Church's relationship with its children."[17] Attorney General Reilly reported that the evidence

> . . . reveals that 250 priests and church workers stand accused of acts of rape or sexual assault of children. . . . The facts learned over the past eighteen months describe one of the greatest tragedies to befall children in this Commonwealth. Perhaps most tragic of all, much of the harm could have been prevented.[18]

Reilly made clear that a public record was necessary.

> The mistreatment of children was so massive and so prolonged that it borders on the unbelievable. . . . For decades, Cardinals, Bishops and others in positions of authority within the Archdiocese chose to protect the image and reputation of their institution rather than the safety and well-being of children.[19]

Evidence presented in the Reilly report also made it clear that officials in the Archdiocese were not only well aware of the ". . . extent of widespread sexual abuse of children,"[20] but their reckless omissions and acts placed further children at risk.[21] The report also outlined how officials in the Archdiocese avoided reporting information to police.

This report of betrayal by the Church hierarchy shocked the world. Survivors who had experienced the cruel reaction from Boston Church officials initially felt vindicated and hoped it would trigger a more compassionate and just response to their plight. While the state's statutes of limitation, as well as the protections of charitable immunity, prohibited most survivors from filing lawsuits, hundreds of survivors participated in a process of mediation and settled with the Archdiocese of Boston. Many survivors, originally gratified by settlements received early in this decade, have been compelled to change their impression when Church officials failed to expose documents and have begun to put known predators back into ministry.

HELP FOR VICTIMS?

Church officials claim they minister to victims no matter when the abuse occurred. This may be true for some. But more questions need to be answered about what exactly is provided and whether everyone in need is receiving services.

One of the concerns expressed frequently is whether, in fairness, innocent Catholics who donate should bear the consequences and now have to pay for the damages Church leaders inflicted on victims many years ago. A key point this argument fails to consider is that the Catholics in the pews have already paid. Their donations have paid for defense lawyers, public relations firms, and insurance policies. Most of all, they have paid with the lives of thousands of us—the Catholic sons and daughters who were raped, sodomized, and sexually assaulted. If Church officials really cared about the innocent Catholic parishioners who donate, they would safeguard their constituents' children and cleanse their church by ridding it of predators and those who enable them.

Another concern expressed is that churches will be forced to close their doors or limit services due to the actions of a "few" bad priests. When Church officials plead that the Church has to make cutbacks in order to compensate victims for the trauma they sustained, questions should arise. It is obvious that until the Catholic hierarchy actually opens its books and allows independent accountants to review the financial records, no one but the Church hierarchy really knows whether the Church can afford to help the victims of clergy sex abuse.

Church officials' statements that they have to cut social services to the poor in order to pay survivors have insulted many of us. It is, first, insulting because it begs the question of who is more worthy. Are the homeless more worthy than the victims who were raped by priests? Perhaps more insulting is the fact that it is just not true. Approximately 90 percent of the monies used by dioceses for social services are actually tax dollars funneled through the Church by government. Therefore, it is clear that they cannot cut the social programs to assist victims. The government money is earmarked for the social services.

Many also question why the dioceses should have to compensate victims for what individual priests did. As has already been illustrated, bishops clearly enabled the predators by moving these dangerous men from parish to parish, intentionally and knowingly. That is what makes them liable. The driver of the getaway car is just as guilty as the bank robber. Basic law holds that those who help in the commission of the crime are just as culpable as those who perform the act.

EXTERNAL PRESSURE

At least 1,000[*] priests have been permanently removed from ministry since 2002, and that alone makes the Church safer. However, the only time bishops have acted to remove a predator is when they were forced to do so by external

---

*Figure of 1,000 comes from adding the following: 700 from report issued in 2004, http://www.bishop-accountability.org/usccb/natureandscope/general/2004-02-28-Goodstein-AbuseScandal.htm, During 2004, 43 diocesan priests or deacons were permanently removed from ministry and 66 to lead a life prayer and penance (pp. 13 and 25); http://www.bishop-accountability.org/usccb/implementation/report_on_2004.pdf, 2005 report: 18 diocesan and 12 religious priests and deacons permanently removed (pp. 44 and 51) and 66 diocesan and 12 religious priests and deacons to lead permanent life of prayer and penance (pp. 44 and 51); http://www.bishop-accountability.org/usccb/implementation/report_on_2005.pdf, 2006 report: 27 diocesan and 4 religious priests or deacons permanently removed (pp. 23 and 33) 65 diocesan and 7 religious priests or deacons previously identified also permanently removed (pp. 23 and 36); http://www.bishop-accountability.org/usccb/implementation/report_on_2006.pdf, 2007 report: 24 diocesan and 5 religious priests or deacons permanently removed and 51 diocesan and 12 religious priests or deacons previously identified also permanently removed (pp. 39 and 52); http://www.bishop-accountability.org/usccb/implementation/report_on_2007.pdf, 2008 report: 20 diocesan and 11 religious priests or deacons permanently removed and 33 diocesan and 13 religious priests or deacons previously identified also permanently removed (pp. 4 and 50); http://www.bishop-accountability.org/news2009/03_04/audit_report_2008t.pdf, 2009 report: 13 diocesan and 2 religious priests or deacons were permanently removed and 21 diocesan and 7 religious previously identified also permanently removed (pp. 38 and 51); http://www.bishop-accountability.org/usccb/implementation/report_on_2009, 2010 report: 13 diocesan and 1 religious priests or deacons were permanently removed and 38 diocesan and 12 religious priests or deacons previously identified were permanently removed (pp. 40 and 49); http://www.bishop-accountability.org/news2011/03_04/2011_04_11_United States_Reporton.pdf, for a total of 1297. Considering some are deacons, safe to say at least 1,000 priests.

sources. It is through the efforts of courageous survivors, diligent prosecutors and law enforcement officials, and tenacious reporters who dig for and expose the truth that the predator priests get removed from ministry. I am unable to find even one occasion where Church officials acted appropriately and publicly removed a predator without external pressure.

Church officials boast of how they have conducted background checks and provided education and training to tens of thousands of employees and volunteers who work with children in Catholic institutions, but this is merely common-sense risk management. Many other agencies providing services to children began these types of services decades ago. "Virtus," the education program most dioceses employ, was developed by insurance providers. While it is fair to assume that this makes the Church safer, it is also obvious that most predators who pose a risk to children will pass the background checks. Since Church officials shielded them from law enforcement for decades, they do not have the criminal histories that would appear on a background check.

PROMISES TO SURVIVORS

Church officials publicly claim to offer many services to survivors and family members. Yet services frequently come with strings attached and are not provided to all survivors. Victims' assistance ministers frequently split hairs and refuse to provide services to those abused by members of religious communities and direct victims to leaders in those communities even when they know the victims will receive little, if any, assistance.

Church officials claim that they will pay for counseling for survivors and family members yet require many to sign releases giving Church officials access to their medical records in order for Church officials to pay. Regardless of whether survivors sign the waivers, counseling is frequently cut off after six months. Many Church officials act like third-party insurers, looking over the shoulders of therapists claiming they are monitoring the quality of services given to survivors. Survivors are insulted and betrayed by this type of intrusion. The last ones who should be involved in the healing process for survivors are Church officials.

Even though Church officials acknowledge that survivors suffer over their lifetimes, they still limit the amount of counseling and support they will provide. The determining factor as to when counseling is cut off is arbitrary. A survivor in Philadelphia had attended counseling for a brief period of time and then, five years later, wanted to resume therapy. The Archdiocese refused to pay, claiming she is not serious about wanting therapy.[22] Further, Church officials make clear they are helping survivors out of their generosity, not because the survivors deserve help. Even one decade after all the alleged reforms and improvements by Church officials, survivors still report feeling that Church officials treat them as enemies rather than as victims deserving justice.

POLICY AND ADHERENCE

In response to the media exposure of clergy abuse sweeping across the United States in 2002, the USCCB instituted its Charter for the Protection of Children and Young People. The new policy was weak and watered down. A significant problem was the lack of a mechanism to ensure compliance and no consequence for bishops who did not follow it. Over the past decade, this deficiency in policy has been borne out; bishops failed to follow the policy, and none has suffered any consequences.

The Cardinal of Chicago, Francis George, was one who breached the policy. In 2006, he acknowledged his wrongdoing, saying:

> ... For the many missteps in responding to the accusations of sexual abuse of minors by Father McCormack, I must accept responsibility. And I do. For the tragedy of allowing children to be in the presence of a priest against whom a current allegation of sexual abuse has been made, I am truly sorry.[23]

The admission that he knowingly allowed a sexual predator to continue to work with children is unusual for its candor but appalling in its ironic consequence. George was elected president of the U.S. Conference of Catholic Bishops after he made this admission. The fact that Cardinal George allowed a child molester to continue to work in his Archdiocese was clearly not a factor for the other bishops in choosing a leader. Alternatively, maybe it was. It begs the question of whether bishops appreciate and honor fellow bishops who protect predators and the reputation of the Church rather than innocent children at risk.

The same question should be asked about how the pope gives promotions. In 2009, Bishop Peter Sartain of Joliet ordained a troubled seminarian, Alejandro Flores, who was found to have "young-looking male porn" on his computer just weeks previously. Six months later, Flores was arrested for abusing a boy. Ironically, Flores pled guilty to the charges on the same day in September 2010 that the Vatican promoted Sartain to head the Archdiocese of Seattle. While it is seemingly possible that Vatican officials were unaware of Sartain's recklessness when they announced his promotion, they certainly became aware of it later and still did nothing to discipline Sartain.

Sartain's actions were a clear violation of the Charter. Sartain was not punished. He was rewarded instead. This case provides a clear example of how corrupt bishops remain viable through movement in the Church structure.

Obviously, a more appropriate response by the Vatican would have been to discipline Sartain for mishandling a clergy sex case. As long as no complicit bishop pays consequences, it is safe to assume they will continue to take risks, leave predators in ministry, and thereby leave children at risk.

WRITTEN POLICY: *CRIMEN SOLLICITATIONIS*

One of the most haunting insights that has become known over the past decade is that the pope and his emissaries have known of the atrocities, worked hard to conceal them, and established written policies that permit and perpetuate the crimes. The exposure of this truth has been devastating to some survivors.

In 2003, the existence of a written Vatican policy titled *Crimen Sollicitationis*"[24] was confirmed. This document, published in March of 1962, was sent with the title *Instruction on the Manner of Proceeding in Cases of Solicitation, the Decree* to all cardinals, archbishops, bishops, and heads of religious congregations by the Supreme and Holy Congregation of the Holy Office[25] from the Vatican. It mandated how to handle clerics who sexually abuse children as well as those accused of bestiality and homosexuality. It is shocking that the document exists at all, as it provides an admission that clergy abuse was a problem throughout the Church and that the highest Church officials were aware of it.

Deplorably, the policy does not require that predators be excommunicated once found to have committed sexual violence but, rather, those who report the abuse beyond the Church officials or otherwise expose the secret are faced with the threat of excommunication. Section 11 of the document[26] states that

> ... each and everyone pertaining to the tribunal in any way or admitted to knowledge of the matters because of their office, is to observe the strictest secret, which is commonly regarded as secret of the Holy Office, in all matters and with all persons, under the penalty of excommunication *latae sententiae, ipso facto* ...

Two sections later, the document makes clear that this includes the accusers, too. "The oath of keeping the secret must be given in these cases also by the accusers or those denouncing [the priest] and the witnesses" (section 13).[27] Yet the punishment for the predator is not nearly as serious. The most serious punishment for the most grievous cases is merely for the priest predator to be laicized (section 61).[28]

Some Church officials maintain that this policy has since been superseded by subsequent changes in Church policies in 1983 and 2001. Even granting this, it is hard to find solace in the fact that, for a 20-year period, the official Vatican policy was to keep clergy sex crimes secret.

Of course, the further question arises. If, in fact, real changes occurred in 1983 and 2001, why have we seen so little improvement in the handling of abuse cases by Church leaders over this span? Policy changes may have been made; but functionally, the emphasis on secrecy and cover-up persists.

EUROPE

As the decade following the eruption of the sex abuse scandal in the United States Church neared its end, similar scandals began to make headlines in Europe. It began in Ireland, where reports from investigations there became public in 2009. It was not surprising when these investigations revealed reports similar to those conducted in the United States. The same policy of cover-up and deception is followed by European Church officials. Two major reports from Ireland show it.

THE RYAN REPORT

Released in 2009 after a nine-year process, the results of the Ryan report were appalling. Approximately 2,000 witnesses reported widespread abuse in schools run by Catholic officials in Ireland for six decades ending in 1999. Sarah Lyall of the *New York Times* compared the reports of abuse of the boys to "... the records of a P.O.W. camp."[29] She put them together in a litany:

Punching, flogging, assault and bodily attacks, hitting with the hand, kicking, ear pulling, hair pulling, head shaving, beating on the soles of the feet, burning, scalding, stabbing, severe beatings with or without clothes, being made to kneel and stand in fixed positions for lengthy periods, made to sleep outside overnight, being forced into cold or excessively hot baths and showers, hosed down with cold water before being beaten, physical assaults by more than one person, and having objects thrown at them.[30]

The reports of sexual abuse in the schools tell of widespread horrific experiences.

Witnesses reported sexual assaults in the forms of vaginal and anal rape, oral/genital contact, digital penetration, penetration by an object, masturbation and other forms of inappropriate contact, including molestation and kissing. (section 9.76)[31]

There are many similarities in the Ryan report to those issues found in the United States. Church officials in Ireland chose to protect predators and reputations rather than the children.

THE MURPHY REPORT

The Murphy Report, released in November 2009, was similar. The report found,

> The Dublin Archdiocese's preoccupations in dealing with cases of child sexual abuse, at least until the mid-1990s, were the maintenance of secrecy, the avoidance of scandal, the protection of the reputation of the church, and the preservation of its assets.[32]

Murphy went on:

> All other considerations, including the welfare of children and justice for victims, were subordinated to these priorities. (section 1.15)[33]

The Commission heard complaints by more than 320 children involving at least 172 priests. Church officials told the Commission that they were not aware of the extent of the problem and that they were on a "learning curve" of sorts. Commission members did not believe them. "Having completed its investigation, the Commission does not accept the truth of such claims and assertions" (section 1.14).[34] In fact, "the authorities in the Archdiocese of Dublin and religious orders who were dealing with complaints of child sexual abuse were all very well educated people . . . This makes their claims of ignorance very difficult to accept" (section 1.17).[35]

The U.S. bishops used the same excuse and statements about their "learning curve" when they were caught covering up for priest predators in the mid-1980s when the first cases were filed, again in the early 1990s, and still again in 2002.

The Murphy Commission found that the effort to maintain secrecy led Church officials to cover up the crimes and that was more important than protecting children. "There was little or no concern for the welfare of the abused child or for the welfare of other children who might come into contact with the priests" (section 1.35).[36]

BEYOND IRELAND

Soon victims in other European countries came forward. In January of 2010, Jesuits officials at first admitted that seven boys at the Jesuit High School in Berlin had been sexually abused and then, within days, admitted that more than 30 boys were molested by several priests, and the Jesuits had known about the abuse for decades but still kept predators in ministry. By the end of January, survivors were speaking up all over Germany.

Then reports of abuse started making headlines in Belgium, the Netherlands, Austria, and England, and by the summer of 2010, they were spreading to nearly every country in Europe. Survivors in Europe found that Church officials in their countries also put the secrecy of the Church over the safety of the children. It seems Church officials there followed the same policy as those in the United States, and it was the policy promulgated by the Vatican.

VATICAN INVOLVEMENT

In March 2010, many were stunned when documents were exposed showing that top-ranking Vatican officials, including the present pope, were among those who kept predators among unsuspecting parishioners. Documents from Wisconsin confirmed that then-Cardinal Joseph Ratzinger, now Pope Benedict XVI, had the opportunity remove a predator priest accused of abusing more than 200 deaf children from ministry but failed to do so.

Shortly thereafter came reports of a case from the Archdiocese of Munich, previously run by then-Cardinal Ratzinger, alleging that a predator priest had been returned to ministry during Ratzinger's tenure with no warning to the parishioners. Even though the priest had been convicted of abusing children in the 1980s, he was not removed from ministry until 2010, when a brave victim spoke out.[37]

SUGGESTED REFORMS

Church officials continue to value their secrecy over children's safety. Lofty words and fancy public relations campaigns do not protect children. Only action protects children. Make no mistake: the so-called reforms touted by Church officials are the bare minimum. They tinker around the edges of the crisis without attacking root causes. Their approach makes for positive public relations but little substantive change. Responses to the crisis by the Church hierarchy's response should be viewed with deep skepticism and the realization that every step has been begrudging, belated, and only taken after intense public and parishioner pressure.

If Church officials really want to make the Church safe, they would:

1. Insist that predators be removed from active ministry immediately.
2. Punish bishops who ignore or conceal sex crimes and make clear that any bishop who does this in the future will be immediately fired.

3. Release the names, work histories, and whereabouts of all the credibly accused predator priests and post them on the Internet so employers, parents, and neighbors can protect children.

4. Issue proclamations frequently telling parishioners that it is their Christian and civic duty to report any information they have about known or suspected clergy sex crimes, regardless of when they may have occurred, to police.

5. Establish mechanisms and awards to give recognition and appreciation to whistleblowers.

6. Open up Vatican and diocesan files with information about sex crimes and cover-ups and turn them over to police. Church officials should actively cooperate with police and prosecutors to bring the predators to justice.

These types of action will break the chains of secrecy and protect children today and into the future.

NOTES

1. Pennsylvania First Judicial District: Criminal Trial Division. (2003b, September 23). Misc No. 01-00-8944: Report of the Grand Jury after Review of Original Proceedings dated September 26, 2001 (Supervising judge C. Darnell Jones and District Attorney Lynne Abraham), 1. Retrieved May 1, 2010, from http://www.bishop-accountability.org/reports/2003_09_25_First_Philadelphia_Grand_Jury_Report.pdf.

2. *Ibid.*, 4.

3. *Ibid.*, 4.

4. *Ibid.*, 1–2.

5. *Ibid.*, 16.

6. Pennsylvania First Judicial District: Criminal Trial Division. (2003a, September 17). Misc No. 03-00-239: Report of the Grand Jury (Supervising judge Gwendolyn N. Bright and District Attorney Lynne Abraham), p. 30. Retrieved May 1, 2010, from http://www.bishop-accountability.org/reports/2005_09_21_Philly_Grand Jury/Philly_00.pdf.

7. *Ibid.*, 36.

8. *Ibid.*, 55.

9. Pennsylvania First Judicial District: Criminal Trial Division. (2011, January 21). Misc No. 0009901-2008: Report of the Grand Jury (Supervising judge Renee Cardwell Hughes and District Attorney R. Seth Williams), 119. Retrieved May 1, 2010, from http://www.bishop-accountability.org/reports/2011_01_21_Philadelphia_Grand_Jury_Final_Report_Clergy_Abuse_2.pdf.

10. *Ibid.*, 80.

11. *Ibid.*, 76.
12. *Ibid.*, 87.
13. *Ibid.*, 93.
14. *Ibid.*, 104.
15. *Ibid.*, 115.
16. *Ibid.*, 44.
17. Massachusetts Commonwealth: Office of the Attorney General. (2003, July 23). The Sexual Abuse of Children in the Roman Catholic Archdiocese of Boston: A Report by the Attorney General Thomas F. Reilly. Retrieved May 1, 2010, 1, from http://www.bishop-accountability.org/resources/resource-files/reports/ReillyReport.pdf.
18. *Ibid.*, 1–2.
19. *Ibid.*, 2–3.
20. *Ibid.*, 3.
21. *Ibid.*, 30.
22. Pennsylvania First Judicial District: Criminal Trial Division. (2011, January 21). Misc No. 0009901-2008: Report of the Grand Jury (Supervising judge Renee Cardwell Hughes and District Attorney R. Seth Williams). Retrieved May 1, 2010, from http://www.bishop-accountability.org/reports/2011_01_21_Philadelphia_Grand_Jury_Final_Report_Clergy_Abuse_2.pdf.
23. Falsani, Cathleen, "Cardinal: I Should Have Done More." *Chicago Sun-Times* (2006, March 21). Retrieved May 1, 2010, from http://www.bishop-accountability.org/news2006/03_04/2006_03_21_Falsani_CardinalI.htm.
24. Vatican Press (1962, March 16). *Instruction on the Manner of Proceeding in Cases of Solicitation.* Retrieved May 1, 2010, from http://www.vatican.va/resources/resources_crimen-sollicitationis-1962_en.html
25. *Ibid.*
26. *Ibid.*
27. *Ibid.*
28. *Ibid.*
29. Lyall, Sarah, "Report Details Abuses in Irish Revolution." *New York Times* (2009, May 20), A1. Retrieved May 1, 2010, from http://www.nytimes.com/2009/05/21/world/europe/21ireland.html.
30. *Ibid.*
31. Commission to Enquire into Child Abuse (2009, May 20). Record of Abuse: Female Witnesses. CICA Report Vol. III Confidential Committee. Retrieved May 1, 2010, from http://www.bishop-accountability.org/reports/2009_05_20_CICA/PDFs/CICA-VOL3-09.pdf.
32. Murphy, Judge Yvonne. (2009, November 26). Commission of Investigation: Report into the Catholic Archdiocese of Dublin. Retrieved May 1, 2010, from http://www.bishop-accountability.org/reports/2009_11_26_Murphy_Report/.
33. *Ibid.*

34. *Ibid.*
35. *Ibid.*
36. *Ibid.*
37. Kulish, Nicholas, "How a Molesting Case Emerged Decades Later." *New York Times* (2010, April 1), A4. Retrieved May 1, 2010 from http://www.nytimes.com/2010/04/02/world/europe/02church.html.

Chapter 13

Sexual Abuse by Catholic Clergy: The Spiritual Damage

Thomas P. Doyle

Sexual abuse by Catholic clergy is especially traumatic because of the devastating effect on the victim's spirituality. Unfortunately, the official Church's focus has been on the emotional and psychological damage, failing to comprehend the spiritual trauma experienced by victims.[1] This trauma is grounded in the victims' beliefs about the nature of the Catholic Church, their relationship to it, and the nature and role of clerics in their lives. The experience of sexual violation by a cleric often results in a deep sense of confusion about these key elements of the Church in their lives. With the confusion, there is a sense of alienation from the Church and from God.

Victims of Catholic clergy are usually from devout families with an intimate and docile relationship to the institution. Generally, such families have embraced the traditional theology of the priest as one who represents Christ and, for this reason, is deserving of special deference and respect. The official teaching of the priest as an *alter Christus* or "another Christ" is commonly interpreted to mean that the priest takes the place of God not only in the liturgy but also at all times.[2]

The victim's spiritual trauma begins with the sexual violation by the abusing cleric. It is compounded by the response of Church officials, especially bishops. Most victims do not disclose childhood sexual abuse, and the minority who do often wait years before finding the strength to speak. Disclosure, for a Catholic victim, is especially difficult because of the associated shame and guilt but most often because the victim remains convinced that he or she will not be believed.

Disclosure was often made to a pastor or even a bishop with the sincere expectation that the victim would be believed and helped. Regrettably, the pattern of response that the victims encountered over the past two decades has been quite opposite of their expectations and, consequently, has been a source of revictimization and more trauma. There is scant evidence that bishops or other clerics have proactively set out to provide sympathetic pastoral care to victims and their families. The common response has been negative and toxic. Victims have been told that they were mistaken, or they were provided with thin excuses that minimized the cleric's actions and dismissed the victim's experience. Most often, they have been enjoined to remain silent and to avoid speaking to law enforcement agencies or the media, all based on the promise that the "Church would take care of it." Church officials have utilized everything from gentle persuasion to threats of excommunication. In an ironic twist, the victims have often been portrayed as enemies of the Church, unwilling to forgive and motivated by revenge to hurt the Church.[3] Bishops have generally concerned themselves with the Church's image and with the welfare of the abuser.[4]

The sexual abuse was always perpetrated by an individual cleric. The bishops' defensive and less-than-compassionate response is perceived by the victim as the *Church* inflicting the harm. The Church they believed would help them has, in fact, rejected them, and this, in turn, causes a strong emotional reaction and deep spiritual confusion.

The foundational issue is the belief about the nature of God. Most victims have been imbued with the traditional teaching of God as a theistic being who rewards good behavior and punishes sins. They have tended to identify the *Church* with the clergy and hierarchy and have been taught that to offend a cleric is to offend God. The institutional Church is presented as a *perfect society* and, therefore, incapable of causing suffering or doing wrong. Additionally, some victims believe the priest is incapable of sin, thereby erroneously assuming the guilt for the sexual violation forced *on them*. Some believe God is punishing them for an unknown sin. Others see the abuser as evil and cannot comprehend how a loving God could allow His special messenger to violate them.

The doctrine of forgiveness has been a source of toxic belief, spiritual confusion, and alienation. Church officials often ask victims to forgive their abusers and to forgive the Church for its often-inadequate response as well. Forgiveness is generally confused with feeling some degree of benevolence. To the victim, this often translates into acting as if the event did not happen, and to the offender, it implies deliverance from responsibility for the abuse. Churchmen or others who urge forgiveness fail to comprehend the depth of pain experienced and fail to understand that when victims are unable to *feel* forgiveness, they are revictimized. Margaret Kennedy has summed it up well:

> The institutional Church hinders its own growth toward pastoral authenticity by using forgiveness to push the abuse into the shadows. Churches use the concept of forgiveness to short circuit the survival empowerment process . . . The Church cannot bear to hear about child sexual abuse, so the quicker a child forgives, the easier it is for the listener. What many want is silence and forgiveness is seen as the key to this silence.[5]

Authentic forgiveness is quite a different matter. It happens when the victim sheds the emotional control the abuser held even years after the tragic event and moves beyond the point where the sexual assault dominates feelings and emotions, continuously disturbing the ability to love and be at peace. Forgiveness is happening when the victim controls his or her anger rather than being devoured and obsessed by it. At this point, the abuser and the enabling Church system have lost control over the victim.[6]

Priest abuse differs from incest or abuse by anyone else precisely because of the victim's belief about the nature of the priesthood. [7] The priest is viewed not only as a representative of God but *as* God by many victims hence the belief that God is the abuser.[8] The descriptive language used by the official Church can easily lead a person to the belief that the priest is the closest thing to God on this earth.[9]

The concept of God, the nature of the Church, and the identity of the priest form a devastating source of trauma for abuse victims. They believe in a *theistic* God with human emotions and reactions who actually does things in their lives. The Church is God's special enclave on earth and its clergy are his personal representatives, complete with some of his powers. He shows himself through the priests and bishops. If a cleric is kind, it is often seen as God's kindness manifested through him. Conversely, a priest's anger toward someone can be misinterpreted as God's displeasure, possibly punishment for some wrongdoing.

The priest's power over his victim, grounded in the erroneous belief about the nature of the priesthood, can create a toxic trauma bond between victim and perpetrator.[10] The bond is fortified by religion-based fears. During the grooming process, the abuser develops the "relationship" with his victim, who often experiences feelings of "specialness" at receiving the coveted attentions of a priest. Once sexual contact is initiated, different feelings develop, including confusion, fear, shame, and guilt. In spite of these conflicting feelings, many victims remain trapped because the trauma bond only grows stronger with the passage of time. The existence of this bond explains why victims tolerate repeated acts of abuse or appear be in a relationship with the abuser. The bond is also the reason why victims are often afraid to disclose their abuse and why they experience persistent fear, shame, and isolation. Dr. Mary-Gail Frawley-O'Dea described clergy sex abuse as an especially destructive form of incest since the priest is framed as a spiritual father superior even to the physical father.[11]

The fear is compounded by deep confusion over the morality of the sexual actions. Some victims experience involuntary sexual pleasure from the abuse. Catholic children are taught that all sexual acts outside of marriage are mortally sinful and that spiritual relief comes through the intervention of the priest in the sacrament of confession. If the priest is the cause of the sin, then the victim's sole avenue for relief is gone and their sense of guilt and fear of divine punishment is compounded.[12]

If a male or female victim sees himself or herself as heterosexual and experiences sexual abuse by a member of the same sex (priest or nun, for example), their moral confusion and sense of isolation and shame are intensified in light of the Church's official teaching on homosexuality.

THE SYMPTOMS OF SPIRITUAL TRAUMA

An initial symptom of spiritual trauma is the radical change in feelings toward priests. Some victims report serious confusion grounded in the deep respect and reverence for the priest, which is now compromised by the sexual abuse. The priest was an icon of the transcendent, a tangible way to be in touch with God. The confusion and betrayal often lead a victim to intense anger and even revulsion, which brings even more confusion if the victim believes that anger at a priest will result in God's wrath. Some see their perpetrator in every other cleric—often a painful reminder of their abuse. Many also feel profoundly betrayed by priests in general because no other cleric stepped up to protect or support them.

The priest is central to every Catholics' spiritual well-being. The faithful have been taught that participation in the Church and its rituals is essential for salvation. It is also a source of emotional security in finding God's favor in this life. The only way to spiritual salvation is through Jesus Christ, and the proper place for encountering Christ is in the Catholic Church.[13]

Victims often exclaim that their sexual abuse robbed them of God. For some, the estrangement from priests means estrangement from the Church and its sacraments, which in turn, means estrangement from God. Others equate the abuse with rejection by God. Either way, the liturgical rituals become a source of isolation, pain, anger, and revictimization. For some, they are a painful revisitation of the initial violation and for others, a harsh reminder of God's rejection.

Catholic victims have often been taught that unquestioning trust in priests is equated with trust in God. When a priest-abuser betrays that trust, victims can easily feel that God has betrayed their trust since the two are intertwined. Cut loose from priests, many victims erroneously believe they are consequently cut loose from God. The betrayal by the trusted priest is enmeshed with a sense of betrayal by the institutional Church, the guarantor of spiritual/religious security, as well as a betrayal by the sacraments, personified in the priest.

An essential element in the Catholic Church's sacramental system and educational mission is the core belief in the sacred and unique nature of the priest. It is not an understatement to say that a Catholic's perception of the priest on all levels—emotional, cognitive, and spiritual—is that of a man in whose essence God resides in a special, powerful way. When a priest sexually violates a minor or an adult, the shock to the victim's spiritual and emotional system is beyond adequate description. Most victims, minor or adult, cannot process the reality of sexual violation by a priest, the embodiment of Christ and the ultimate symbol of purity.

ATTITUDES ABOUT THE CHURCH

For many, the Church is identified with clerics, rituals, and the security of familiar Church buildings. Many cannot distinguish between the Church as a sociopolitical institution and the Church as a spiritual community. Victims experience emptiness because they are emotionally unable to participate in the sacramental liturgies and other familiar rituals. This is no small issue because the major life events are all commemorated in the Church's sacramental ceremonies. The emptiness experienced is the void left from spiritual loss. This pain is especially acute when connected to the more emotion-laden life events such as baptism, marriage, and death. Many victims have experienced intense spiritual pain at being emotionally unable to attend the funerals of loved ones or not being able to have children baptized.

Catholics are surrounded by the visible symbols of their belief in God and in God's presence in their lives through the medium of the visible Church. The ritual of the sacraments, the liturgical vestments worn by clerics, the statues, rosaries, and stained glass windows—all are symbols that remind the victim of God's presence in the Church and, thereby, in his or her life. Sexual abuse destroys their trust in the Church's representatives, and it fragments the symbols of belief. Bishop Geoffrey Robinson sums it up thus:

> The power that has been abused is a spiritual power that allows a person to enter deeply into the secret lives of others. The link between the minister and the god can be impossible to break and it can easily seem as though the very god is the abuser. The abuse shatters the power of the symbols of that belief, e.g., the picture of a priest holding a host aloft becomes a mockery. The search for perfect love within that system of belief can become impossible.[14]

The official Church's response to the victims is pivotal to their spiritual balance. Many cannot simply separate their experience with the abuser from their relationship with the Church and with God. The abuser is in a far more powerful position in the Church than the abused victim. When the bishops appear to support the cleric-abuser, the victim experiences further betrayal and isolation. For many victims, the most trusted source of comfort in times of trouble has abandoned them or, worse, turned against them.

Victims initially turned to the civil law as a last resort when they could no longer tolerate the frustration of dealing with the twisted and manipulative response from Church authorities. Although there have been exceptions, for most victims the Church has been an uncaring, unresponsive, and dishonest institution. The deep-seated sense of rejection by God was communicated to victims by the Church's response.

This sense of rejection is intensified when segments of the lay community turn against victims or their family members. When victims or their families have "gone public" and engaged the Church in an embarrassing legal battle, common responses in the community are defensiveness and denial.[15] Victims are naturally bewildered and shocked that laypeople, especially parents, would support a man who has sexually assaulted vulnerable children or adolescents. The disclosure of abuse rocks the belief system of many in the community because it threatens the symbols that give them spiritual security. They refuse to believe that a priest has committed such a heinous act because they *cannot* believe it. There is often a defensive reaction whereby the abuse victim is treated as a criminal. The threat to the security of their dependent spirituality is often more serious to the members of the community than the victim's allegation of sexual abuse against a priest. The reality of sexual abuse committed by a priest and the consequent cover-up by the bishops brings an emotional trauma many cannot bear.

The betrayal by the clergy and the lay community is a powerful step in the complete disintegration of the victim's religious world and spiritual system.

Sexual abuse has been aptly described as *soul murder*. Those who remain secure in their association with God fail to comprehend this concept. Victims, betrayed by the clergy, isolated from the Church community, and cut off from meaningful support, fall deeper into despair. The rupture of their relationship with God appears final. This deep spiritual loss leads to additional anxiety, depression, and hopelessness.

Sexual assault by a Catholic cleric and the betrayal by the Church seriously damage or completely destroy the victim's relationship with Catholicism. They can also severely damage the possibility of finding spiritual refuge anywhere. The victim's life and world, which once included a spiritual dimension that provided security and a source of meaning for the more profound and deeply influential moments in life, is radically altered. The severe disillusionment is not only with the institutional Church but also with the concept of a loving God. The signs, symbols, rituals, and persons that represented spiritual security have become harsh reminders of betrayal and abuse. After sexual abuse, many victims experience something they never experienced before: the empty feeling that this spiritual bond is worthless because the earthly signs of it are all wrapped up in the betrayal.

The spiritual pain suffered from the sense of abandonment often turns into depression or even despondence. The abused person continually encounters situations that require some form of spiritual support such as deaths, births, illnesses, or losses. Prior to the abuse, this support was channeled through rituals and external symbols or from the clergyman turned to for support. However, what was once a source of security is now a source of pain. Frustration and anxiety result from the futility of seeking a source of spiritual assistance and finding none.

Because of the Church's insistence that there is no other way to experience the presence and love of God except through the medium of the visible institution and its ministers, with few exceptions, abused and betrayed Catholics have nowhere to turn. Their religious system is severely limited by this dependent spirituality and, thus, they are unable to respond to the trauma of betrayal and loss.

The breaking point in coping can also come also from limitations and deep flaws in the ecclesiastical system that provided orientation and balance. The orienting system of general beliefs, practices, relationships, and emotions can anchor people through stormy times.[16] Sexual abuse and betrayal by priests and members of the hierarchy can rupture that system and deprive the victim of his or her anchor.

Once the shock of what has happened begins to wear off, victims experience a variety of emotions, often beginning with anger directed at the abuser and extending to the Church leaders who failed to respond in a compassionate manner. It becomes more firmly entrenched as the victims learn that the Church authorities actually enabled the abuser. The anger can be deepest and therefore most debilitating if it is grounded in the spiritual betrayal and resulting loss. For most Catholic victims, the external Church, with its customs, devotions, teachings, and regulations, exerted a powerful control over most aspects of their lives. This control does not evaporate even if the victim separates himself or herself from the Church. The tentacles reach deep into the emotions and the soul and, thus, enable the anger to retain such a strong hold.

HEALING THE WOUNDS

Anecdotal experience with Catholic abuse victims over the past two decades has shown that most counseling situations did not respond to the spiritual trauma. When the institutional Church finally began to respond to victims, it generally offered psychological but not spiritual counseling. Indeed, it appears that Church authorities, all of whom are clerics, were hardly cognizant of the nature and effects of the spiritual trauma. There is little evidence that the popes and the bishops ever offered anything more than prayer or ritual. There is no available evidence that any Church office, from the Vatican to local dioceses, ever put into place programs or policies to assess the spiritual damage and, consequently, to respond to it. The late Pope John Paul II publicly acknowledged victims on several occasions but offered only prayer as a healing remedy. His letters and speeches, always addressed to bishops, never spoke directly to victims:

> So then, venerable brothers, you are faced with two levels of serious responsibility: in relation to the clerics through whom scandal comes and their innocent victims, but also in relation to the whole of society systematically threatened by scandal and responsible for it. A great effort is needed to halt the trivializing of the great things of God and man. I ask you [the bishops] to reflect together with the priests, who are your co-workers, and with the laity, and to respond with all the means at your disposal. Among these means, the first and most important is prayer: ardent, humble, confident prayer . . . Yes, dear brothers, America needs much prayer—lest it lose its soul.[17]

In his first public recognition of the scandal, the late pope's call to prayer was mingled with his attempt to shift blame to the secular society. The promise of prayer for victims is really a long-practiced tactic for distancing the cleric from the person requesting help or relief. In this case, the pope's words provided no relief for victims and, consequently, were meaningless to those for whom they should have provided comfort.

There is no available tradition or font of information about healing the spiritual wounds of clergy sexual abuse. Consequently, one can only look at the damage and its sources and respond to each aspect of the trauma. It goes without saying that any therapist working with victims should be well aware of the idiosyncratic nature of sexual abuse by clergy and by Catholic clergy in particular.

The traditional core elements of Catholic spirituality—participation in liturgy, fidelity to doctrine, and docile obedience to the clergy—provide no solace for a victim in dire need of healing. Yet the Church leadership cannot see fit to listen to victims and search for an understanding and response that comes from them rather than one imposed on them. In spite of good intentions, the official responses continue to betray a blindness to the dependent spirituality that is responsible for the pain and not a path to healing.

Many of the victim-oriented penitential liturgies or "healing Masses" have actually reactivated the trauma associated with the abuse. Even the suggestion of such services, in spite of good intentions, indicates a lack of comprehension of the nature of the spiritual and emotional damage from clergy abuse. Liturgies, performed primarily by clerics, include expressions of regret and sorrow and end up by giving the clerics the feeling that they have "done something" and possibly even satisfied any obligation they had toward victims. Yet these rituals have little if any long-term healing effect on victims, most of whom avoid them. Like the abuse itself, the clerics command the dominant role by expecting the victims to return to the environment of their abuse. The Church confuses gesture or ritual with substantial healing. In reality, the liturgies are symbolic and quickly forgotten, but they illustrate the continuing attempts by clerics to maintain control over the scandal they have caused.

The first level of response should be to the victim's self-destructive belief system. The immediate concern should be the concept of a priest. The victim needs guidance and support in shedding the magical notion that the priest is somehow the personal representative or stand-in for God. The dependence on the priest and on the clerical system needs to be first challenged and then replaced with a deeply rooted sense of personal spiritual autonomy. This "adult spirituality" will bring freedom from the misplaced guilt that burdens so many victims.

Perhaps the most fundamental and radical dimension of the healing process is re-imaging the notion or image of God. Upon it hinges the victim's concept of Church, sin, and even self. It is possible to move from a theistic Supreme

Being to a concept of God that does not lend itself to toxic beliefs about guilt, suffering, sin, and punishment.[18] Such a transition is easiest on the cognitive level but much more challenging to the emotions. Many victims continue to feel guilt because they have exposed a priest or sued a diocese. This is all grounded in the irrational belief that God resides in a special way in the institutional Church.

Once a clergy abuse victim begins to accept a compassionate, nonjudgmental Higher Power that is not under the control of the ordained officeholders of the Church, he or she will be able to move to the level of healing - that is separating the visible, institutional Church from the Higher Power. This should include an examination of the emotional ties associated with the victim's relationship to the Church. Once the variety of feelings is acknowledged, it is perhaps time to cognitively examine the historical and doctrinal bases for the Church's contention that it was founded by God, is controlled by God through clerics, and provides the only authentic source of spiritual security. As they examine the concept of the Higher Power, victims realize that what they have believed in and feared was not an authentic reality but someone else's vision of what God was all about.

RESPONDING TO THE LOSS OF RELIGION

The victim's anger at the Church needs to be acknowledged and affirmed as a healthy response to the abuse. This might be the appropriate time to examine (or re-examine) the radical distinction between organized religion and spiritual security and strength. The toxic belief that God will be displeased because of anger toward the Church must be replaced with a more realistic belief that the Church has actually been a barrier to a secure relationship with the Higher Power. The victim needs to know that the visible Church is not the only pathway to God. The spiritual recovery process offers a unique opportunity for a spiritual maturity that provides the emotional security needed for whatever choices the victim makes about the place of religion or a higher power in his or her life.

AFFIRMING THE CHURCH'S RESPONSIBILITY

The institutional Catholic Church has, thus far, avoided accepting its responsibility for the culture of clergy sexual abuse and cover-up, and until it does so, it will continue to be incapable of understanding, much less leading, the way to spiritual healing. The progress claimed by the bishops is measured by policies, programs, background checks, and review boards, none of which reflect an awareness of the profound spiritual damage done to victims and so many others.

The institutional leadership will remain incapable of seeing the profound spiritual damage it has wrought so long as it adheres to the narcissistic self-definition of a *perfect society*.[19]

The Church's responsibility is directly related to the educational process that formed Catholics from childhood to adulthood. The victims need to see this as preconditioning, as a prelude not only for the grooming for the abuse itself but also for the subsequent guilt and shame they experienced as a consequence of the violation of their bodies and souls.

FINDING AN AUTHENTIC SPIRITUALITY

Most clergy abuse victims did not realize that they had a spiritual dimension until it was taken from them. The final phase of healing involves the discovery and acceptance of an authentic, life-giving spirituality. God or the Higher Power is re-imaged from an omniscient super person to a source of love and benevolent power that is not subject to the human limitations or interpretations of churchmen. An authentic spirituality is a relationship with a Higher Power or an institutional Church that is not a source of pain, fear, and guilt but an enhancement of joy and balance in one's life. Such spirituality requires a healthy sense of self-worth if it is to take root and grow. The path to emotional and spiritual health is often arduous and even bewildering at times. Yet it can bring freedom from spiritual pain and a new and hope-filled future.

NOTES

1. J. Kramer, "The Church Needs a Study of Human Sexuality." *National Catholic Reporter* (2002, November 1), 5–7.
2. *Catechism of the Catholic Church* (Vatican City: Libreria Editrice Vaticana, 1994), 387.
3. J. Balboni, *Clergy Sexual Abuse Litigation* (Boulder, CO: First Forum, 2011). See Chapter 4, "The Road to Litigation," pp. 49–74.
4. United States Conference of Catholic Bishops. *A Report on the Crisis in the Catholic Church in the United States* (Washington, DC: Author, 2004), 96–101.
5. M. Kennedy, "Christianity and Child Sexual Abuse: The Survivors' Voice Leading to Change." *Child Abuse Review* 9 (2002): 133.
6. G. Robinson, *Confronting Power and Sex in the Catholic Church* (Victoria, Australia: John Garrett, 2007), 220–225.

7. K. DeGuilio, "Interview with Dr. Leslie Lothstein." *National Catholic Reporter* (2002, August 9), 3.

8. B. Blaine, "Many of Us Feel as if We Had Been Raped by God," in "Abuse's Impact Can Be Lifelong," by L. Ungar. *Delaware News Journal.* (2002, June 13), A3.

9. Catechism of the Catholic Church. 387 and John Paul II, *Letter to Priests: Holy Thursday,* 2002.

10. J. Julich, "The Stockholm Syndrome and Child Sexual Abuse." *Journal of Child Sexual Abuse* 14 (2005): 107–129. Also P. Carnes, *The Betrayal Bond* (Deerfield Beach, FL: Health Communications, 1997).

11. M. Frawley-O'Dea, *Perversion of Power* (Nashville, TN: Vanderbilt Press, 2007), 98–99.

12. Julich, *op. cit.,* 120.

13. John Paul II. *Dominus Jesus* (Vatican City: Libreria Editrice Vaticana, 2000), Nos. 13, 14, 16, 20, 21, 22.

14. Robinson, *op. cit.,* 218.

15. Frawley-O'Dea, *op. cit.,* 185–190.

16. K. Paragament, *The Psychology of Religion and Coping* (New York. The Guilford Press, 1997), 341.

17. Pope John Paul II. "Letter to the Bishop of the United States." June 11, 1993. *Origins,* 23.

18. J. Spong, *Why Christianity Must Change or Die* (San Francisco: Harper-Collins, 1999); and J. Spong, *A New Christianity for a New World* (San Francisco: Harper-Collins, 2001).

19. T. Doyle, "Clericalism and Catholic Clergy Sexual Abuse," in *Predatory Priests, Silenced Victims,* edited by M. Frawley-O'Dea, pp. 147–162 (Mahwah, NJ: The Analytic Press, 2007).

Chapter 14

A Priest's Perspective on the Crisis

Richard Vega

The news conference about clergy sexual abuse conducted in Boston in January 2002 was like a stone thrown into a pond. There was a quick ripple effect throughout all of the dioceses in the United States. For a time, one could not open a newspaper or catch the local or national news broadcast without the lead story being a new allegation against a Catholic priest. The stories were often linked to the notion that a diocesan official had known of the situation for years but had done nothing more about it than to quietly shuffle accused priests to other assignments within the diocese.

As the details of the Boston news conference began to reach the various corners of the country, there was an initial sense among us that this large number of allegations could not be real. The idea that so many priests had somehow violated the trust that children and families had so freely given to them seemed incredible.

For centuries, the Catholic priest has been told that he is the *alter Christus*, another Christ. The priest is the model, the image, and the personification of Christ to others. Throughout seminary formation, priests are repeatedly instructed to "see that you believe what you read, that you teach what you believe, and that you practice what you teach."[1] At his ordination, a priest is reminded that through the sacramental laying on of hands, the priest is "configured" to Christ.

So the reporting must be a mistake. But it was not.

Now, the image of Christ as revealer was being tarnished by the image of the priest as an abuser.

SEEKING SOLUTIONS: THE BISHOPS GO IT ALONE

The anger, fury, and whirlwind of activity from survivors, victims, their families, the Catholic faithful, and priests reached its climax in the June 2002 meeting of the U.S. Conference of Catholic Bishops (the Conference) held in Dallas, Texas. Media outlets camped outside the bishops' hotel, where protestors carried signs stating that the "bishops didn't get it." Inside the building, the bishops attempted to deal with the unprecedented storm that had hit the Church in America. Amid this activity, all of us waited anxiously for signs of pastoral leadership from our bishops.

The result of the bishops' gathering was the publication of the *Charter for the Protection of Children and Young People*.[2] As I spoke with priests around the country when the document appeared, there was consensus that presbyteral councils and even individual priests were betrayed. It was as though the bishops knew that "something had to be done," but they did not understand they should have consulted with us priests—their closest collaborators in ministry—before they acted. We had been left out of the discussion about what steps to take to address the crisis. Yet we were being held to standards of accountability that the bishops had not established for themselves.

The *Charter*, this course of action, was being imposed upon priests, but there had been no input from those of us whose lives were to be most affected by its creation. This was not a case of priests wanting to "get out" of any requirements on us or avoiding sanctions for the guilty. The opposite was true—many of us saw ways of strengthening the procedures being mandated. Yet we simply were not asked.

The Decree on the Ministry and Life of Priests, *Presbyterorum Ordinis*, paragraph 7, states:

> All priests share with the bishops the one identical priesthood and ministry of Christ. Consequently the very unity of their consecration and mission requires their hierarchical union with the order of bishops. Bishops, therefore, because of the gift of the Holy Spirit that has been given to priests at their ordination, will regard them as their indispensable helpers and advisers in the ministry and in the task of teaching, sanctifying and shepherding the people of God. [Bishops] should be glad to listen to their priests' views and to consult them and hold conference with them about matters that concern the needs of pastoral work and the good of the diocese. . . . and by their advice could effectively help the bishop in the management of the diocese.[3]

Presbyterorum Ordinis acknowledges that no one office—be it that of bishop or priest—let alone no one individual can bear that weight alone. Paragraph 7 continues:

There is all the more need in our day for close union between priests and bishops because nowadays apostolic enterprises must necessarily for various reasons take on many different forms. And not only that, but they must often overstep the boundaries of one parish or diocese. Hence no priest is sufficiently equipped to carry out his mission alone, and as it were, single-handed. He can only do so by joining forces with other priests, under leadership of those who are rulers of the Church.[4]

The rite of ordination to the priesthood acknowledges the unique ontological as well as the working relationship between a bishop and his priests. In the sample homily in the rite, the bishop is to say that "priests are [the] established co-workers of the Order of Bishops, with whom they are joined in the priestly office and with whom they are called to the service of the people of God."

The promises made by a priest to his bishop at ordination underscore the unique working relationship that they share:

Do you resolve, with the help of the Holy Spirit, to discharge without fail the office of priesthood in the presbyteral rank, as worthy fellow workers with the Order of Bishops in caring for the Lord's flock?[5]

The Code of Canon Law then sets forth the manner by which a bishop can seek the wisdom and advice of his priests:

A presbyteral council is to be established in each diocese, that is, a body of priests who are to be like a senate of the bishop, representing the presbyterate; this council is to aid the bishop in the governance of the diocese according to the norm of law, in order that the pastoral welfare of the portion of the people of God entrusted to him may be promoted as effectively as possible. . . . The presbyteral council enjoys only a consultative vote; the bishop is to listen to it in matters of greater moment.[6]

The issue of sexual abuse was a "matter of greater moment" as important as any there has been or will likely be in the life of the Church. It is an issue that directly or indirectly impacted every member of the Christian community. By 2002, it seemed to many priests active in the meetings of the National Federation of Priests' Councils (NFPC) that the closest collaborators to the bishops were now the lawyers who were guiding the bishops through the legal ramifications of the abuse crisis. Priests were sidelined in the conversation. In anticipation of their meeting in Dallas, each diocesan bishop could have brought the collective wisdom of his presbyteral council to bear on the document that would touch upon the life of every priest serving the Church in the United

States. Unfortunately, no such consultation took place prior to the bishops' unveiling of the document in Dallas.

In addition to the development of the *Charter*, the bishops established a National Review Board, and individual dioceses began to establish local review boards to assist the bishop in reviewing sexual abuse allegations made against priests. It was thought that the inclusion of the laity on these boards would bring some transparency to the proceedings and handling of the cases. However, the National Review Board and the Bishops' Conference had strong differences of opinion as to the direction and purpose of the Board. These differences quickly came to light in the media. Again, priests were on the sidelines, and our questions and our concerns emerged.

IMPLEMENTING THE *CHARTER*: SOUL SEARCHING IN THE PRESBYTERATE

The cases revealed in Boston in 2002 were not the first allegations of sexual abuse leveled against Catholic clergy. Before that we priests would hear rumors at our local diocesan gatherings or informal clergy gatherings. In 1985, former Louisiana priest Gilbert Gauthe was convicted of 34 counts of child molestation, yet that still seemed an exception. But then throughout the 1990s, abuse cases gained public notoriety in the archdioceses of Milwaukee and Chicago. In 1998, the case of former Dallas priest Rudy Kos was national news. By the time the scandal erupted in Boston, public and national exposure allowed us to see the bigger picture and put whatever local rumors we priests had heard in our own dioceses in perspective.

Through its member presbyteral councils, the NFPC began to hear that many priests feared for the people in their parishes: Had any of their parishioners been abused in the past? How do we find out if anyone has been harmed? What do I do if I find out that someone is a victim? The conversation among priests at NFPC meetings revealed that many priests were wracking their memories about brother priests and former seminarians, wondering: Have I missed warning signs? Have I overlooked clues? Could I have prevented an incident of abuse or provided pastoral care to a victim but missed the chance?

Some priests thought back to their own school days and wondered if these acts had been going on around them, perhaps involving their friends or even their own brothers or sisters. Others recalled painful memories of being abused themselves as adolescents or children. Eventually, one bishop, Thomas Gumbleton of Detroit, admitted publicly that he had been abused by a priest as a young man. He has since become an outspoken advocate for the abused.[7]

All of us dreaded the next newspaper or television news story that would announce that another priest was accused of sexually abusing a child. Priests were uncertain about what to believe and were often shocked when we heard allegations about individuals whom we knew. The accused were sometimes men we had served with, individuals whom we had esteemed. Others were our contemporaries and peers who studied with us in the seminary, and some were our deceased brothers who could no longer speak for themselves.

These allegations and events took a toll on the clergy. There was a sense of devastation, betrayal, sadness, and loss. The priestly spirit and zeal waned and weakened among the Roman Catholic priests of our country. Some said it appeared that there was a low-grade depression among the clergy of the country. Many of us went about our priestly duties—but as if in slow motion.

Yet most of us, realizing the horror of what had been perpetrated against the victims, felt reluctant and unable to speak up about what we were experiencing. As vivid as it was to us, our demoralization paled in comparison to what the victims suffered and continued to feel. And some of us were deeply afraid that the sight of the Roman collar, a word or phrase we might utter, a gesture we might make, or even our very existence as priests might unintentionally compound the pain of survivors.

There were attempts among groups of priests and our various organizations to try to understand what was going on, to see the big picture. Bishops were not forthcoming about the identity of perpetrators but began to remove priests from ministry across the country. With each removal, there were many questions from fellow priests but few answers from the bishop or his advisors. As we watched our brother priests be removed from ministry and, at times, be sent away, we wondered: Where are they going? For how long? Is this punishment? Is this rehabilitation?

And there were other questions: If the bishop—and we as church in general—had mishandled the care of abuse survivors and their families, how would the bishop—and we as church in general—deal with falsely accused priests? What would happen to those priests whose past behavior was questionable but against whom no accusation had been made? And, of course, what was to happen to those priests who were guilty of such grievous behavior and crimes?

The automatic removal of the accused and the subsequent lack of information about their cases angered most priests in active ministry, as reported to the NFPC by member councils in meetings as early as September 2003. At times, it seemed that there was more information coming from the media than from our local chanceries. What was the truth and what was media speculation?

Of course, there were some bishops who were quite open with their presbyterates. They spoke plainly and truthfully and informed them of the situation. Others asked for patience and more time to respond, but there were some who never responded to the inquiries of their priests. Chaos, confusion, and uncertainty were common in the days following the explosion of the scandal in Boston.

As the bishops left Dallas in 2002 and began to implement the *Charter*, there was a general uneasiness among priests. Guidance was needed in expressing care and concern for survivors and victims. To make matters worse, it soon became apparent that there was no consistency from diocese to diocese as to the implementation of the *Charter* and its interpretation.

CONCERNS ABOUT ADJUDICATION

Priests deeply feared being falsely accused of sexual misconduct. As some priests told us at the National Federation of Priests Councils: "One call to the bishop about me and it's all over." That fear was (and is) compounded by the continued lack of clarity as to what establishes a "credible allegation" of sexual abuse and other concerns such as: What are the rights of a priest who has been accused of sexual abuse or sexual impropriety? What are the responsibilities of the bishop toward the priest who was accused but found to be innocent? And, perhaps the most beguiling question, what is the responsibility of the bishop toward the priest who has been found to be guilty?

Some priests who are under investigation for sexual abuse have complained about the length of time it takes to process a case, especially if there are no criminal proceedings that are concurrent with the accusation. Canon lawyers have complained that bishops and their intermediaries have, many times, been unresponsive to inquiries to gather information or to relay pertinent information about the case to those defending our brother priests. When a response does come from the Congregation for the Doctrine of the Faith (CDF), which currently has jurisdiction for these cases, enough information simply is not relayed in a timely manner to all concerned parties. In cases where the CDF has indicated that there is insufficient evidence to support the accusation and asked that the priest be returned to active ministry, often the decision is ignored in the diocese for fear of repercussions, the priest is remanded to a house of prayer and penance or even left without an assignment of any kind, and the hard work of reconciliation is not even attempted.

Recently, there has been increased concern by priests about laicization without priest participation or due process. Pope Benedict XVI has permitted bishops to seek laicization of priests without their consent or involvement.

The overwhelming concern here is that this bungling is a further attempt to make the problem "go away" rather than an earnest effort at sorting out the truth, seeking justice, and ministering healing.[8]

CONCERNS ABOUT PASTORAL CARE
FOR THE ACCUSED

There are cases in which the CDF has found a priest guilty of sexual impropriety and has ordered him placed in "a house of prayer and penance." There are no known objective criteria for operating these facilities, and practices seem to vary widely from diocese to diocese.

These facilities seem to operate under the radar. At least one letter received by the NFPC from a priest residing in one such facility, as well as anecdotal evidence from a survey of member councils that the NFPC conducted in 2009, raises the question of whether the basic civil rights of the priest-residents are being violated. There are those who believe that there is an underlying pressure for priest-residents to apply for laicization. Just as some sex offenders who are not priests are deemed psychologically unfit and remanded to mental institutions indefinitely, there is a fear that houses of prayer and penance will become facile dumping grounds for some priests. Concerns about the standards of monitoring and availability of professional care lead priests to ask whether this practice may do more harm than good.

Any abuse is reprehensible and cannot be tolerated. Yet there are significant differences of severity among inappropriate acts. Civil law establishes a gradation for offenses and sets forth various levels of punishment for the type of offense. The *Charter*, however, makes no distinction between forms of inappropriate behavior. There is but one punishment: dismissal from ministry and the clerical state. This has been a source of consternation for many priests.

As brother priests were removed from pastoral ministry, another concern surfaced. Once removed, whether guilty or not, the man was on his own. The 2009 NFPC survey revealed that many NFPC member councils questioned the wisdom of this. If a priest removed from ministry is innocent, it is unjust to deprive him of necessities and imperative to restore his name and reputation. Yet little provision is made for this in the *Charter* or in diocesan practices.

An even thornier issue concerns those who were guilty of sexual abuse. What should the Church do with a priest who was convicted, served a prison sentence, and was released? What obligation does the institutional church have to him, especially if he has known no other way of life or occupation than the priesthood? Most important, would we be failing the victims and survivors if the institutional church merely washed its hands of the guilty men while they were still in prison, requested their laicization and then, when they were released, simply said, "This man is no longer our responsibility. Let him make his way in the world and follow the local laws for sex offenders. We will not supervise, support, or monitor him in any way"?

It is common today to read or hear in the news about sex offenders who fail to register in their communities, violate their probation, fall through the cracks of state systems, and even game the system to continue gaining access to children. If former priests are to be consigned to this system, then what about restorative justice for the survivors and the victims? What about reconciliation and rehabilitation for the guilty?

ROME MISREAD THE CRISIS

Another disconcerting element in the sexual abuse crisis was the attitude and position of officials of the Roman Curia. Many of these officials believed that the sexual abuse crisis was an American issue—the result of our lax moral and sexual values and our permissive society. The Roman Curia also seemed to believe that media were persecuting the Church in the United States.[9]

All of this thinking seemed to take a turn in 2010 when the Church in Europe began to acknowledge the sexual abuse crisis that was gripping the continent. While there had been some previous indication that sexual abuse was occurring in the Church in Austria, the issue was downplayed and minimized. When the crisis did explode in Europe it seemed to take its heaviest toll on the Church in Ireland.

After the experience in the United States, one would think the Roman Curia would have learned something from our miscues and our mistakes and been much more proactive in dealing with the crisis. It appeared that many of the same issues that had been raised in 2002 were again being raised. There was an impression that there was no transparency about the subject of sexual abuse and that nothing had been learned from the American experience. With the exception of the resignation of some Irish bishops, the Church was starting anew, and this was an insult to the survivors and devastating to priests.

PRIESTS AND BISHOPS—A DECADE LATER

Prompted by the suffering of the victims and survivors, many priests have questioned whether the Church has failed to live out the values of the kingdom of Jesus in response to those priests who have been found guilty of pedophilia or stand accused of sexual abuse. Have bishops and priests demonstrated the compassion, forgiveness, and restorative justice that the gospel compels us to preach? Many believe that we have failed to live up to the gospel mandate. Cutting off communication with our brother priests, failing to provide pastoral ministry to priests who are guilty and incarcerated, leaving those who stand accused but whose cases are ambiguous or unresolved in limbo—these are surely not gospel responses. And, in the long run, are these the best actions for healing the victims and survivors of abuse?

As the bishops gathered in November of 2010 for their biannual meeting, one of their agenda items was a review of the *Charter* and the *Essential Norms*. A few bishops, learning from the past, sought the wisdom and insight of their priests, using the 2009 questions from the NFPC to organize discussions within their presbyteral councils. As of March 1, 2011, the United States Conference of Catholic Bishops has not issued any public statements about its discussion and review of the *Charter* or the *Essential Norms*.

It appears that the relationships between priests and bishops continue to be strained by the current handling of accusations of sexual abuse by priests. Yet to select men to become priests who are fully integrated human beings and to deal with the complex psychosexual issues of a celibate priesthood, we must enter into an honest conversation about human sexuality. We must have a formation process that allows us to be honest about who we are. We must understand how we are the instruments that God has chosen to serve the Church.

Priests exercise the role of Christ as pastor and head of the church in proportion to their share in authority. In the name of the bishop, they gather the family of God as sisters and brothers endowed with the spirit of unity and lead it in Christ through the Spirit to God the Father. For that to happen, for the gospel to be lived, bishops and priests together need to renew the trust and cooperation essential to the bishop-priest relationship.

NOTES

1. From the rite of ordination of priests, no. 123, in United States Conference of Catholic Bishops, *The Roman Pontifical: Rites of Ordination of a Bishop, of Priests, and of Deacons*, second typical edition (Washington, DC: Author, 2002).
2. United States Conference of Catholic Bishops *Charter for the Protection of Children and Young People* (Washington, DC: Author, 2002).
3. Decree on the Ministry and Life of Priests, *Presbyterorum Ordinis*, no. 7. The translation used here is from A. Flannery (Ed.), *Vatican Council II: The Basic Sixteen Documents* (Northport, NY: Costello Publishing Company, 1996).
4. *Ibid.*

5. From the rite of ordination of priests, no. 124, in United States Conference of Catholic Bishops, *The Roman Pontifical: Rites of Ordination of a Bishop, of Priests, and of Deacons*, second typical edition (Washington DC: Author, 2002).

6. Canon Law Society of America (trans.), *Code of Canon Law: Latin-English Edition* (Washington DC: Canon Law Society of America, 1983), Canon 495 §1 and canon 500 §2.

7. See Sadowski, D. (2009, October 14). Banned from public, Gumbleton speaks privately. National Catholic Reporter, p. 5. http://ncronline.org/news/banned -public-gumbleton-speaks-privately accessed on June 27, 2011.

8. The authority to forcibly laicize priests was announced by the Vatican in a letter to the world's bishops on April 18, 2009, but was not made public in the United States until June 3, 2009. See http://www.catholicnews.com/data/stories/cns/ 0902539.htm, accessed March 1, 2011. While it was said in 2009 that the new procedure for forced laicization was not to be used in instances of allegations of sexual abuse, in 2010, a retired priest of the archdiocese of New York was forcibly laicized for events that happened 30 years prior. See http://www.firstthings.com/ onthesquare/2011/01/the-priesthood-and-justice, accessed on March 1, 2011. For more on the growing suspicion that forced laicization is compounding the problem and not addressing the crime it seeks to address, see http://ncronline.org/news/ accountability/campaign-builds-rethinking-zero-tolerance-sex-abuse, accessed on March 1, 2011.

9. For a recent example, see http://www.huffingtonpost.com/2010/04/01/vatican -lashes-out-at-new_n_521544.html, accessed on March 1, 2001.

Part V

CLERGY SCREENING, FORMATION, AND TREATMENT

Psychological Screening of Clergy Applicants: Keeping Those Who Might Harm Children and Others Out of Ministry

Thomas G. Plante

The Roman Catholic Church, as well as many other religious and nonreligious groups and organizations (e.g., police officers, firefighters), have used psychological testing and screening for decades to evaluate their applicants to these important and trusted positions. They must do so in order to maximize the chances that only those applicants who are psychologically healthy, fit for duty, and generally free of significant psychiatric disorders and behavioral troubles who might be at risk for harming vulnerable others are not admitted to their trusted ranks. The results of these psychological evaluations conducted for the Roman Catholic Church are not used by psychologists (or other mental health professionals) to instruct Church officials (such as vocation and formation directors, seminary presidents and rectors, or bishops and religious-order provincials) about who they should or should not admit to formation programs, seminary, and ministry. The Church generally does not like having others tell it how to manage its affairs, including who it should admit to seminary and priestly formation. Rather, the psychological evaluations should provide Church decision makers with thoughtful, insightful, and hopefully helpful information concerning the psychological and behavioral functioning as well as an at-risk profile of applicants to formation and ordained ministry. What Church leaders do with this information is completely up to them.

Since the clergy sexual abuse crisis in the Roman Catholic Church entered the public consciousness in such a significant way during the winter of 2002, it has become that much more important to be hypervigilant to ensure that those who might be at risk of sexually exploiting children (e.g., pedophiles, ephebophiles) never enter ministry and never wear the Roman collar as priests, brothers, or deacons. One of the best ways to avoid clergy sexual abuse in the Church is to prevent those with predilections for sexually exploiting children and teens from ever entering leadership and ministry roles in the Church to begin with. I, for one, have been conducting these psychological screening evaluations for a wide variety of dioceses and religious orders in the Roman Catholic Church (as well as for the Episcopal Church) for 25 years, completing more than 600 evaluations to date.

The purpose of this chapter is to reflect on the role that psychological screening evaluations play in the Roman Catholic clergy sexual abuse crisis in the United States and elsewhere and to articulate some of the current and future issues and areas of concern that are still unresolved a decade after the crisis unfolded and after the 2002 *Dallas Charter* was published.[1]

PSYCHOLOGICAL SCREENING EVALUATIONS OF CATHOLIC CLERGY APPLICANTS MEANS PREVENTION

While there is little that we can do about clergy sexual abuse in the Church that happened in the past, there is a great deal that we can do to prevent it from occurring in the future. One of the principal components of prevention is to greatly minimize the chances that those who are at risk of harming and exploiting children in the Church never have the opportunity to do so by screening out those who may engage in sexual and other exploitive behaviors. A variety of techniques can be used to maximize the chances that only psychologically healthy men will enter the priesthood (and other ministries) in the Church. Legal background checks, for example, can identify those who have already committed sexual crimes, as well as other problematic criminal behaviors. Medical evaluation, securing a credit history report, recommendations from trusted others, and interviews conducted by Church officials all assist in the evaluation and screening process as well.

Psychological testing is a useful tool in the battery of assessments used to evaluate the functioning of the applicant. Psychological assessment, like any health or medical test, is not completely free of predictive error. Just as not every mammogram, for example, accurately finds cancer when it exists, psychological testing can't predict correctly 100 percent of the time who will later harm a child. All tests have limitations with false positives (i.e., detecting a problem when none exists) and false negatives (i.e., failing to detect a problem when one exists). Yet state-of-the-art research and clinical practices clearly indicate that psychological evaluations and testing can be appropriately and professionally used to examine psychological, psychiatric, behavioral, and other troubles and risk factors as well as to determine whether an applicant is likely to be psychological healthy and fit for ministry.

While individual psychologists as well as individual dioceses and religious orders may have particular tests and processes that they prefer, the vast majority of these evaluations include several important components. These include the following:

1. *Clinical interview.* The psychologist conducts a clinical interview with the applicant to ask questions about his upbringing, history of psychological, behavioral, relational, work, medical, legal, and psychiatric history, the stresses and traumas experienced thus far in life, his coping ability, relational history, and so forth. An examination of possible risk factors (e.g., conviction of sexual crimes, impulse control disorders) or previous troubles (e.g., psychiatric hospitalizations, alcoholism, history of sexual, physical, or emotional abuse) can occur during the interview. The interview also examines the applicant's social skills and attempts to identify any particular areas of psychosocial risks or concerns. Generally, the interview is semistructured, with particular questions asked for all applicants but enough freedom and time to deviate from the interview protocol when unique issues or areas of concern emerge. For example, if an interviewee admits that he has been victimized by child abuse or neglect, additional follow-up questions are offered to help better understand the nature of the victimization as well as whether he has adequately healed from the experience.

2. *Objective psychological testing.* The psychologist usually administers standard reliable, valid, and objective psychological and personality tests that are scored and compared with national norms. The tests most typically utilized include the Minnesota Multiphasic Personality Inventory (MMPI-2),[2] the Millon Clinical Multiaxial Inventory (MCMI-III),[3] and the 16 Personality Factors (16PF)[4] tests. These instruments have been used successfully for decades and have an enormous amount of quality research to demonstrate their reliability, validity, and utility for use with clergy applicants as well as with the general population. Some of these instruments focus on the assessment of psychopathology or personality and psychological problems and disorders (i.e., MMPI-2), while others focus more specifically on personality dysfunction and concerns (i.e., MCMI-III), and others focus not on pathology but on personality style and psychological strengths (i.e., 16PF). These tests offer national norms and so individual responses can be assessed relative to the general population. Thus, one can determine how unusual or unique his psychological conflicts and troubles might be relative to others.

3. *Additional projective or cognitive testing. if and when necessary.* These additional testing instruments might include either projective psychological tests

or a cognitive/intellectual evaluation. In addition to the clinical interview and objective psychological testing, most evaluations might include at least some projective testing instruments. Typically, these might include a sentence-completion or word-association test or perhaps the famous Rorschach inkblot test[5] or Thematic Apperception Test.[6] These projective instruments are often used to enhance the clinical interview and examine psychological themes that may be harder to assess through clinical interview or objective questionnaires and techniques. Cognitive and intellectual testing (such as IQ testing), typically using the Wechsler Adult Intelligence Scale, Fourth Edition (WAIS-IV),[7] or other instruments, are incorporated into the evaluation if and when concerns about cognitive and intellectual functioning have arisen. For example, a young man interested in seminary who has not completed a rigorous academic program at the college level or beyond may not be able to complete the academic rigors of seminary education. Additionally, if the applicant is from another country and culture where English is not his first language, questions concerning his ability to adequately function in both oral and written English can be evaluated by additional educational or cognitive testing.

The results of the testing and interview processes are then written in a report to be sent to the appropriate person within each diocese or religious order (e.g., vocation director, seminary rector, bishop, provincial) for review and use as he sees fit.

Perhaps a useful way to think about the psychological evaluation process is like a physical examination that we participate in regularly with a doctor. The physical examination does not always find disease when it is present. It is a screening process to examine the signs and symptoms of disease by a series of questions asked by a doctor in combination with the use of laboratory tests (such as blood, urine, and X-ray testing) to obtain a closer look at the physical functioning of the patient. The psychological screening evaluation is very similar to a physical examination. If psychological or behavioral dysfunction is present, the combination of the clinical interview and the psychological tests administered will likely (but not always) find it. Once dysfunction is observed, the psychologist can determine if the applicant's troubles would put him at high risk for harming others in ministry or perhaps significantly interfere with his formation to become an ordained clergy member.

Conducting these evaluations helps to prevent significant problems later on. While not perfect in every way, the evaluation helps to minimize the chances that those who have a predilection for exploiting or violating children and other vulnerable people are spotted before they have a chance to enter the formation and, later, ordination process. Additionally, those who either have or previously have had significant psychiatric, psychological, behavioral, or relational troubles (e.g., severe anxiety, depression, impulse control, or thought disorder, addictions to gambling, alcohol, substances, sex, or pornography) are identified. The more the Church knows about the previous and current psychological functioning of the applicant, the better it is able to make an informed decision to accept the person into formation and, ultimately, ordained ministry. It can use this information with data obtained about the applicant from multiple sources (e.g., academic record, criminal background checks, medical evaluation) to make informed choices about who to admit and who not to admit for seminary.

THREE CURRENT CHALLENGES IN CLERGY APPLICANT SCREENING EVALUATIONS

Several important issues and concerns need to be better addressed if the psychological evaluation process will be used in the most productive and useful manner possible for the benefit of the Church. In this next section, I will reflect on critical and unresolved issues regarding (1) culture and language, (2) homosexuality, and (3) lack of communication and collaboration between religious groups.

Culture and Language

Anyone active and engaged in the Roman Catholic Church knows that an increasing number of priests in the United States were born and/or trained (formed) and ordained outside of the country. As vocations to the priesthood for those born and raised in the United States continue to dwindle, priests who are from other countries and cultures have been filling the needs of priestly ministry in the United States. While this has led to a more diverse and universal Church, it creates several problems as it relates to the clergy sexual abuse crisis.

First, conducting psychological screening evaluations of international priests already ordained to the priesthood before their arrival to the United States is not universal in all dioceses and religious orders. Since many of these men were also not evaluated or screened from a psychological, psychiatric, or behavioral perspective in their home countries, an increasing number of priests in America have had no psychological, psychiatric, or behavioral screening at all. Second, criminal background checks, credit histories, and other typical and generally easy-to-accomplish background evaluations in the United States are not possible in many other countries, especially in the developing world where so many international priests come from. Third, even when psychological screening evaluations are conducted, differences in language and culture make conducting these evaluations extremely challenging and sometimes impossible. For example, while some of the psychological tests, such as the MMPI-2, can be administered in different languages (e.g., Spanish), many tests do not have versions available in many of the languages that are needed to evaluate international priests (e.g., Vietnamese). Few qualified psychologists are available who can conduct culturally competent evaluations of men from a wide range of cultures and languages as well. Finally, many of the intimate questions asked during the clinical interview (e.g., sexual history) are culturally inappropriate and often offensive to ask of men from particular countries and cultures.

Homosexuality

The Church has made clear that homosexual men are not welcomed in seminary and ordained ministry. The Vatican released an instruction during November 2005 stating that men who have a homosexual orientation should not be admitted to seminary or to holy orders.[8] It is unclear if the Vatican instruction, released several years after the clergy sexual abuse crisis in the American Church unfolded and just one year after the John Jay College of Criminal Justice published its comprehensive research report finding that 81 percent of clergy abuse victims were boys, was a response to the clergy sexual abuse crisis.[9] Nonetheless, homosexual men are not welcomed to become priests in the Church. Yet research from a variety of sources suggests that somewhere between 25 and 45 percent of priests in the United States are, in fact, homosexual in orientation.[10] Since quality research from many sources suggests that only about 5 percent of American men are homosexual, the proportion of priests (and perhaps, thus, formation and vocation directors, seminary presidents and rectors, bishops, cardinals, and so forth) who are homosexual is at least 5 times and perhaps as much as 10 times larger than the national average for men. This contradiction (i.e., banning homosexual men from ordained ministry yet having a very large number of them as ordained ministers) seems to be unaddressed by the Church at the local and international levels.

The American Psychological Association and other professional mental health organizations (e.g., the American Psychiatric Association) have consistently issued policy statements reporting that homosexuality is *not* associated with sexual crimes against children or other psychological disorders or dysfunction.[11] Empirical research on homosexual men in the priesthood also supports these policies by finding that these men are no more likely to experience psychological, psychiatric, or behavioral dysfunction than heterosexual men.[12]

Psychologists conducting screening evaluations are, therefore, in a bind as to how to evaluate applicants' psychosexual development and functioning if stating that their sexual orientation is homosexual will disqualify applicants for the priesthood.[13] Thus, a "don't ask, don't tell" policy seems to be functioning at the present time. This creates trouble in that a vigorous and complete evaluation of an applicant's psychosexual functioning, maturity, and development is often stymied. Even if an evaluation of an applicant's sexual history and experiences is conducted, it may not appear in a written report due to concerns that homosexual orientation might prevent the applicant from being considered for ordination in the Catholic Church.

Communication and Collaboration between Religious Groups

Although most dioceses and religious orders throughout the United States employ psychologists to conduct psychological screening evaluations for those interested in entering seminary and ordained ministry, there are currently no universally agreed upon standards as to who should conduct these evaluations, what the evaluations should consist of, and how to collaborate and consult with others who also conduct these evaluations. Furthermore, while there are some empirical research studies available to guide psychologists in conducting these evaluations with Catholic clergy applicants,[14] there certainly are not enough given the importance of this task for the Church. Thus, most psychologists employed by the Church to conduct psychological evaluations are operating somewhat in the dark, doing what might seem reasonable, appropriate, and professional in their own minds without any standards of practice or organized collaboration in this area. Additionally, no national database currently exists that allows professionals to organize and analyze psychological testing and screening data of clergy applicants and examine potential patterns of responses that might prove useful in future work. Although many psychological data have been collected on clergy applicants, there is no systematic way to describe and interpret this information.

THE FUTURE

As we move forward into the second decade following the 2002 *Dallas Charter* and this remarkable period in the American Roman Catholic Church history, it is critical that we use the best that psychological science and practice have to offer to ensure that all men who wish to become priests, brothers, and deacons are psychologically fit for duty. While no one is perfect, these men must be free of significant psychiatric and psychological dysfunction that would put them at risk of harming and exploiting vulnerable children and others. Those who have sexual predilections toward children or suffer from dysfunction that places them at high risk of harming children, youth, or vulnerable others should not be entrusted with ordained ministry representing the Church to the faithful. We owe it to the public and to the faithful to do all that we can to ensure that children are safe within the care of the Roman Catholic Church.

While it may not be possible to stop every priest who is intent on harming and exploiting a child, we can use all of the state-of-the-art tools that are available to us to minimize the risk. These include a thoughtful psychological evaluation in addition to appropriate background checks used in a professional and confidential manner. Since the best predictor of future behavior is past behavior, we must be careful to make sure that those who have engaged in any behaviors that might harm children and vulnerable others are not able to secure the trust of and access to these persons. If we are to prevent priests and other clergy from potentially harming children and others under their pastoral care, we must be sure that they are as psychologically healthy as possible and, thus, fit for duty. We can do this. We must do this. How can we not do this?

NOTES

1. United States Conference of Catholic Bishops, *Charter for the Protection of Children and Young People* (Washington, DC: Author, 2002).
2. A. Tellegen and B. Kraemmer, *Minnesota Multiphasic Personality Inventory (MMPI-2): Manual for Administration and Scoring* (Minneapolis: University of Minnesota Press, 1989).
3. T. Millon, C. Millon, R. Davis and S. Grossman, *Manual for the Millon Clinical Inventory-III* (Minneapolis, MN: Pearson, 2008).
4. R. B. Cattell, A. K. Cattell and H. E. P. Cattell, *Sixteen Personality Factors Questionnaire* (5th ed.) (Champaign, IL: Institute for Personality and Ability Testing, 2002).
5. J. E. Exner, *The Rorschach: A Comprehensive System: Vol. 1. Basic Foundations* (4th ed.) (New York: Wiley, 2003).
6. H. A. Murray, *Thematic Apperception Test* (Cambridge, MA: Harvard University Press, 1943).
7. D. Wechsler, *Wechsler Adult Intelligence Scale* (4th ed.) (Minneapolis, MN: Pearson Assessments, 2008).

8. Congregation for Catholic Education, *Instruction Concerning the Criteria for the Discernment of Vocations with Regard to Persons with Homosexual Tendencies in View of Their Admission to the Seminary and to Holy Orders* (Vatican City: Author, 2005).

9. John Jay College of Criminal Justice, *The Nature and Scope of the Problem of Sexual Abuse of Minors by Catholic Priests and Deacons in the United States, 1950–2002* (New York: Author, 2004).

10. Plante, T. G., "Homosexual Applicants to the Priesthood: How Many and Are They Psychologically Healthy?" *Pastoral Psychology* 55 (2007): 495–498.

11. American Psychological Association Division 44/Committee on Lesbian, Gay, and Bisexual Concerns Joint Task Force on Guidelines for Psychotherapy with Lesbian, Gay, and Bisexual Clients, "Guidelines for Psychotherapy with Lesbian, Gay, and Bisexual Clients." *American Psychologist* 55 (2000): 1440–1451; American Psychological Association, "Ethical Principles of Psychologists and Code of Conduct." *American Psychologist* 57 (2002): 1060–1073; R. E. Fox, "Proceedings of the American Psychological Association, Incorporated, for the year 1987: Minutes of the Annual Meeting of the Council of Representatives." *American Psychologist* 43 (1988): 508–531.

12. Plante, "Homosexual Applicants to the Priesthood."

13. T. G. Plante, "Ethical Considerations for Psychologists Screening Applicants for the Priesthood in the Catholic Church: Implications of the Vatican Instruction on Homosexuality." *Ethics and Behavior* 17 (2007): 131–136.

14. Plante, T. G., "Ethical Considerations for Psychologists"; T. G. Plante, "A Collaborative Relationship between Professional Psychology and the Roman Catholic Church: A Case Example and Suggested Principles for Success." *Professional Psychology: Research and Practice* 30 (1999): 541–546.

Chapter 16

Seminary Formation in Light of the Sexual Abuse Crisis: *Pastores Dabo Vobis*

Gerald D. Coleman

In their chapter on the incidence of clerical sexual abuse, Terry, Schuth, and Smith point out that the role priestly formation played in the sexual abuse crisis is "crucial." They demonstrate that most of the allegations of abuse were against priests who attended seminaries prior to the 1970s. In those years, seminarians had minimal human and sexual formation, coupled with little preparedness to understand and resist inappropriate sexual impulses. These seminarians lacked understanding of victimization and their own future positions of power. These problems allowed the crisis to escalate.[1]

At the close of the Year of the Priest (June 2010), Pope Benedict XVI echoed this same assessment and vowed "to make every possible effort in priestly formation to prevent anything of the kind from happening again." A seminal document that lays out the blueprint for an enlightened seminary formation is *Pastores Dabo Vobis* [*I Will Give You Shepherds*] (*PDV*), the 1992 apostolic exhortation of Pope John Paul II. This is the most influential document on priestly formation in recent times.[2] While its content was referenced in the 1992 *Program of Priestly Formation* (*PPF*) by the United States Conference of Catholic Bishops (USCCB), it only became fully incorporated into the fifth edition of the *PPF* in 2006.

This exhortation was issued before public awareness of the clergy sex abuse crisis in the United States, but it has since informed every official document and response to the crisis. Chapter 5 lays out the four pillars that form the cornerstone of all priestly formation: human, spiritual, intellectual, and pastoral. While each of these anchors is critical and interrelated, *PPV* emphasizes that "The whole work of priestly formation would be deprived of its necessary foundation if it lacked a suitable human formation."[3] This point is underscored in the exhortation's note of *special importance*:

> In order that his ministry may be humanly as credible as possible, it is impor-
> tant that the priest should mold his human personality in such a way that it
> becomes a bridge and not an obstacle for others in their meeting with Jesus
> Christ ... (T)he priest should be able to know the depths of the human heart,
> to perceive difficulties and problems, to make meeting and dialogue easy, to cre-
> ate trust and cooperation, to express serene and objective judgments. (no. 43)

PDV enunciates a series of human qualities that must be cultivated by a seminarian, including the capacity to relate to others and affective maturity, through an education for sexuality, true friendship, and an authentic depth of obedience to moral obligations. It is now important to situate certain events that took place before the issuance of major magisterial documents about priestly formation.

BACKGROUND

In early 1992, the president of the USCCB set forth five guidelines on how bishops might handle the problem of clerical sex abuse.[4] Within a year, the bishops brought together a number of experts to discuss this issue. This effort culminated in the formation of a Joint Study Commission with Vatican offi-
cials. In a letter to the U.S. bishops in 1993, John Paul II wrote that the clergy sex abuse problem was the result of an "irresponsibly permissive society, ... hyper-inflated with sexuality." He named American society as the "real culprit" behind the crisis and said at World Youth Day in August 1993 that " ... at a time when all institutions are suspect, the Church has not escaped reproach."[5]

The U.S. bishops established reviews of diocesan policies on sexual victimi-
zation, descriptions of treatment centers, ways to care for victims/survivors, and reporting mechanisms. The bishops attempted to deal with the *effects* of clerical sex abuse, but neither they nor the Vatican dealt with its root *causes*. However, as clergy sex scandals spread to Ireland, Germany, Canada, Australia, Britain, France, Mexico, Poland, and Oceania, the notion that a permissive American society was responsible for clergy sex abuse began to lose credibility, prompting John Paul II to ask forgiveness for the institutional Church in so far as it was culpable for child sex abuse. In 2001, the Vatican issued two documents defining child sex abuse as a "grave offense" against Church law and issued guidelines on how to deal with the problem.[6]

In 2002, John Paul's spokesman, Joaquin Navarro-Valls, shifted the blame of the sexual crisis from American society in general to homosexuals in particular. He said that "People with these inclinations just cannot be ordained."[7] The Pope subsequently summoned to a Vatican meeting all the American cardinals, the leadership of the U.S. bishops, and the heads of several offices of the Holy See. By convening this summit (April 23–24, 2002), the Vatican sent a strong signal that it viewed the clergy sex abuse scandal as a grave crisis for the entire church.

In his 2002 Holy Thursday letter to priests, the Pope wrote of sin, compassion, penitence, and forgiveness, emphasizing the need for priests to be "true ministers of mercy." He claimed that the sex abuse scandal casts a "dark shadow of suspicion . . . over all the fine priests who perform their ministry with honesty and integrity." To those priests involved in the sexual abuse of children, the Pope held out his trust "in the healing power of grace" and the necessary search for holiness. As the U.S. bishops prepared to meet for their biannual meeting in Dallas, they were urged by the Vatican to avoid rushing to judgment and to consider all proposals calmly and without emotion or anger.[8]

MAJOR RESPONSES

Meeting of John Paul II and the Cardinals of the United States

When the U.S. cardinals and the leadership of the USCCB met in 2002 with the pope and various Vatican officials, John Paul II expressed his grief that the sex scandal was caused by priests and religious.[9] This fact makes "the Church herself . . . viewed with distrust, and many are offended at the way in which the Church's leaders are perceived to have acted in this matter." The Pope called the crisis "by every standard wrong and rightly considered a crime by society; it is also an appalling sin in the eyes of God." He professed his "profound sense of solidarity and concern" for the victims and their families.

Saying that "a great work of art may be blemished, but its beauty remains," the Pope encouraged bishops and priests not to forget the power of Christian conversion and the possibility of a "radical decision to turn away from sin and back to God." He added, however, that "there is no place in the priesthood and religious life for those who would harm the young." He named "a deep-seated crisis of sexual morality" as the primary "symptom" of the abuse problem affecting the church and concluded that this crisis "must lead to a holier priesthood."

The day following this meeting, the U.S. cardinals and the USCCB leadership issued a communiqué with six proposals, one of which was "an Apostolic Visitation of seminaries and religious houses of formation, giving special attention to their admission requirements and the need for them to teach Catholic moral doctrine in its integrity."[10]

VATICAN SYMPOSIUM ON PEDOPHILIA AND SEMINARY ADMISSION GUIDELINES

On April 2 through 5, 2003, under the auspices of the Pontifical Academy for Life, the Vatican sponsored a meeting featuring eight of "the most qualified experts on the theme, including specialists in recuperative therapy of people affected by this problem."[11] The eight experts included one American, Dr. Martin Kafka, professor at McLean Psychiatric Hospital in Belmont, Massachusetts, the teaching hospital for Harvard University. Homosexuality was described as a "risk factor" for the sexual victimization of children since the majority of cases in the American crisis involved males between ages 14 and 17 "victimized by adult gay priests." The symposium members emphasized, however, that homosexuality does not *cause* abuse because a risk factor is not a cause. The experts used the analogy that priests who abuse minors tend to do so five to seven years after ordination, making "being recently ordained" another risk factor. But this does not mean that this factor causes abuse any more than homosexuality does.

Three points emerged regarding zero-tolerance policies: the complexity of individual cases, the risk factor of stress when a priest is stripped of his livelihood and support system, and the danger of letting an abuser loose on the community without support and assistance.

Following this symposium, reputable sources indicated that the Congregation for Catholic Education was working on its third draft of a document on the admission of homosexuals to Catholic seminaries. The original impetus for this document came from some American bishops, who urged the Vatican to take a strong stand against the admission of homosexuals in the wake of the U.S. sex abuse crisis. It is said that John Paul II expressed a generally negative view about admitting men with a homosexual tendency to the seminary and houses of formation.[12]

Priesthood Candidates and Homosexuality

The instruction, *Priesthood Candidates and Homosexuality*, was issued in 2005 by the Congregation for Catholic Education.[13] The document points out that "the present instruction is . . . made more urgent by the current situation"—a reference to the clergy sex abuse of children. The document reiterates previous Vatican teaching that "homosexual tendencies are found in a number of men and women," and these tendencies are "objectively disordered." The Congregation indicates that three categories of men cannot be admitted to the seminary or holy orders: those who practice homosexuality, those who have deep-seated homosexual tendencies, and those who support the gay culture.[14] One exception is given: the case where homosexual tendencies represent only a "transitory problem—for example, . . . an adolescence not yet superseded." However, this problem must be "clearly overcome" at least three years before ordination to the diaconate.[15]

The instruction highlights the importance of "human formation as the necessary foundation of all formation." Affective maturity is the bedrock of authentic human development. The Congregation places the "primary responsibility" for a seminarian's formation on the candidate himself and stresses that it is "dishonest for a candidate to hide his own homosexuality in order to proceed, despite everything, toward ordination." Such a posture is named "a deceitful attitude."

GUIDELINES FOR THE USE OF PSYCHOLOGY IN THE ADMISSION AND FORMATION OF CANDIDATES FOR THE PRIESTHOOD

In 2008, the Congregation for Catholic Education issued guidelines about the use of psychology in seminary admissions and formation.[16] The central point of *PDV* is again restated: the human dimension is the foundation of all formation, and the seminarian and priest must be a bridge and not an obstacle for others in their meeting with Jesus. Citing the Congregation's earlier document *A Guide to Formation in Priestly Celibacy*, the guidelines admit that errors have been made in discerning priestly vocations and, too often, "psychological defects, sometimes of a pathological kind" reveal themselves only after priestly ordination. Detecting these defects earlier is the goal in order to "avoid many tragic experiences."

Seminary formators, for example, spiritual directors and advisors, under the overall guidance of the rector or religious superior, play the necessary and critical role in the candidate's formation. However, recourse to experts in psychology is seen as useful for evaluating a candidate's "psychic state" and "human dispositions," although these experts can only offer formators "an opinion" about a candidate's diagnosis.

The guidelines indicate that today's candidates for the seminary are affected by "an emerging mentality characterized by consumerism, instability in family and social relationships, moral relativism, erroneous visions of sexuality, the precariousness of choices and a systematic negation of values especially by the media." These factors have left the candidate with "psychological wounds." In addressing these concerns, the Congregation judges that "therapy should be carried out before [a candidate] is admitted to the seminary or house of formation." It is also necessary to "evaluate [a candidate's] sexual orientation."

Citing its 1996 *Instruction to the Episcopal Conferences on the Admission to the Seminary of Candidates coming from other Seminaries or Religious Families*, the Congregation insists that

> It is contrary to the norms of the church to admit to the seminary or to the house of formation persons who have already left or, *a fortiori*, have been dismissed from other seminaries or houses of formation without first collecting the due information from their respective bishops or major superiors, especially concerning the causes of the dismissal.

REPORT ON VATICAN VISITATION OF U.S. SEMINARIES

The mandated visitation of seminaries and houses of formation was initiated in 2002 by the U.S. cardinals and the officers of the USCCB, and all apostolic visitators were approved by Vatican authorities. The visitations commenced in 2005, and the Congregation for Catholic Education released its report on these visitations in December 2009.[17] The report admits that its findings can claim only to be a snapshot of the seminary at the time of the visit, and all the problems were likely not unearthed. The visitators were all bishops and priests working under the direction of Archbishop Edwin R. O'Brien, then archbishop of the military ordinariate. Laypersons attached to these visits were considered resource persons who had no direct voice in the drawing up of the reports.

The final report lists 10 general conclusions that subsequently have affected seminaries and houses of formation:

1. In some seminaries, the church's doctrine on the distinction between ministerial and hierarchical priesthood needs to be emphasized more. It is also noted that problems can arise when seminaries offer theological education to nonseminarians.
2. Almost universally, bishops and major superiors demonstrate interest in and support of their seminaries, which is critical since "there is no institute more important in the diocese or province than the center for priestly and

religious formation." The "most encouraging" result is the fact that seminary superiors are good and holy men who "genuinely are doing all they can to prepare men well for the priesthood." Rectors in particular are pointed out as having "an irreplaceable role." When the rector is weak, so is the fabric of the seminary. It is an error when the rector is travelling too much, for example, for fundraising purposes. The report significantly indicates that the "formation faculty must be priests," and the majority of the teaching faculty must be priests. When disharmony was apparent, it was "almost always due to one or more educators being less than faithful to the magisterium of the church." Laity should never be routinely permitted to enroll in classes and should not be admitted to seminary living spaces, such as the dining room, chapel, library, and living quarters.

3. Admission to a seminary or house of formation affirms only that the candidate has potential for ordination. Only subsequent years of education/formation can ascertain whether the candidate can be ordained. The propedeutic period as envisioned in *PDV* is almost nowhere to be found in diocesan seminaries, and bishops must review this fact. Bishops should not delegate too much of their responsibility for acceptance of candidates to others, especially their vocation directors. It is a good thing that candidates are scrutinized twice before admission, once by the diocese and once by the seminary. The seminary must never lower its standards due to a lack of vocations.

4. Seminarians are universally found to be generous, intelligent, full of zeal, pious, faithful to prayer, and loyal to the church's magisterium—even though many are weighed down from "the problems of our time," for example, coming from broken families. In the past, some seminarians evidenced "difficulties in the area of morality," and this usually meant "homosexual behavior." The instruction on the admission of candidates with homosexual tendencies is underscored.

5. Almost all seminaries emphasize the human development called for in *PDV*. The external forum formation advisors assist seminarians in addressing the four pillars of priestly formation. At times, however, some seminarians have been "obliged to divulge matter that belongs to the internal forum." It is important to monitor seminarians in their use of alcohol, a curfew, and the Internet. Bishops and seminary authorities should put more importance on how seminarians spend their summers. The internal forum needs to be more carefully safeguarded.

6. In diocesan seminaries, liturgical norms are generally obeyed, although this is not always the case at religious centers of formation. All seminaries should celebrate lauds and vespers daily, as well as the daily celebration of the Eucharist (including weekends). The Sacrament of Reconciliation should be celebrated twice monthly, and there should be in place the appropriate recitation of the rosary, novenas, and Stations of the Cross.

7. Academic standards are generally high, and seminarians take their studies seriously. There is now the requirement of a minimum of 30 credits in philosophy. Too many electives create *lacunae* in the teaching of Mariology and patristics. It is rare for seminarians to have a proper grounding in Latin. Some theology teachers demonstrate reservations about areas of magisterial teaching, especially in the field of moral theology. In some schools of theology run by religious, dissent is "widespread." Ordination is restricted to men alone.

8. Most seminaries have a well-rounded program of pastoral formation, even though there are a number of priests who mentor seminarians who lack this training. "Programs of pastoral formation should be under the direction of a priest."

9. Nonordained and non–Catholic faculty members are barred from voting on a seminarian for Holy Orders. At times, seminarians have been ordained over reasoned objections from seminary superiors.

10. When possible, the seminary should provide ongoing formation for the newly ordained.

In its general conclusion, the Congregation points out three positive facts: there is much more stability in U.S. seminaries than in the 1990s, the overall judgment of the visitation is positive, and diocesan seminaries are generally healthy.

PROGRAM OF PRIESTLY FORMATION

The fifth edition of the *Program of Priestly Formation (PPF)* was promulgated in August of 2006.[18] The Foreword mentions that this edition is "greatly influenced by the Apostolic Exhortation of John Paul II, *Pastores Dabo Vobis* (1992)," and notes the "special benefit" of increased requirements for philosophical studies and the lengthening of the pre-theology period. This fifth edition has also been influenced by the series of voluntary seminary visitations that have been taking place since 1995.

The PPF carefully spells out admission requirements and standards and stresses the need for "sufficient human formation for admission." The seminary or house of formation is not to be understood or seen as "the place for long term therapy or remedial work," as this must take place prior to admission. Vatican documents are cited as authority for background checks for candidates and how to regard the admission of "candidates with same-sex experiences and/or inclinations . . . "

Formation is not to be understood as equivalent to a secular sense of schooling but, rather, a "foremost cooperation with the grace of God." In order to have a proper understanding of a "solid moral character," the PPF lists a number of human qualities that must be evident in a candidate, for example, a free, prudent, and discerning person, a man of communion who demonstrates authentic affective maturity and who "respects, cares for, and has vigilance over his body."

Of special import, this edition gives clear norms that must guide a seminarian's progress in his human, spiritual, intellectual, and pastoral formation (no. 280 ff.). In light of norms set out in the report on the Vatican Visitation of Seminaries, the PPF states that "As a general rule, professors for significant portions of the course of studies in the major theological disciplines ought to be priests" (no. 347). This edition also contains an important addendum regarding norms about readmission of seminarians to a seminary or house of formation.

SEMINARY RESPONSES

Even before the outbreak of the sex abuse crisis, U.S. seminaries were beginning to strengthen admission standards and put into place stronger education and formation programs about human sexuality. Interviewing psychologists were given clear outlines of questions and concerns, and seminary admission committees took the written results from these interviews seriously without making them the only data considered for admission. After the abuse crisis, seminaries generally pursued the topic of sexual abuse and those operated by the Sulpicians expended great efforts in publishing materials for seminarians and faculty regarding sexual abuse. Examples of these publications include *Policy for Sulpicians on the Sexual Abuse of Minors*, *Policies and Procedures Regarding Child Abuse and Harassment*, *Policy Regarding the Proper Use of the Internet*, *Formation in Sexuality and Priestly Celibacy*, and *The Mentoring and Advising of Seminarians*.

Most seminaries mandate workshops on sex abuse and sexual harassment every year for faculty, students, and staff, as well as instruction on the reporting laws of the state where the seminary exists. Seminarians are required to watch the online course *Shield the Vulnerable*, a program that helps the viewer "recognize, report, and prevent abuse." Fingerprinting is required in the application process. Rectors of seminaries give regular conferences to the seminary community on sexual abuse and sexual harassment, and the academic program normally offers courses in these subjects.

The vocation director for the Archdiocese of San Francisco reports that

every year in a seminarian's formation, he will receive information about what constitutes child abuse and sexual harassment, how it can be identified in a victim, the criminality of such behavior on the part of the perpetrator, the emotional and spiritual harm experienced by victims and the reality of the scandal caused to the faithful when a priest violates his vow of celibacy.

POPE BENEDICT XVI

In addition to personal meetings with clergy sex abuse survivors, Pope Benedict XVI has addressed this crisis on several occasions. The Pope's recurring message can be discerned in his comments to reporters aboard the papal plane en route from Rome to Lisbon during May 2010 trip to Portugal:[19]

> attacks against the pope or the church don't come just from outside the church. The suffering of the church also comes from within the church, because sin exists in the church . . . The greatest persecution of the church doesn't come from enemies on the outside, but is born in sin within the church. The church has a deep need to re-learn penance, to accept purification, to learn on the one hand forgiveness but also the necessity of justice.

He repeated this assertion in his homily at the Vatican on June 29, 2010.[20]

In his Letter to Catholics of Ireland,[21] the Pope evaluated the clergy sex abuse crisis in general.[22] He referenced the "rapid transformation and secularization of Irish society" and emphasized that too often, sacramental and devotional practices, such as frequent confession, daily prayer, and annual retreats, have been neglected, as well as the misguided tendency to avoid penal approaches. This overall context provides a window "to understand the disturbing problem of sexual abuse." He addressed priests and religious who sexually abused children and told them of the "shame and dishonor" they have brought on other priests, and the "immense harm" done to victims. The Pope bluntly wrote, " . . . take responsibility for the sins you have committed" by giving an account of your actions, conceal nothing, openly acknowledge your guilt, submit yourselves to the demands of justice, "but do not despair of God's mercy."

The Pope's approach is substantially different from a high-ranking member of the Congregation for the Doctrine of the Faith, who declared that priest-abusers must be weeded out of the clergy as the "remedy to such scandals offered by God as the 'Divine Surgeon' is to 'cut out [disease] in order to heal' and to 'amputate in order to restore health.' "[23]

NORMS CONCERNING THE MOST SERIOUS CRIMES

In 2001, John Paul II issued *Sacramentorum sanctitatis tutela*, which gave the Congregation for the Doctrine of the Faith responsibility to deal with and judge serious crimes within canon law, with particular emphasis on the problems of sex abuse. On July 15, 2010, these norms were revised to bring "rigor and transparency" to how the church deals with clergy sex abuse.[24] These revisions address, for example, the process of laicization for the formal removal of a priest from the priesthood, extending the statute of limitations for sex abuse cases, with the possibility of waiving it on a case-by-case basis, and adding the acquisition, possession, or distribution of child pornography as a grave crime under Church law.

REFLECTIONS

Virtually all official responses to the clergy sex abuse crisis are grounded in John Paul II's exhortation *I Will Give You Shepherds*. The four pillars for priestly formation form the bedrock for the proper education of priests. The clergy sex abuse in the United States was studied by American bishops and Vatican officials before 2000, and the crisis was situated in a permissive society inflated with erroneous notions of sexuality. There was little, if any, acknowledgement of the root causes of this crisis. There was even a certain calmness in the way clergy sex abuse was understood and addressed, believing the problems causing the abuse were mainly spiritual in nature, a belief that enabled a certain serenity about supporting spiritual retreats as an avenue for dealing with offenders, along with some psychological assistance in dealing with a spiritual problem rather than an addiction or crime. This erroneous concept made it easy or comfortable for bishops and personnel officers to transfer offending priests to another assignment.

The symposium on pedophilia and seminary admission guidelines, coupled with the instruction on candidates and homosexuality, evidence the belief that homosexuality and child sex abuse are not the same reality. At the same time, however, concerns persist that priests who sexually abuse teenage boys (the majority of reported cases) were, in fact, homosexuals. For example, during his April 2010 visit to Chile, Cardinal Tarcisio Bertone, Vatican Secretary of State, claimed that "many psychologists and psychiatrists have shown that there is no link between celibacy and pedophilia, but many others have shown . . . that there is a relationship between homosexuality and pedophilia."[25]

In the past decade, Vatican and American Church officials have set out certain unambiguous norms about what sort of candidate can be accepted to the seminary and then be ordained to the priesthood. While these stricter norms might be interpreted as an accusation against American seminaries for being too lenient in the past, the Vatican Visitation now reports on the overall strength of seminaries and their faculty and students. While some noteworthy concerns were raised, as a general rule, diocesan seminaries were especially lauded for their strengths and high standards.

U.S. seminaries have taken the problems connected with clergy sex abuse seriously and have put into place excellent policies, programs, and educational/formational workshops to help seminarians and faculty to properly understand sex abuse and harassment. The 2009 annual report by the U.S. Conference of Catholic Bishops points out that there has been a significant drop in the number of priests and deacons against whom credible allegations of abuse have been made. This positive report rests to some degree on official Church norms laid out in the last 10 years, as well as the strengthening of seminary programs.

Pope Benedict XVI clearly grasps the enormity of the sex abuse crisis and looks not only at external factors contributing to the abuse but also at internal factors in the church itself. The 2010 *Norms Concerning Most Serious Crimes* is a good example of the Pope's commitment to transparency and honesty.

It is obviously crucial that seminarians understand the issues surrounding clergy sex abuse and incorporate authentic truthfulness about their human and spiritual growth into their lives. If seminary formation programs do not insist on and facilitate such interior knowledge and outward transparency, no amount of norms, documents, and regulations will head off future crimes against children and vulnerable others.[26]

In statements, speeches, pastoral letters, and interviews, bishops in various parts of the world have begun to raise provocative questions about whether something intrinsic to the Church—its clerical culture—has either caused or abetted the clergy sex abuse crisis.[27] In 2008, Jesuit George B. Wilson laid out this case in *Clericalism: The Death of Priesthood*."[28] Wilson references the works of Jean-Jacques Olier, S.S., which became the "way of life" of seminarians for centuries. While Olier's writing's were pastoral, baptismal, and mystical, his successor's revisions were clerical and ascetic: the priest was a man apart and a cleric separated from laypeople. Seminarians should be trained to keep themselves distinct from laypersons and separate from the spiritual life of ordinary Christians. This attitude dominated the seminary system from 1676 to 1966.[29]

While the causes for the clergy sex abuse tragedy are many, clericalism cannot be discounted as a factor. Seminaries must disabuse its students of a self-exaltation created by status and privilege that elevates them above others in the Church. The distinction between ministerial and hierarchical priesthood is theologically important, but it should not be overshadowed by a dysfunctional human formation that fosters narcissism, elitism, entitlement, arrogance, and a lack of a true sense of boundaries. The various documents mentioned above stress the central role of the priest in the formation of seminarians, for example, formators must be priests, the majority of a theological faculty must be priests, only priests can vote for a seminarian's progress toward ordination, and a seminarian's pastoral work should be supervised by a priest. While these norms ideally create in a seminarian a healthy sense of priestly identity, caution must be raised about formation programs that fashion a type of priest who sees himself as better than everyone else.

NOTES

1. See C. W. Baars, *The Role of the Church in the Causation, Treatment and Prevention of the Crisis in the Priesthood*, unpublished paper (1971). Retrieved March 7, 2011, http://www.bishop-accountability.org/reports/1971-11-Baars-TheRole .pdf.

2. Pope John Paul II, "Pastores Dabo Vobis," *Origins* 21, no. 45 (1992): 717–759.

3. See G. D. Coleman, *Catholic Priesthood and Human Development* (Liguori, MO: Liguori Press, 2006).

4. See J. R. Formicola, "Catholic Clerical Sex Abuse: The Vatican, the American bishops, and U.S. Church State Relations," *Journal of Church and State* 46, no. 3 (2004): 479–502.

5. W. D. Montalbano, "Pontiff Assails U.S. Church, Sex Abuse by Priests." *Los Angeles Times* (1993, August 15), A1.

6. M. Henneberger, "Vatican to Hold Secret Trials in Pedophilia Cases." *New York Times* (2002, January 9), A8.

7. R. Howell, "Vatican Focuses on Gay Priests." *Newsday* (Queens edition, 2002, March 21), A6. This point is also made by Benedict XVI, *Light of the World* (San Francisco: Ignatius Press, 2010), 151–153.

8. V. L. Simpson, "Crisis in Church/Official Response: Vatican Takes Cautious View of US Bishops' Proposals." *Boston Globe* (2002, June 8), A14.

9. John Paul II, Address to the cardinals of the United States, (2002, April 23), retrieved on March 7, 2011, from http://vatican.va/holy_father/john_paul_ii/ speeches/2002,april/documents/hf_j.

10. U.S. Cardinals and the Leadership of the N.C.C.B., *Final Communique* (2002), Retrieved on March 7, 2011, from http://www.vatican.va/roman_curia/cardinals/ documents/rc_cardinal_20020424_fi. In his December 2010 Christmas message to the Cardinals, Benedict XVI insisted that the moral theory of proportionalism was responsible for the crisis.

11. Pontifical Academy for Life, Symposium on Homosexuality (2003). Retrieved on March 7, 2011, from http://www.nationalcatholicreporter.org/word/pfw0411 .htm.

12. A 1999 report from a committee of the German Bishops' Conference provided additional reflections for the Congregation for Catholic Education regarding

criteria when a homosexual candidate cannot be admitted. Retrieved on March 7, 2011, from http://huk.org/texte/priesterweihe.htm.

13. Congregation for Catholic Education, "Priesthood Candidates and Homosexuality." *Origins* 35, no. 26 (2005): 429–431.

14. T. G. Plante and G. D. Coleman, *Sexuality, Candidates and the Priesthood* (2005). Retrieved on March 7, 2011, from http://www.com/psyrelig/plante2.html.

15. See L'Osservatore Romano Reprints, *Christian Anthropology and Homosexuality*, 38 (Vatican City: Libreria Editrice Vaticana, 1997).

16. Congregation for Catholic Education, "Guidelines for the Use of Psychology in the Admission and Formation of Candidates for the Priesthood." *Origins* 38, no. 23 (2008): 357–363.

17. Congregation for Catholic Education, "Report on Vatican Visitation of U.S. Seminaries." *Origins* 38, no. 33 (2009): 520–529.

18. United States Conference of Catholic Bishops, *Program of Priestly Formation*, 5th ed. (Washington, DC: Author, 2006).

19. Pope Benedict XVI, *Comments to Reporters on the Papal Plane en Route to Portugal* (2010). Retrieved on March 7, 2011, from http://ncronline.org/print/18259.

20. Pope Benedict XVI (2010), *Homily at the Vatican*, http://ncronline.org/print/118946, retrieved on March 7, 2011.

21. Pope Benedict XVI, *Letter to Catholics of Ireland* (2010). Retrieved on March 7, 2011, from http://www.zenit.org/phprint.php.

22. See Russell Shorto, "The Irish Affliction." *New York Times* (2011). Retrieved on March 7, 2011, from http://www.nytimes.com/2011/02/13/magazine/13Irish-t .html?_r=1@emc=eta1&pagewant.

23. C. J. Scicluna, *Homily at the Altar of the Chair of Peter* (2010). Retrieved on March 7, 2011, from http://ncronline.org/print/18525.

24. Allen, J. L. (2010, July 15). "Vatican Revises Church Law on Sex Abuse." Retrieved on June 27, 2011 from http://ncronline.org/news/vatican/vatican -revises-church-law-sex-abuse?page=1. See "Congregation for the Doctrine of the Faith" (2010, July 22); "Revised Norms on Dealing with Clerical Sex Abuse of Minors and Other Grave Offenses." *Origins* 40, no. 10 (2010): 145–152; "Historical Introduction for the Revised Norms on Dealing with Clerical Sex Abuse of Minors and Other Grave Offenses." *Origins* 40, no. 10 (2010): 152–154; and F. Lombardi, "The Significance of the Revised Norms." *Origins* 40, no. 10 (2010): 154–155.

25. Cardinal T. Bertone, "Comments by Cardinal on Sexuality Create a Stir." *New York Times* (2010, April 15), A4. Bertone's statement finds an echo in the May 4, 2010, CBS News/*New York Times* poll indicating that 30 percent of Catholics polled believe that "homosexuality is a major contributing factor" to child sex abuse. This belief finds troublesome support in an unnuanced paper published by Human Life International Research Director Brian Clowes. LifeSite News claims that this paper closes "the book on the question of whether homosexuality in the priesthood is a root cause of the clerical sexual abuse crisis."

Clowes affirms that it is: Retrieved on June 27, 2011, from http://www.lifesite news.com/news/archive/ldn/2010/apr/10041916.

26. See The Linacre Institute, *After Asceticism: Sex, Prayer and Deviant Priests* (Bloomington, IN: Author House, 2006).

27. "Some Bishops Questioning Clerical Culture (2010)." Retrieved on June 27, 2011, from http://ncronline.org/news/accountability/some-bishops-questioning -clerical-culture.

28. G. B. Wilson, *Clericalism: The Death of Priesthood* (Collegeville, MN: Liturgical Press, 2008).

29. *Ibid.*, 111.

Chapter 17

The Response of Religious Institutes of Men to the Crisis of Sexual Abuse in the Roman Catholic Church in the United States

Monica Applewhite and Paul Macke

The Roman Catholic Church is divided into geographic areas called dioceses and archdioceses that are overseen by the bishops, archbishops, and cardinals. Within and across dioceses, however, there exist numerous other Catholic organizations that function fairly independently of the dioceses. These include but are not limited to religious institutes of priests and brothers that have existed within the Church since men and women first heard the call of the desert in the third century AD.

Today's religious institutes include societies of apostolic life, congregations of brothers and priests, monastic communities, clerical institutes of priests, and many other forms of men's consecrated life. Each institute is led by major superior, who may be an abbot in a monastery, a provincial in a province, or even a president in some relatively new institutes. In the United States, bishops are members of the United States Conference of Catholic Bishops (USCCB), whereas the leaders of men's religious institutes belong to the Conference of Major Superiors of Men (CMSM).

A DISTINCTIVE APPROACH TO THE CRISIS

When the USCCB issued the *Charter for the Protection of Children and Young People (Charter)*[1] in June 2002 in response to the sexual abuse crisis, the religious communities in the United States included 23,000 brothers and priests. In August of that year, CMSM issued an Assembly Statement titled *Improving Pastoral Care and Accountability in Response to the Tragedy of Sexual*

Abuse.[2] This statement began the initiative that would soon be known as the Instruments of Hope and Healing.[3] This was the response of the men's religious institutes to the sexual abuse crisis, and from the beginning, was distinctive in terms of commitment, collaboration with victims' groups, education, mental health, and psychological perspectives and accountability.

THE COMMITMENTS

The CMSM's *Assembly Statement* of 2002 was not a full-scale plan for all religious institutes like the *Charter* but, rather, a series of commitments made by the provincial superiors to develop the plan. The commitments they made were:

- ◆ To research and design needed services for members to respond promptly to any allegation of sexual abuse
- ◆ To research and design further services whereby its members can establish independent review boards
- ◆ To research and design mechanisms of public accountability
- ◆ To seek consultation with experts in the protection of children to develop programs of prevention, especially educational programs
- ◆ To research currently available resources and design needed services for effective care, treatment, and follow-up supervision of religious members who have abused
- ◆ To initiate dialogue with appropriate groups for the creation of programs for healing, reconciliation, and wellness for all those affected by sexual abuse

To fulfill these commitments, the executive leadership of CMSM analyzed the options, met with experts, and began their program of change between August 2002 and August 2003. In the spring of 2003, they contracted with Christian Brothers Services and Praesidium, Inc. to provide the educational programs, standards, and system of accountability for the men's religious orders and congregations in the United States. Their initiative became known as Instruments of Hope and Healing, and institutes representing more than 95 percent of male religious signed up to become part of program.[4] It is worth noting that the characteristically low-profile religious leaders by and large had the luxury of deliberating without the same level of attention and scrutiny that was placed on the bishops' planning session in the summer of 2002.

COLLABORATION WITH VICTIMS' GROUPS

By mid-May of 2003, plans for the annual General Assembly of Major Superiors, to be held in Louisville, Kentucky, were underway. The conference staff received a phone call from representatives of LinkUp, a sexual abuse sur-vivors' group based in Louisville. The LinkUp initiated this contact in order to inform the Assembly of a planned demonstration at their upcoming meeting. A cordial conversation was followed by a second and a third. By the day of the General Assembly, an entirely different event had been planned. Now a prayer service would be held by the members of the LinkUp and the members of CMSM.

On the day of the prayer service, about 30 members of the LinkUp gath-ered outside the Galt House Hotel grounds. They held candles and recited prayers while they waited with trepidation to see whether any of the provin-cials, abbots, or other leaders would join them. The group had invited Church leaders to events before, but none had ever shown up. A few minutes after the appointed hour, the LinkUp contingent watched with amazement as the doors of the hotel opened up and the Major Superiors began to emerge. One LinkUp member described the moment, "Once they started coming out, we couldn't believe it, because once they started coming . . . they just kept coming. They tripled our numbers. We had no idea."

More bewilderment mixed with relief followed as survivors and religious leaders took turns speaking to the crowd gathered there. Among them was a survivor who prayed for reconciliation and to have a voice within the Church and a provincial who shared his own history of abuse and gratitude for the courage of those assembled. After more than two hours, a tenuous but signifi-cant relationship began. It was a relationship based on personal contact between Church leaders and those who had been harmed within the Church. The experience of shared prayer and the hope for reconciliation with survivors left a deep impression on the major superiors and laid the groundwork for the actions that followed.

EDUCATING THE LEADERS

Another distinctive aspect of the approach by men's religious communities was that the major superiors decided that they would begin meeting their commitments by educating themselves in a variety of areas related to preven-tion and response. They viewed videotaped accounts of abuse made by mem-bers of the LinkUp in which the survivors explained why they had waited for many years to report their abuse and what they were hoping someone from the Church would say to them. The survivors also described what happened when they actually came forward and made suggestions as to how the Church could help them heal. Hearing the words of victims describing their injuries and how they had been treated by Church authorities had a profound effect on the major superiors of men and strengthened their commitment to finding better ways to respond.

CMSM general assemblies and regional meetings became the forum for the educational programs that were held throughout 2003 and 2004. In addition to pastoral care, other topics included appropriate response and reporting, methods for prevention, handling internal investigations, use of review boards, supervising those who have abused, and educating the general membership of the religious community.

MENTAL HEALTH AND PSYCHOLOGICAL PERSPECTIVES

Religious institutes of men have many ties to the world of mental health and psychology. This background informed and shaped the response by religious men to the question of sexual abuse. As a whole, religious communities steered away from the criminal justice perspective prominent in the *Charter* and sought psychological and sociological explanations and solutions. Instead of law enforcement officers, religious superiors sought social workers, psychologists, and clinicians to advise in the development of their standards and protocols. Many religious were educated and credentialed in mental health and social services, including psychologist Reverend Ray Carey, who had spent more than two decades using behavioral interviewing techniques for screening new religious community members. Vicars, provincial assistants, and other trusted members with relevant training and experience were selected for key roles in the institutes to respond to allegations, conduct internal investigations, maintain records, and supervise sexual offenders.

While the mental health perspective was enormously helpful toward advancing the response of the religious to victims, it was not always consistent with the efforts to appropriately supervise and hold accountable those members of the institutes who had themselves been abusers. Many of those members had been through treatment programs in the 1980s and had been declared "low risk" or "very low risk" to abuse again. Some of the religious who sexually offended had been working with the same therapists for more than 5, 10 or even 15 years.[5] The majority of offenders had received a clean bill of health from a clinical provider at some point in the past. In 2002 and 2003, many of these therapists fought against the idea of "supervision" or increased oversight of the religious who had sexually offended.[6]

With their close ties to the mental health field and backgrounds steeped in psychology, superiors struggled with the competing perspectives. On one hand, the major superiors had a mandate to manage risk: the public clamored for justice for the crimes that had occurred in the past; the media reported daily on the whereabouts and activities of priests and religious offenders; and the bishops had announced they were laicizing all priests who had sexually offended.

On the other hand, religious superiors were taught to respect the recommendations of experts. They were hearing from clinicians who claimed it was virtually impossible for a particular religious member to ever abuse again. Unfortunately, the majority of clinical providers that had been trusted by religious did not specialize or have experience working with sexual offenders.[7] They did not know that the treatment of sexual offenders had advanced dramatically after the mid-1990s and that predictions of recidivism based purely on clinical judgment and signs of remorse had since been found to be slightly less accurate than chance.[8] The educational program addressing support and accountability for religious who have abused would later answer many questions and prove to be essential to the development of standards for supervision of sexual offenders.

ACCREDITATION

In 2002, as the U.S. Catholic bishops faced intense scrutiny in the wake of an enormously public failure of integrity and leadership, corporate America was suddenly facing large-scale questions of its leadership, honesty, and abuses of power in the wake of disclosures about the misleading accounting practices and outright deceit of one of the most credible publicly held corporations in the history of the United States: Enron. Gone were the days when organizations were loosely held accountable for the mistakes of their leaders. Now corporate leaders were being held accountable for the mistakes made on their watch—actions that they knew of or should have known about. After 2002, an era began in which anything short of absolute transparency could be considered a cover for blatant abuses.

It was in this environment that the bishops began their deliberations on the solutions for ending the public mistrust of the Church's handling of priests who sexually abuse minors. During their conference in Dallas in 2002, the U.S. bishops recognized that a critical flaw in each of their reform efforts previously endorsed in 1992[9] through 1996[10] was that their plans lacked systems of accountability—ways to be certain that every diocesan ordinary was following the same set of rules. Their *Charter* and the corresponding canonical *Essential Norms*[11] approved by Rome at the request of the U.S. bishops corrected that problem by now holding each bishop accountable to the same set of standards. Later, the Gavin Group, Inc. was enlisted to develop and implement an external system of diocesan audits to ensure uniform adherence to the *Charter*, and the lay National Review Board was established to oversee the process.

For the major superiors, it was apparent that any system of reform intended to restore trust and rebuild identity would need to build in a methodology to hold the religious institutes accountable to a set of guidelines or standards. Audits to be conducted within one year seemed too fast for some institutes and almost too slow for others. The idea of scheduling an audit before the institute felt ready or before the religious had an opportunity to "do things right" did not appeal to the major superiors.

Because many religious are familiar with and work within many educational and health care institutes, ideas from those organizations began to flow into conversations regarding accountability. An accreditation program, similar to those programs utilized by university and hospital systems but distinctly different from the audit process used by the dioceses, was proposed and adopted. Praesidium, Inc. was selected to become the accrediting body for the men's religious institutes in the United States and its territories. An advisory council of religious was created to work with Praesidium on the development of accreditation standards covering three broad areas: prevention, response, and supervision. The advisory council was critical to the process of developing standards because the religious orders, congregations, and societies of apostolic life presented such diverse forms and styles of life.

IMPLEMENTING THE INSTRUMENTS OF HOPE AND HEALING

The following examples illustrate some of the ways in which the religious institutes have implemented the standards of prevention, response, and supervision according to their core charism of living the evangelical counsels of poverty, chastity and obedience in a community setting.

Education: Expanding the Content

Standard 5 of the Accreditation program requires that: *The Institute will educate its Members regarding the prevalence, identification, and prevention of sexual abuse of minors, giving special attention to topics that are of unique relevance to religious.*

In order to meet this standard, every member of each community of men is to receive three hours of professional education in the area of sexual abuse prevention and response every three years. Within the Society of Jesus (Jesuits), this meant that professors, deans, and university presidents were required to participate in continuing education programs regardless of their own backgrounds or experience working in the field.

The first round of education focused on the sexual abuse of minors, the effects of abuse, characteristics of perpetrators, the warning signs that another religious could be crossing boundaries, and what to do if abuse is suspected. By 2005, some of the provinces were looking ahead to the reaccreditation process that is required every three years, and the Jesuits recognized this as an opportunity to expand the educational program by addressing other ethics violations and the issues surrounding the exploitation of adults. They requested that Praesidium expand the list of subjects approved for education and developed a national program for all of their members. A panel of experts created a new Hope and Healing educational program, and the Early Responders Distance Learning Center at St. Joseph University in Philadelphia contributed by putting together the video production and training manuals.

The Jesuit leadership promoted this training not so much as a requirement for accreditation but as an educational tool that religious men can use to help themselves to better live with their religious commitments. In the past, the topics addressed in the Jesuit program of education would have been considered taboo or at least very difficult to confront directly. The program's developers were happily surprised that, overall, men in religious communities were pleased to be able to privately discuss topics such as chastity, celibacy, and boundaries in professional ministry with one another. One Jesuit provincial told this writer (Paul Macke, S. J.) that the best parts of the training were the many intimate conversations that followed among Jesuits in the dining and recreation rooms of the community. The program makes community members more aware of the warning signs exhibited by a member who might act out inappropriately and demonstrates that it is each individual member's responsibility to intervene with another who may be at risk rather than just waiting for the superior to take action. It is widely perceived within the Jesuit community that this training and others like it will lead to greater self-knowledge and new wisdom toward preventing boundary violations with both adults and minors.[12] The Jesuits in the United States have made the Hope and Healing training available to the entire CMSM membership and to various dioceses interested in the program. As cases have recently come forward from Germany, Ireland, and Latin America, they are also receiving inquiries from religious communities around the world.

Without the extensive educational efforts in 2003 and 2004, it is unlikely that an initiative such as this enhanced educational program could have gained the momentum and interest needed to see the new program through to fruition. Due to the success of this program among the vast majority of religious men who have participated, there is an expectation of continued openness and attention to other new programs that address interpersonal behavior, boundaries and ethics in ministry.

Response: A Survivor's Graveside Service

> Standard 10 of the Accreditation program requires that: *Representatives of the Institute will make a significant effort to promote the healing process for individuals who allege being sexually abused as a minor.*

To meet this standard, the religious institutes are required to offer to meet in person with anyone who alleges abuse and must be able to document their attempts to assist in the healing of any individual who reports abuse. Some professionals believe they should know instinctively how to help a survivor of abuse find healing, but often, a better way is to ask and listen to the answer. Religious leaders are sometimes fearful of making a mistake when they are involved in pastoral care with those who have been abused, but the greatest gains have been made when the core ideals of the community guide their efforts and show the way forward.

Several communities have engaged in unique initiatives for healing when typical means are either not available or not deemed meaningful for the survivor. One example was experienced in a monastery in the winter of 2005.

Following the Rule of St. Benedict, monks welcome guests to the monastery with care and hospitality. Each guest must be respected and the reason he or she has come to the monastery understood, regardless of status, wealth, or faith. It was this dimension of the Rule that Abbot Thomas[13] considered when a new arrival asked the guest master if he could speak with the abbot about sexual abuse. The monastery had been through some difficulties in 2002 when media reports about one of the monks who sexually offended became national news. Compared to other organizations, their time in the limelight was brief, but the experience left both the abbot and prior uneasy about their abilities to manage sexual abuse matters properly. Still, Abbot Thomas arranged to meet with the guest, Michael,[14] a man in his 50s, who had been abused by a monk.

At the Abbot's request, Michael told him his story about being abused. The Abbot grieved that a monk had caused the harm that Michael described and asked how he could help him. Michael wanted to arrange a meeting with the monk who had abused him many years ago, but that was not possible because the monk was now deceased. Disappointed and exhausted, Michael became emotional and began to express his anger that no one from the monastery had prevented the perpetrator from harming children.

Later, Michael calmed down and came to realize that his respect for the monastic life was separate from how he felt about his abuser. He believed that he had at last reached a point in his life and healing where he was ready for closure. He proposed that the Abbot conduct a prayer service at the grave of the monk who had abused him.

Although he was hesitant, Abbot Thomas agreed to the prayer service and asked Michael who should attend. Together, they decided to invite the monks and the other guests who were staying at monastery at the time. The next day, during a heavy snowfall, Abbot Thomas, Michael, 14 monks and five guests walked to the monastery's cemetery. When they arrived, Abbot Thomas began with prayer, then led the small group through the three songs that Michael requested be sung. They were familiar songs from his youth, a time before his pain, and they symbolized a reclaiming of his contentment and faith. It had taken him many years to stand in this place and feel welcome and solid.

Michael felt nervous but in control as he read a letter he had written to his abuser. The monks and other guests reached out and touched his shoulders as he talked about his betrayal and what he had lost in his life. The monks and the guests, moved to tears by Michael's words, felt changed when he finished and Abbot Thomas said a final prayer. Later, Michael expressed his gratitude to the Abbot and revealed that this graveside service had finally freed him of 30 years of fear and shameful daily memories.

Supervision: A Friar's Experience of Accountability

> Standard 21 of the Accreditation program requires that: *Individuals who supervise members who have Safety Plans will be physically and emotionally capable and adequately trained to perform the duties involved in supervision.*

As of 2010, about one-third of individuals who supervise members who have Safety Plans are hired professionals who are not members of religious communities. In 2003, however, when supervision was first initiated on a large-scale basis, virtually all supervisors were religious members. Brother Steven[15] was one such member. As a member of a mendicant community for 22 years, Brother Steven valued the friar's life: shared living, community prayer, and fraternal support for his work with impoverished families in an urban setting. In the autumn of 2003, the provincial of his community selected him to supervise two other friars who had sexually abused minors during the 1970s. Brother Steven was shocked to learn that two of his brothers had abused children and, worse, that they were both living in the community where he was the local superior. Thinking about members of his community in this light was both painful and repugnant to him and he mentally resisted the idea of becoming involved.

As recommended in the Standards, the provincial directed Brother Steven to review the friars' files so that he would understand their offenses. After more than two decades in pastoral ministry, Brother Steven did not expect to be surprised by what he read, but he was. One of the friars had abused multiple children, been involved in sexual misconduct with adults he had served in ministry, and had improperly used community and parish funds. The friar's file also contained letters of complaints and demands he had made to each provincial even before he professed final vows. Because this friar was so rarely in the community space, Brother Steven had never seen the anger or frustration expressed in the man's correspondence.

The other friar's file contained one allegation and little else. There was no documentation of an investigation, psychological treatment, or other information about the abuse with the exception of a short note written by the provincial decades earlier that the friar had admitted to an improper relationship with a 15-year-old youth. It would have been difficult to imagine at the time that this note would lead to his removal from public ministry and a requirement for sexual offender supervision in a post–2002 environment.

The idea that these two friars would need to be watched for the rest of their lives seemed strange and unforgiving to Brother Steven. Nevertheless, he accepted the role. Over the next three years, he attended several educational programs to learn more about sexual offenders. He wrote supervision plans for them, met with each of them once a week, and worked hard to keep up with how they spent their time. Supervising them was not easy; Brother Steven still had a full-time assignment and both friars were not performing ministry, leaving them with a considerable amount of unscheduled time to fill.

The friar with multiple offenses was extremely difficult to engage in a system of accountability. He fought his controls at every turn, creatively interpreted the requirements of his written plan, and frequently manipulated other community members to take up his cause for ending his supervision. The other friar was less open about resisting supervision, but he was no less difficult to hold accountable because he spent a great deal of time with many families he maintained close relationships with, some of whom had children. He did not disclose his whereabouts unless pressured to do so, and although Brother Steven did not want to isolate the friar, he did he want to permit him to cultivate the same type of relationship that became abusive 35 years ago.

At meetings with other supervisors, Brother Steven came to realize that his experience was not unique and that supervising other community members was a very challenging role. Over time, he increasingly came to identify himself with the role and found that even when it was difficult he had, in fact, become good at supervising. He developed a thicker skin with respect to the men he was supervising as well as other critics in the community. He gained a better sense of when the friars were attempting to deceive him.

As a member of the provincial council, Brother Steven now finds himself dedicated to preserving the systems of support and accountability for the two friars who still live in his community, despite the concerns by other friars who question whether such accountability is necessary. He no longer views the role of supervision as being at odds with his vocation but as a deeply involved, ever-present reminder of the commitment to fraternal support he made when he vowed to live the life of a friar.

THE GOOD NEWS

Despite the vast differences in how men live religious life in the United States, thousands of religious have embraced the principles, education, and accreditation standards that make up the Instruments of Hope and Healing. Although the program has been voluntary from the beginning, institutes representing 95 percent of religious men in the United States have enrolled,[16] and many have successfully achieved their accreditation. As awareness of the accreditation has process grown, so too has the pressure on institutes that do not participate in this system of accountability. In future years, it is possible that religious institutes must be accredited in order for its members to serve in public ministry. Given the reality of how complicated it is for religious leaders to hold their own members accountable, this additional level of accountability has been essential to the full implementation of standards. In both spirit and action, the majority of men's religious institutes have embraced and lived these transformative changes brought forth through their distinctive approach.

NOTES

1. United States Conference of Catholic Bishops, *Charter for the Protection of Children and Young People* (Washington, DC: Author, 2002).

2. Conference of Major Superiors of Men, *Improving Pastoral Care and Accountability in Response to the Tragedy of Sexual Abuse* (Silver Spring, MD: Author, 2002).

3. Conference of Major Superiors of Men, *Instruments of Hope and Healing* (Silver Spring, MD: Author, 2003).

4. Conference of Major Superiors of Men, *Group Work Plan—August 2003 to August 2004: Participating Institutes* (Silver Spring, MD: Author, 2003).

5. Monica Applewhite. Personal Knowledge. 2003–2005.

6. *Ibid.*

7. *Ibid.*

8. H. E. Barbaree, M. C. Seto, C. M. Langton and E. J. Peacock, "Evaluating the Predictive Accuracy of Six Risk Assessment Instruments for Adult Sex Offender." *Criminal Justice and Behavior* 28 (2001): 490–521.

9. National Conference of Catholic Bishops, *Five Principles* (Washington, DC: Author, 1992).

10. National Conference of Catholic Bishops, *Restoring Trust Volumes 1–3* (Washington, DC: Author, 1994–1996).

11. United States Conference of Catholic Bishops, *Essential Norms for Diocesan/ Eparchial Policies Dealing with Allegations of Sexual Abuse of Minors by Priests or Deacons* (Washington, DC: Author, 2002).

12. Paul Macke, S. J. Personal Knowledge. 2010.

13. Not his real name.

14. Not his real name.

15. Not his real name.

16. Conference of Major Superiors of Men.

Chapter 18

Understanding the Treatment of Clerical Sex Offenders

Gerard J. McGlone

Psychological treatment of religious and priest (clerical) sexual offenders in the past 10 years has undergone some important, significant, and interesting developments. There have been three major developments that have transpired in these years, and these will be the focus of this chapter. The first of these developments is the *Dallas Charter*[1] and its impact on treatment. The second is the development in the actual treatment of clerical and nonclerical offenders, and the third is the development of the role of risk assessment and its implications for the clerical sexual offenders. Before talking about aspects of these developments, certain initial caveats need to be provided.

INITIAL CAVEATS

The first caveat is that when one sees or hears stories about abuse and abusers, there often seems to be little sympathy, little understanding, and little tolerance. As a member of a treatment team and as a priest, my bias and my belief reside in the efficacy of treatment and in the possibility of forgiveness. Such beliefs do not explain away, nor do they ever mean to condone, any crime or any sin. In the treatment of sex offenders, one often hears the saying, "there is no cure, but these conditions are manageable." This current analysis is an attempt at understanding a complex, perplexing societal and ecclesial problem.[2]

Second, the rise in our society of elements that view sex offenders as subhuman or even lepers can be seen in various stories in the media. The frenzy after both the 2002 crisis and the current crisis in other parts of the world has served us in many ways in the field of child maltreatment, but it also has had some significant downsides.[3] It seems to be a both a public policy disaster and an inhumane event when convicted sex offenders cannot find any residence other than a tent under a highway or causeway. If we in this field know that stress can be a situational trigger for the clear majority of sex offenders to reoffend, it seems both illogical and imprudent to increase stress through punitive and politically popular residency sanctions against them.

Additionally, many writers have chronicled the history of neglect by the leadership of the Roman Catholic Church. The current chapter does not condone inaction, nor should it be seen as in any way justifying the Church leader's neglect of their primary role as shepherd, which is to protect and defend the flock—especially the young in their care. Most Catholics in the pews and most nonoffending priests in the pulpits continue to be dismayed at the lack of accountability in their own leadership. Many see systemic sin and criminal behaviors being tolerated if not ignored.[4]

The press cries "cover-up," and the Church is yet again reactive in a new moment of crisis management in a seemingly endless saga. Some would claim this is a continuation of anti–Catholic bias and that there are many organizations equally guilty of the same offense. Many others claim that they see lawyers dictating a pastoral response that leaves the People of God without that which they have always wanted—a shepherd. This tension and the wide spectrum of debate must be acknowledged in any discussion of this topic.[5]

Finally, there have been several amazing developments in the Church since the *Dallas Charter* was approved by the bishops in June 2002. Enormous strides have been made to keep the Church and her children safer: hundreds of thousands of adults have been trained in child protection and safety; and the research supported by the United States Conference of Catholic Bishops (USCCB) is singular and extraordinary in its transparency and in its possible effects in our society.[6]

These are but a few of the many accomplishments of the Church thus far, but as the data suggest, much still needs to be done. Nonetheless, as a faith community, we can be quite proud of these actions for they are yielding some significant and measurable gains. These efforts are clearly helping the field of child protection and maltreatment enormously—but at what price?

If we do not model forgiveness in our Church and faith community, what do we abandon and what will we lose? One cannot help but recall the late Cardinal Avery Dulles's lament, if not warning, at the same Dallas meeting in 2002 when he predicted that the *Dallas Charter* could irrevocably damage the priest–bishop relationship. Some now wonder if he was right. Now that we know that 98 percent of the clerical sex offenders are not pedophiles after all, is it time to reconsider the *Charter's* zero-tolerance policy?[7] Most solid psychologically based research points to the mental health benefits of forgiveness. Can we figure out a way to be forgiving as well as accountable and protective of our children? Our tradition has a long and sacred deposit of faith that now makes scientific sense. Can we, at least, pose this question? This writer believes that it is time.

UNDERSTANDING THE PROBLEM OF CLERICAL SEX OFFENSES

One of the first and most important developments since Dallas deals with a more descriptive picture of the nature and the scope of the problem that contextualizes treatment today.[8] Terry, Mercado, and Smith (2008) have allowed us to view the full dimensions of the issues in light of the John Jay College of Criminal Justice Nature and Scope study and the effect of the *Dallas Charter's* zero-tolerance mandates. Concretely, this research continues to inform treatment and direct discharge planning and has confirmed what the treatment centers and the treating psychologists have known for some time: there is an enormous heterogeneity within this clerical sex offender population. This heterogeneity demanded and still demands a varied and far more nuanced response to a very complex and challenging clinical reality.[9] These study data confirm that the "one size fits all" treatment approach simply does not work and clearly is not appropriate with this clerical population. Additionally, the annual diocesan audits conducted since the *Charter* was implemented in 2002 and the USCCB's response to the problem have had some positive effects worthy of additional discussion and analysis.

Second, this period has also seen important developments in the theoretical underpinnings of the treatment process in the advent and use of the Good Lives Model (GLM), in the fine-tuning of the Response Needs Model (RNR) treatment modality, and the Relapse Prevention (RP) model. This chapter will update and review these new developments, their impact in the field of sex offender treatment and explain how this might be seen specifically in the treatment of clerical sexual offenders. Third, the other large and most important development has occurred in the area of risk-assessment procedures, instruments, and utilization of the posttreatment safety plans for these men. These very significant changes will also be discussed in this chapter.

The John Jay Study "The Nature and Scope of Sexual Abuse of Minors by Catholic Clergy in the United States, 1950–2002" has given us enormous data that are descriptive and useful. The study is a tribute to the research team at the John Jay College and the USCCB for sponsoring it. It estimates essential prevalence and incidence data about this problem between the years 1950 and 2002 and also describes the reality facing treatment providers. Researchers estimate that about 4.2 percent of the priest population and about 2.7 percent of the religious brothers and priests in the years 1950 through 2002 were sexual offenders. The reason for this significant discrepancy between the groups is still unknown at this time.

The data seem to also suggest that clerical sexual offenders tend to be divided into three main groups, or types. The members of the first group comprise the vast majority of offenders (about 88.8 percent) and are nondiagnosable or what, for the purposes of this chapter, are termed the "undifferentiated" clerical sex offenders. They are not easily diagnosed with a paraphilic disorder or a sexual disorder and typically had one victim or incident. If no disorder fits them, what are they? More central to this chapter, what do we treat?

The second type is the ephebophilic group comprised of about 10 percent of the men. They would best be categorized as being ephebophiles or hebophiles—or those attracted to adolescents. The third and final group, categorized as pedophiles, made up about 2.2 percent of the total. Notably, this group and these men (approximately 150) accounted for about 30 percent of the victims and clearly had a diagnosable sexual disorder. Perhaps with better screening these men could have been prevented from abusing children,[10] however, there is no standard screening test that the field uses to distinguish these men. Had there been such a test it would have been used to screen candidates for the priesthood as well as to screen candidates for all other occupations.

About 80 percent of all reported victims in the John Jay study were adolescent males. This has often been offered as proof that the majority of offenders were homosexual. This fact is simply not supported by the data and ignores the basic situational factor that there were no altar girls until 1994 in most U.S. dioceses thus limiting the opportunistic offender's access to girls. *Understanding this data is critical in any discussion of treatment and treatment outcomes. Some of the clerical sex offenders did not fit into any diagnosable sexual disorder. Part of the difficulty in accurately diagnosing clerical offenders is that situational and systemic issues are often ignored. Simply put, treating a pedophile is very different from treating someone who is not a pedophile; one cannot treat what one does not know.*

LATEST PREVALENCE

Within this picture, one must place the changing treatment realties that have shifted dramatically in the past 10 years, as has the prevalence of the problem. It is quite obvious in the recent data released by the USCCB that there are fewer and fewer cases of clerical sexual abuse in the U.S. Catholic Church being reported each year. If these data are to be taken seriously, the overall current prevalence rates seem to be lingering around .04 to .05 percent of all religious and diocesan priests in the United States.[11]

Two issues quickly emerge. First, the recent data compiled by the Center for Applied Research in the Apostolate (CARA) for the USCCB suggests that half of all the new allegations sexual abuse were made against international clergy.[12] Additionally, the figures clearly indicate that the more recent surge of international clergy (about 8,000 to 12,000 is an estimate of the total number), now estimated to be about 15 percent of the total number of priests in the United States, needs to examined far more closely and more seriously. This is a source of grave concern. For many reasons, most of these clergy never have any psychological screening evaluations,[13] unlike the typical seminarian in the United States (McGlone, 2010).

Second, and more germane to this chapter, these data indicate, and it seems logical, that most treatment facilities have seen and continue to see far fewer inpatient referrals for sexual offender treatment than in the past five to six years. This clearly is significant and is good news in what can be an overwhelmingly complicated clinical reality. This also means that treatment centers are not seeing as many clerical offenders in treatment.

APPROACHES TO TREATMENT

Most inpatient and outpatient providers of psychological treatment for this clerical population use a multidimensional and multifaceted approach. This means that practitioners often view the problem and the person within a unique theoretical or broader systemic framework. This is often called the bio-psycho-social-spiritual orientation. In this framework, the medical, biological, psychological, environmental, and situational factors are seen within the full context of the spiritual and pastoral realities of the individual.

Sex offender treatment has progressed significantly in the past 10 years, and its effectiveness is hotly debated.[14] The three modalities most often used in inpatient facilities are intensive individual (whether psychodynamic and/or cognitive-behavioral), psycho-educational group, and intensive group or milieu therapies. Therapists often employ a cognitive-behavioral treatment focus in individual treatment that attempts to look at the unique distortions for the offending behaviors. Some research indicates that this clerical population does exhibit unique distortions related to their sexual offending behavior.[15] Dynamic treatment is also used to address the more long-standing internal defenses and unresolved attachment needs of the offender. Recent research has shown some promise for this most traditional form of treatment in general. However, it seems counterindicated in sex offender treatment. Research supports other types of more multidimensional forms of treatment for this population.

TYPES OF SEX OFFENDERS

For several years, clerical and lay offenders have been divided into two general types: situational and preferential.[16] Within these groupings or typologies, one often sees co-varying or co-occurring disorders of a sexual and nonsexual nature. Treatment would follow based on how the offender was diagnosed and whether there were any co-morbid conditions.

The situational offender typically has more environmentally based triggers: for example, grief in the loss of a parent, particularly the loss of the mother; burnout; situational stress and anger management; naïve sexual knowledge; poor sexual boundaries; and immature sexual development; and, therefore, had similar treatment solutions. These offenders, who comprised the clear majority of all clerical offenders, were also more generally amenable and open to treatment than the preferential offender and typically had very few (or even one) victims.

The preferential offender seems more fixated and more emotionally similar to his victims, more self-focused or self-centered, more dependent or needy in his interpersonal relationships, and more driven by his sexual urges toward children. Providers often thought them to be narcissistically disordered, but research has yet to support that theory. There has been some support for more dependent like features in these more serial-type offenders.[17] This means that these men tend to look more compliant and even more attached to unhealthy relationships. These men typically had many more victims, were less open to treatment, and were more convinced that their offending behavior was consensual and helpful to their victims than the opportunistic offenders.

ASSESSMENT OF THE OFFENDER

The purpose of an extensive assessment phase is essential in determining the full nature of what the man's problem(s) may be and how treatment might be best directed toward addressing the more prevalent or pressing issues. At the St. John Vianney Center, assessments last at least 30 days, beginning with extensive medical and psychiatric evaluations along with extensive evaluations by a team of psychologists, pastoral counselors, and social workers. Clinicians are often very concerned in the initial phase of treatment and assessment about suicidality and the man's tendency to think that his life has no meaning. This was and is a special concern in light of the *Charter*'s zero-tolerance policy. It goes without saying that revelations and ongoing information gathered from as many sources as possible often accompany treatment and assessment. Experienced practitioners in the sex offender field expect and depend on ongoing and constantly adaptable facets of assessment. More information, possibly more offenses or problematic behaviors, and more relevant data are often revealed in the treatment process itself. In light of this, the initial assessment phase is critical to the formulation of any treatment plans and goals. These assessments provide structure and focus to the treatment process. Individual, milieu, and group therapies are typical for most cases. These modalities often spring out of an integrated understanding of what sexual offending might be for the person.

Clerical offenders tend to compartmentalize these aspects of their being. Sometimes the assessment is the first attempt to bring these aspects together for the person. One typical goal of most treatment is to address this tendency to compartmentalize in an attempt to have the person see himself and others as whole human beings. Treatment has often lasted anywhere from six to nine months in most inpatient treatment centers. The various modalities used and the issues that typically are addressed vary according to each treatment plan and each therapist's expertise.

TREATMENT OF OFFENDERS

Most inpatient and outpatient treatments have utilized the Relapse Prevention (RP) Model for most of these offenders and disorders.[18] The diagnosis and the use of this model have advanced significantly in this 10-year period. The premise in this model is that this disease is like any addiction and should be treated as such. This sexual addiction model was and is still controversial in the field.

Two major critiques of this approach have surfaced that seem rather compelling. First, for some, it seems inappropriate and actually counter therapeutic to have the offender self-identify as a sex offender in each and every group session using the traditional Alcoholics Anonymous-type introduction—"Hi, my name is Bill, and I am an alcoholic." For years, offenders would often be asked to do the same and detail their offenses in the group settings. Second, a relapse is a major concern for any addict. Addictions are disorders of relapse and are seen as more problematic in the context of sexual offending. One relapse cannot apply in this new arena of offenders. Simply put, the language and the format seem to not have made the translation helpful.[19]

Research is getting better at pinpointing what may make up the conditions under which a person offends. We are far from understanding all the causes, and there are many debating theories, but some of the situational factors seem more clear.[20] Today, most centers use intensive psychodynamic individual therapy, which tends to help with the more longstanding personality and family issues that the person may present.[21] Additionally, most centers employ cognitive-behavioral and behavioral forms of treatment when these seem both appropriate and possible. Most research indicates that these methods seem to be showing enormous promise and efficacy.[22]

The Good Lives Model (GLM) is most often employed in or for group treatment. These emphases combine to offer the most effective treatment programming that has been solidly researched within the field.[23] This development has come out of the positive psychology movement.[24] It attempts to align the virtues and the values of the individual in light of his ability to engage with whatever discharge plan he might receive in the future. Unlike the relapse prevention model, which is still utilized by many, this approach attempts to substitute more systemic manners of behavior that would allow the person to look at his fulfillment and happiness outside of how he used to see himself being fulfilled through his abusive cycles and behaviors. Hanson and Marshall propose this theoretical model to be adjunctive in their theory of treatment.[25] In other words, this model can combine what has already been done in the traditional psychodynamic and cognitive-behavioral approach with more relevant issues related to better or more positive images of self, the use of spirituality, the practice of virtues and those aspects of what the person sees as a "good" life.

SEXUAL HISTORY OF THE OFFENDER

A clerical child abuser sometimes has a history of being sexually abused. In the John Jay 2006 Supplemental Report, single-incident clerics were found to be less likely to have a recorded history of abuse (physical/sexual abuse as well as substance abuse) than clerics with more than one incident. The group of single-incident clerics included 4.2 percent who had suffered physical or sexual abuse as children, compared to 8.8 percent for clerics with multiple incidents.[26] It should be noted that these rates are well below the rates for male nonclerical victims of sexual abuse *only* (one in six males before the age of 21, or 16.6 percent).

For those who were abused, the question becomes how does this man integrate or not integrate this fact into his sexuality, his celibate capacity, and his sexual fantasies or attractions? Overall, the John Jay study found an overall rate of 9 percent of clerical sexual offenders with a history of being sexually abused. This means that most men who have been abused do not end up being abusers but that those who abuse may have a history of traumatic experiences. Other studies have found that priest nonoffenders have higher rates of being sexually abused as children yet have no history offending against children.[27] To suggest that anyone who has a history of being sexually abused should be excluded from consideration for admittance to the priesthood seems rash and ill advised. There is little evidence to support an assumption of predictability such as in the myth of a "victim to victimizer" so commonly believed by many.[28] It seems prudent to question what significance this event has in the person's sexual identity, but the data do not support use of a childhood history of sexual abuse as an exclusionary criteria for candidacy to religious life and priesthood. It does necessitate further investigation, and it may be a risk factor that needs attention and further inquiry. A large percentage of the pedophile priest group report being sexually abused, and this issue clearly warrants serious attention and care in assessment of candidates.

POST–DALLAS

These assessment processes were enhanced enormously during the initial surge of clerical offenders seeking treatment in the beginning of the crisis in 2002 and 2003 as well as from the more detailed and concise allegations of victims at the time. It was apparent from the initial and subsequent surge of clerical offenders coming into treatment that the veracity of the allegations and the standards of credibility were and are clearly different from what was expected in a court of criminal law. In most cases, the law was simply inadequate. The crimes and incidents had gone beyond most statutes of limitations for criminal conduct. Most, if not all, of the overwhelming majority of these cases were never adjudicated in a court of law. This posed and poses a significant hurdle for treatment centers and those Church officials referring their men to these centers.

The "beyond a reasonable doubt" criminal standard was no longer operational, and the standard of credibility used by most treatment centers and likewise by the National Review Board, most local review boards sponsored by dioceses and religious orders, and the USCCB would set a new standard for most clerical allegations and cases in the United States. As more local diocesan and religious provincial-level review boards adopted a standard that was used in most American civil law cases the credibility issue was placed at the forefront in the treatment providers' assessment processes. These evidentiary standards are obviously different for criminal cases.

This level of evidence was simply stated on the oft-quoted variable that "51 percent of the evidence" seemed or was likely to indicate that the allegation was credible. This is an essential new and important development that many are not aware of and do not understand. It actually is a stricter standard than U.S. criminal law would imply or use. This became and is the current evidentiary standard that is used in most dioceses and in most religious orders today. This issue is important and central to treatment of sex offenders. Treatment must break through the denial process, and anything that the treatment team can use to assist in this difficult process is critical to a better treatment outcome. The treatment programs and modalities that most often effect change and seem to be long lasting and have measurable outcomes would obviously be the most advantageous to use in the field. The field is experiencing a healthy and necessary debate in clarifying the exact nature of which modality and which program are most effective in sex offender treatment.[29] These evidentiary standards seem to have helped in this regard.

RISK ASSESSMENT

The final significant development has occurred in the field of risk assessment. Most religious orders under the standards set forth by the Conference of Major Superiors of Men (CMSM) have adopted very strict plans to monitor and supervise their members who were found to have a credible allegation against them (see Chapter 17, this volume). A few dioceses that run "prayer and penance" programs have also been vigilant in this regard, most notably the dioceses of Chicago and Philadelphia. The recent events in the Archdiocese of Philadelphia seem not to have affected the efficacy of this program.

Essentially, there exist certain permanent (static) and changing (dynamic) factors within risk assessment, and these need persistent updating and ongoing assessment to assure safety. The theory is based upon developmental psychology's insight that as humans, we continue to change, mature, and hopefully grow long into our retirement years; so too would a person with a sexual disorder.[30] Assessment of risk, therefore, is both essential and necessary for any long-term care program for impeded priests and religious. Part of this ongoing assessment would most probably and possibly include a re-engagement in treatment if the situational factors change or if factors within/of the personality necessitate it. Treatment may, therefore, become warranted again.

CONCLUSION

In summary, treatment of the clerical and nonclerical sexual offender has progressed in the past 10 years and continues to do so. There is still much more research to be done and still much more that the Church and society must continue to do to face this ongoing problem. The data that continue to come forth from the Church through the independent researchers at the John Jay College of Criminal Justice will hopefully change a system and structure that have allowed these abuses to take place. The complete sanctity of life that is the tradition of the Church can and must be honored in the sacred duty before her in this crisis.

NOTES

1. United States Council of Catholic Bishops, *Charter for the Protection of Children and Young People* (Washington, DC: Author, 2002).
2. G. J. McGlone, "Understanding the Clerical Sex Offender: A Review of the Research," in *The Dark Night of the Catholic Church: An Examination of the Scandal of Child Sexual Abuse*, edited by B. Geary and J. Greer (in preparation).
3. D. Finkelhor, "The Legacy of the Clergy Sexual Abuse Scandal." *Child Abuse and Neglect* 27 (2003): 1225–1229.
4. T. Doyle, R. Sipe and P. Wall, *Sex, Priests, and Secret Codes: The Catholic Church's 2,000-Year Paper Trail of Sexual Abuse* (New York: Bonus Books, 2006).
5. J. P. Chinnici, *When Values Collide: The Catholic Church, Sexual Abuse and the Challenges of Leadership* (Maryknoll, NY: Orbis Books, 2010).
6. K. J. Terry and A. Ackerman, "Child Sexual Abuse in the Catholic Church: How Situational Crime Prevention Strategies Can Help Create Safe Environments." *Criminal Justice and Behavior* 35 (2008): 643–657.
7. K. J. Terry, *Update and Report to the USCCB Meeting in Baltimore* (Washington, DC: USCCB, November, 2010).
8. J. Tallon and K. J. Terry, "Analyzing Paraphilic Activity, Specialization, and Generalization in Priests Who Sexually Abused Minors." *Criminal Justice and Behavior* 35 (2008): 615–628.
9. J. A. Loftus and R. Camargo, "Treating the Clergy." *Annals of Sex Research* 6 (1993): 287–303.
10. Tallon and Terry, 615–628.
11. Terry, 3.
12. *Ibid.*, 5.
13. G. McGlone, F. Ortiz and R. Karney, "A Survey Study of Psychological Practices in the Screening and Admission Practices of the Candidates to the Priesthood in the U.S. Catholic Church." *Professional Psychology: Research and Practice* 41 (2010): 526–532.
14. T. W. Campbell, "Maximizing Accuracy and Welcoming Scrutiny in SVP Evaluations: An Additional Response to Wilson and Looman." *Open Access Journal of Forensic Psychology* 2 (2010): 337–346.
15. B. Geary, J. W. Ciarrocchi and N. J. Scheers, "Sex Offenders, Spirituality, and Recovery." *Counseling and Spirituality* 25 (2006): 47–71.

16. D. Finkelhor, *The Sourcebook on Child Sexual Abuse* (Newbury Park, CA: Sage, 1986).

17. G. J. McGlone, *Sexually Offending and Non-offending Roman Catholic Priests: Characterization and Analysis*. Unpublished dissertation (San Diego, CA: California School of Professional Psychology, 2001).

18. J. N. Hook, J. P. Hook, D. E. Davis, E. L. Worthington and J. K. Penberthy, "Measuring Sexual Addiction and Compulsivity: A Critical Review of Instruments." *Journal of Sex & Marital Therapy* 36 (2010): 227–260.

19. G. Parent, J. Guay and D. Knight, "An Assessment of Long-term Risk of Recidivism by Adult Sex Offenders: One Size Doesn't Fit All." *Criminal Justice and Behavior* 38 (2011): 188–209.

20. D. A. Andrews and J. Bonta, *The Psychology of Criminal Conduct*, 4th edition (New York: Mathew Bender & Co., 2006).

21. J. Shedler, "The Efficacy of Psychodynamic Therapy." *American Psychologist* 65 (2010): 98–109.

22. M. C. Seto, "Risk Assessment," in *Pedophilia and Sexual Offending Against Children: Theory, Assessment, and Intervention*, edited by M. C. Seto. Washington, DC: American Psychological Association, 2008, pp. 141–66.

23. W. L. Marshall, L. E. Marshall, G. A. Serran and M. D. O'Brien, *Rehabilitating Sexual Offenders: A Strengths-based Approach* (Washington, DC: American Psychological Association, 2011).

24. W. Marshall and L. Marshall, *Can Treatment Be Effective with Sex Offenders or Does It Do Harm? A Response to Hanson (2010) and Rice (2010)*. Retrieved on May 2, 2011, from http://www.sexual-offender-treatment.org.

25. Campbell, 337–346.

26. Terry, K., & Smith, M. L. (2006). The Nature and Scope of Sexual Abuse of Minors by Catholic Priests and Deacons in the United States: Supplementary Data Analysis. Washington, DC: USCCB. Retrieved on June 27, 2011 from http://s3.documentcloud.org/documents/9230/07-12-27-john-jay-study-2006 -supplemental-report.pdf

27. McGlone, G. J. (2004). "Towards an Understanding of the Sexually Offending and Non-Offending Roman Catholic Clergy." *National Child Advocate*, 5, 1–20.

28. M. Cannon, "Invited Commentaries on Cycle of Child Sexual Abuse: Links Between Being a Victim and Becoming a Perpetrator." *British Journal of Psychiatry* 179 (2001): 495–96.

29. G. DeClue and T. W. Campbell, "Still Maximizing Accuracy in Sexually Violent Predator Evaluations." *Open Access Journal of Forensic Psychology* 2 (2010): 322–36.

30. T. Ward and C. Stewart, "The Treatment of Sex Offenders: Risk Management and Good Lives." *Professional Psychology: Research and Practice* 34 (2003): 353–60.

Part VI

CONCLUSION

Chapter 19

Beyond the Decade of Crisis

Kathleen L. McChesney and Thomas G. Plante

As it should, the story of clergy abuse remains a highly emotional one. More than 1,476 children were abused by priests from the Archdiocese of Boston alone. The men and women who came forward with their stories of unimaginable depravity inflicted upon them as children and teenagers have been called modern-day martyrs. These are the people for whom this book is written— the unsuspecting victims of manipulative, deceitful predators who often profaned the sacraments as they committed their atrocious acts.

The remarkable "earthquake" that the Roman Catholic Church experienced in the United States during January 2002[1] should have served as a wake-up call for the Catholic hierarchy around the world. In some countries, like Ireland, it did. Similarly, in Australia, the United Kingdom, and Canada, Church leaders and lay professionals intensified their efforts at removing unfit clergy from ministry and providing healing and support services to abuse victims. Nearly 10 years later, aftershocks of the quake continue to occur as new allegations of systemic abuse are revealed and law enforcement and Church authorities in Europe, Africa, and Latin America react by opening investigations of present and past abuses.

During the past decade, the issue of sexual abuse of children by Catholic clergy and others in the employ of the Church has been taken very seriously by most American bishops. Yet, as pointed out in this book, there continue to be some bishops who put minimal, if any, effort in implementing the provisions of the *Charter*.[2] Some failed to see the need for a comprehensive response in troubled dioceses, and at least one bishop flatly refused to comply with the

Charter's mandate for an external audit. Bishops who ignored the *Charter's* suggested guidelines, child-protection policies, and best practices suffered no consequence or benefit of fraternal correction. Perhaps the fact that bishops can do as they wish and are rarely held accountable for their actions within the Church structure is what continues to anger so many Catholics, as well as non–Catholics, about the clergy abuse crisis.

For a scandal of this magnitude, with its global ramifications on the future of the Catholic Church, one might expect the Holy See to initiate a full-scale crisis-management plan. For those who know the ways of the Church and its tendency to slowly change and seldom communicate, it probably comes as no surprise that the Vatican has not been as proactive about the issue as would be expected of the largest faith community in the world. Pope Benedict's comments during his trip to the United States in 2008 promising to do "all that is possible" to prevent abuse ring hollow now inasmuch as he and the leaders of the Church's key congregations have yet to follow-up his statement with helpful actions.

Perhaps those at the highest levels of the Church, comprising its greatest and last line of defense, still hope to protect the Church from scandal and maintain the moral high ground on all issues of sexuality. Have they noticed that they failed to do either? Do they realize that they need to listen more closely to the victims, to hear their pain, and to engage the laity in helping them to respond more like "church?" Do they understand that they really need to "get this right"? Do they know that to regain their credibility as an ethical church, they will need the help of different types of people—including those within and outside of the Church and those with priestly collars and without?

While the events and responses of the Catholic Church in the United States and, to some extent abroad, are not all good, neither are they all bad. Much progress has been made. Church leaders can point to the great strides in keeping children safe through *Charter*-directed safe-environment programs, zero-tolerance policies, guidance of local and national review boards, regular audits, better screening of clergy applicants, and quality research by the scholars at the John Jay College of Criminal Justice, among others. The Church is far better at protecting children in 2011 than prior to 2002. However, as long as abuse cases can fall between the cracks and bishops can refuse to follow the guidelines outlined in the *Charter* without corrective feedback and accountability, risks to child safety remain.

At the end of this very dark decade in the Church, there is some light. According to the John Jay researchers, the clergy abuse crisis in the Church is primarily a historical problem with peak levels of abuse occurring during the 1960s and 1970s. Significant reductions started to occur in the early

1980s and incidents of new abuse cases have been very rare during the past decade.[3] Policies and procedures generated by *Charter* mandates, external audits of diocesan child-protection procedures, and the close scrutiny of bishops' actions by victim-advocacy groups and the media now provide the kinds of checks and balances that were unheard of in previous decades. This previously concealed place in the Church has been exposed, and secrecy about these cases is harder to maintain than in the past.

On April 4, 2011, Archbishop Diarmuid Martin of Dublin, Ireland, addressed the attendees of the annual Restorative Justice Conference at Marquette University,[4] surprising many with his candor and sincerity and providing hope to others that Church leaders are finally "getting it."

"Mistakes were made," he said.

> It was thought best for the Church to manage allegations of abuse within its own structures and to use secrecy to avoid scandal. That type of avoidance of scandal eventually landed the Church in one of the greatest scandals of its history. Such an approach inevitably also led to those coming forward with allegations being treated in some way as adding to the problem . . . some were never given the impression that they were believed.[5]

The archbishop also called for the Church to analyze and address the culture of clericalism that may have facilitated the abusive behavior and bad decisions made by bishops and superiors that allowed such activity to go on (as have several contributors in this book). He goes on to say that he worries about signs of renewed clericalism, which may be at times "ably veiled behind appeals for deeper spirituality or for more orthodox theological positions."[6] To that end, he adds that men should be selected for the priesthood because of their desire and ability to be of spiritual service to others rather than because of their need for the personal security that is often afforded by the position.

It seems that everyone, Catholic and non-Catholics alike, has very strong opinions about the Church and especially about the clergy abuse crisis. Some who have conflicts or issues with the Church or who maintain a particular conservative or liberal agenda have used this crisis to try to advance their particular goals. For example, those who are in favor of women and married priests or who believe homosexuals should not be allowed in the priesthood find reasons to justify their causes within the clergy abuse story. Flames of centuries old anti-Catholic bias and prejudice have also been reignited with the clergy abuse crisis.

Furthermore, many Catholics, even some victims of clergy sexual abuse, are experiencing "issue fatigue." They are tired of the jokes, the innuendos, the movies and news reports about priests who violated children. Many devout Catholics are embarrassed by their Church and angered by the missteps of particular bishops and the Church in general.

Many members of the clergy are also tired and demoralized, worried that they are just one false allegation away from losing their livelihood and reputation. Many are uncomfortable wearing their clerical attire in public locations like airports and are often viewed with scorn, distaste, and, at-times, aggression. Priests, bishops, and even high-ranking cardinals have been confronted on the streets with accusations from strangers who assume that all priests are pedophiles. Sadly, this darkest decade is not the end of the scandal. It may be just the beginning of a century of tragedies for victims and the Church. Unforeseen and unintended consequences may lie ahead. Where exactly it will all lead remains unclear.

Our initial query at the outset of this book was whether Church leaders have done all that they could during the past decade to make the Church a safer place for children and adequately address the problem of sexual abuse by clergy. The authors of these chapters are thoughtful and knowledgeable individuals who care deeply about the issue. Most have played key roles in this narrative during the past 10 years and beyond. While these experts do not universally agree about whether or not the Church has done everything possible to make it a safer place for the young and the vulnerable or even how the clergy sexual abuse crisis occurred or should be addressed in the future, their perspectives and conclusions are important contributions to understanding this crisis.

Notably, there is agreement among the writers that there is much more to be accomplished. We are not yet able to ensure that children are completely safe in the Church and that those who wish to harm children are no longer allowed to be in ministry. At this point in the Church's history it is imperative that we use state-of-the-art research and best practices to achieve those goals. With this shared sense of purpose, the laity and the clergy can work together and succeed.

We must get this right—failure is not an option. We remain cautiously optimistic that through current and future pastoral efforts, abuse victims will find solace, peace, and support. We also hope that the Church will one day become a holier place—one that is more virtuous and purged of the evil that permeated the souls of over four thousand priests.

Beyond this decade of crisis we look forward to a far better Roman Catholic Church, one in which our collective concern that a member of the clergy might harm a treasured child is the worry of a distant past.

NOTES

1. Boston Globe Investigative Staff, *Betrayal: The Crisis in the Catholic Church* (New York: Little, Brown, 2002).
2. United States Conference of Catholic Bishops, *Charter for the Protection of Children and Young People* (Washington, DC: Author, 2002).
3. John Jay College of Criminal Justice, *The Nature and Scope of the Problem of Sexual Abuse of Minors by Catholic Priests and Deacons in the United States* (New York: Author, 2004); John Jay College of Criminal Justice, *The Causes and Context of the Problem of Sexual Abuse of Minors by Catholic Priests and Deacons in the United States* (New York: Author, 2011).
4. D. Martin, *The Truth Will Make You Free: A Personal Journey*. Keynote lecture presentation at Harm, Hope, and Healing: Marquette University International Dialogue on the Clergy Abuse Scandal, Milwaukee, WI (2011, April 4).
5. *Ibid.*
6. *Ibid.*

About the Editors and Contributors

Thomas G. Plante, PhD, ABPP, is professor of psychology and director of the Spirituality and Health Institute at Santa Clara University as well as an adjunct clinical professor of psychiatry and behavioral sciences at Stanford University School of Medicine. He currently serves as vice chair of the National Review Board for the Protection of Children and Youth for the U.S. Council of Catholic Bishops. He has published 14 books, including *Sin against the Innocents: Sexual Abuse by Priests and the Role of the Catholic Church* (Greenwood, 2004) and *Bless Me Father For I Have Sinned: Perspectives on Sexual Abuse Committed by Roman Catholic Priests* (Greenwood, 1999). As a licensed psychologist in private practice, he has evaluated or treated more than 600 priests and applicants to the priesthood and diaconate and has served as a consultant to a large number of dioceses and religious orders in both the Roman Catholic and Episcopal Churches.

Kathleen L. McChesney, PhD, has a wide range of executive experience in business, government, and faith-based institutions. She has held executive leadership positions in the Federal Bureau of Investigation and the Walt Disney Company and established and served as the first executive director of the Office of Child and Youth Protection of the United States Conference of Catholic Bishops. Dr. McChesney has also taught law-enforcement courses at the King County Police and the FBI's Training Academies. She is co-author of *Pick Up Your Own Brass: Leadership the FBI Way* (Potomac Books, 2011), the contributor of "Pledges, Promises and Actions; The Road to Resolution of the Crisis of Abuse of Children by Catholic Clergy" in the book edited by Thomas G. Plante, *Sins against the Innocents* (Greenwood, 2004) and has published articles and major reports on various law enforcement and child-abuse prevention issues. She has received several prestigious awards, including the U.S. President's Meritorious Achievement Award, the Lifetime Achievement Award for Women in Policing, and the Hildegard Van Bingen Woman for the World Award. She currently operates her own company, Kinsale Management Consulting, which provides leadership and security guidance to businesses and serves on several nonprofit boards.

THE CONTRIBUTORS

Anonymous is an educator living on the east coast of the United States who was abused by a Catholic priest as a young girl. She has been active in recovery efforts and met with Pope Benedict during his visit to the United States in 2008.

Monica Applewhite, PhD, has developed national and international programs for sexual abuse prevention and response in the Catholic and Episcopal Churches, the Salvation Army, and numerous other faith-based organizations. She began work with religious orders and congregations in 1996 and was the principal developer and director of the Instruments of Hope and Healing designed to hold Catholic religious men accountable to the highest standards of child protection and response. This program was adopted by the vast majority of religious institutes of men, allowing Dr. Applewhite to work directly with more than 150 religious institutes in the United States.

In 1988, **Barbara Blaine** founded SNAP, the Survivors Network of those Abused by Priests, the nation's oldest and largest self-help organization for victims of clergy sexual abuse. SNAP's first support meetings were held in a Catholic Worker House in south Chicago where Blaine worked. Through word of mouth and small ads, SNAP grew into an international outreach, educational, and advocacy organization. Today, SNAP has more than 10,000 members and 65 chapters in the United States, Canada, and Mexico, with new groups forming in Australia and Europe. Blaine is herself a survivor of abuse by a priest that she suffered as a young teen.

Judge Terrence A. Carroll currently sits as Distinguished Jurist in Residence at the Seattle University School of Law, where he serves on the faculty as well. He was appointed chair of the clergy abuse board for the Archdiocese of Seattle (Western Washington) following the implementation of the *Dallas Charter*. That board issued a detailed report regarding the history and causes of clergy abuse in the archdiocese. In addition to his judicial background and extensive alternative dispute resolution experience, he has been active in issues relating to police accountability and has served on many community boards and panels.

Mark E. Chopko, Esq., is a partner and chair of the Nonprofit & Religious Institutions practice group of Stradley, Ronon, Stevens & Young, LLP, in its Washington, DC, office. He is engaged in advising religious and nonprofit institutions on structural, risk-management, and risk-avoidance issues and defending them in litigation throughout the United States. He has participated in more than 30 cases in the U.S. Supreme Court. In addition, Mr. Chopko is an adjunct professor of law at Georgetown University. He is coauthor of *Exposed: A Legal Field Guide for Nonprofit Executives* (National Risk Management Center, 2009), and numerous articles on legal topics important to religious and nonprofit organizations. Between 1987 and 2007, he was general counsel to the United States Conference of Catholic Bishops, Washington, DC.

Rev. Gerald D. Coleman, SS, PhD, is a member of the Society of St. Sulpice (Sulpicians) in the United States and the former president/rector of St. Joseph's College, Mt. View, CA (1985–1987) and St. Patrick's Seminary & University, Menlo Park, CA (1988–2004). He is the vice president for corporate ethics for the Daughters of Charity Health System of the West and a lecturer in the Graduate Department of Pastoral Ministries at Santa Clara University, Santa Clara, CA. He writes monthly columns for three Catholic newspapers and has published widely in areas of moral and pastoral theology. His most recent book is *Catholic Priesthood: Formation and Development* (Liguori, 2006), and he was the contributor of "Clergy Sexual Abuse and Homosexuality" in the book edited by Thomas G. Plante, *Sins against the Innocents* (Greenwood, 2004). His lengthy analysis of the principle of gradualism and the use of prophylactics is in the Spring 2011 edition of *Catholic Ethics USA*.

Rev. Thomas P. Doyle, JCD, CADC, a canon lawyer and addictions therapist, has been deeply involved in issues surrounding clergy sexual abuse since 1984. While serving at the Vatican Embassy in 1985 he coauthored (along with F. Ray Mouton and Fr. Michael Peterson) an extensive report on the clergy abuse crisis. He has been actively supportive of clergy abuse victims and their families throughout the United States and abroad. He has served as a consultant and expert witness in civil and criminal cases throughout the United States. He has provided similar pastoral and professional support in Canada and several European countries. He coauthored, along with A. W. R. Sipe and Patrick Wall, a historical account of sexual abuse by the clergy titled *Sex, Priests and Secret Codes* (Bonus Books, 2006).

Rev. J. Cletus Kiley is a priest of the Archdiocese of Chicago, ordained in 1974. In 1997, Rev. Kiley was named Executive Director, Secretariat for Priestly Life and Ministry, for the U.S. Conference of Catholic Bishops. He served as the staff to the bishops' Ad Hoc Committee on Sexual Abuse and, in this capacity, assisted the committee and the response team in the development of the *Charter for the Protection of Children and Young People* in 2002. In 2006, Rev. Kiley was named the president and CEO of the Faith & Politics Institute in Washington, DC. and in 2010 became the Director of Immigration Policy of Unite/HERE.

Rev. Paul Macke, SJ, is a priest of the Chicago Province of the Society of Jesus ordained in 1973. Since 2005, he has been secretary for Pastoral Ministry & Jesuit Life for the Jesuit Conference of the United States based in Washington, DC. Fr. Macke recently developed, with other experts, an educational program for religious focused on professional boundaries in ministry with adults and the use and abuse of the Internet. He is a professional pastoral psychotherapist with more than 30 years of clinical experience.

Monsignor Francis J. Maniscalco has been a priest since 1971 and served the diocese of Rockville Centre as director of religious education; director of the office of family life; and, for eight years, as editor of *The Long Island Catholic*, a weekly diocesan newspaper. Beginning in 1993, he served at the United States Conference of Catholic Bishops as director of media relations, and in October 1995, he was appointed the Conference's Secretary of Communications. He served in that post until September 2006. Monsignor Maniscalco served as a consultor to the Pontifical Council for Social Communications of the Vatican; chaired the Interfaith Broadcasting Commission, which supplies programming of a religious nature to the major TV networks; and served as one of nonindustry members on the board that monitors the TV rating system. In February 2007, Monsignor Maniscalco returned to the Diocese of Rockville Centre as director of the respect life office and public policy adviser to the diocesan bishop and is pastor of St. Thomas the Apostle Parish.

Gerard J. McGlone, SJ, PhD, is currently the executive director at the Saint John Vianney Treatment Center in Downingtown, PA. Fr. McGlone is a Jesuit priest of the Maryland Province of the Society of Jesus (Jesuits), ordained in 1987. He is currently an assistant professor (applied-on leave) at the Georgetown University School of Medicine and Department of Psychiatry. He has been a psychotherapist in many settings while in California, Massachusetts, Maryland, and Pennsylvania for almost 25 years. He consults with dioceses and religious orders extensively throughout the Americas and Europe. He is coauthor of *Creating Safe and Sacred Places* (Saint Mary's Press, 2003) and coauthor of *Instruments of Hope and Healing* (Saint Joseph's University Press, 2009).

Judge Michael R. Merz has been a trial judge in Ohio for 34 years; his work currently focuses on review of death penalty cases. Since 2004, he has served as a member, chair (2007–2009), and consultant to the National Review Board, the lay board established by the U.S. Conference of Catholic Bishops to oversee implementation of the *Dallas Charter*.

James E. Post, JD, PhD, holds the John F. Smith, Jr. Professorship in Management at Boston University. He has held many administrative and teaching appointments in an academic and professional career that spans more than 35 years. He teaches courses in strategic management, corporate governance, and professional responsibility. In 2002, he co-fonded the Catholic lay group Voice of the Faithful in response to disclosures about clergy sexual abuse in the Archdiocese of Boston. He served as president of VOTF from June 2002 to January 2006 and as a member of its board of trustees from 2002 to 2009. He is the author, coauthor, or editor of 20 books and more than 150 papers on the topics of governance, public affairs, and professional ethics.

Bishop Geoffrey J. Robinson, DCL, is a retired auxiliary bishop of the Archdiocese of Sydney, Australia. He was ordained a priest in 1960 and a bishop in 1984. In 1994, he was appointed to the Professional Standards Committee of the Australian Bishop's Conference and remained a member until 2003, for the last six years as its chairman. In this role, he had the task of coordinating the response of the entire Australian Church to revelations of sexual abuse, dealing with issues such as the establishment of a national protocol for responding to complainants, the establishment of a national treatment center, the preparation of a code of conduct for church personnel, preparation of preventative measures and opportunities for education, and assistance for new bishops and religious leaders in this field. In 2004, he retired from his office as bishop. He recently authored the book *Confronting Power and Sex in the Catholic Church* (Liturgical Press, 2008) in an attempt to confront the deeper causes of abuse within the Church. He followed this with the book *Love's Urgent Longings* (John Garratt Publishing, 2010), setting out some of his own personal journey in response to abuse.

Katarina Schuth, OSF, PhD, holds the Endowed Chair for the Social Scientific Study of Religion at the Saint Paul Seminary School of Divinity at the University of St. Thomas and has published extensively on education for Catholic ministry. Educated in both the social sciences and theology, she has earned an MA and PhD in cultural geography from Syracuse University, and a Master of Theological Studies and License in Sacred Theology from the Weston Jesuit School of Theology in Cambridge, MA. Dr. Schuth has written numerous articles pertaining to the Catholic faith and five books: *Priestly Ministry in Multiple Parishes; Educating Leaders for Ministry; Seminaries, Theologates, and the Future of Church Ministry; Reason for the Hope: The Futures of Roman Catholic Theologates;* and *Cooperative Ventures in Theological Education.* She has received numerous awards and serves on many educational nonprofit boards.

Anson Shupe, PhD, is professor of sociology at the joint campus of Indiana University/Purdue University, Fort Wayne, Indiana. He has been following the phenomenon of sexual, economic, and authoritarian abuse across a wide variety of Christian and non–Christian groups for the past two decades. He has authored/coauthored 20 books and edited/coedited another nine volumes, mostly on religious topics, as well as approximately 100 journal, magazine, and encyclopedia/handbook articles. He is currently coauthor (with Christopher S. Bradley) of *Self, Attitudes and Emotion Work: Western Social Psychology and Eastern Zen Buddhism Confront Each Other* (Transaction Publishers, 2010).

A. W. Richard Sipe is devoted full time to research into the sexual and celibate practices of Roman Catholic bishops and priests in the United States. That path includes the study of the sexual teaching of the Church and its effects on behavior, especially sexual abuse of minors by clergy, and the tangle of sexual problems that some people claim are blocking every religious agenda and destroying beyond repair the credibility of the Catholic Church in sexual matters. His seven books include *A Secret World* (Taylor-Routledge, 1990) and *Sex, Priests and Power* (Brunner/Mazel, 1995), which explore various aspects of the questions about the pattern and practice of religious celibacy. He spent 18 years serving the Church as a Benedictine monk and Catholic priest. In those capacities, he was trained to deal with the mental health problems of priests. Both as a priest and married man, he has practiced psychotherapy, taught on the faculties of major Catholic seminaries and colleges, lectured in medical schools, and served as a consultant and expert witness in both civil and criminal cases involving the sexual abuse of minors by Catholic priests.

Margaret Leland Smith is a quantitative criminologist at the Institute for Criminal Justice Ethics at John Jay College/CUNY. She was the key researcher on the national *Study of the Nature and Scope of Sexual Abuse in the Catholic Church from 1950–2002* and data analyst on the *Study of the Causes and Context* *of Sexual Abuse of Minors by Catholic Priests in the United States, 1950–2010.* She is a graduate of Rutgers University.

Karen J. Terry, PhD, is a professor in the criminal justice department and the interim dean of research at John Jay College of Criminal Justice. She holds a doctorate in criminology from Cambridge University and has several publications on sex offender treatment, management, and supervision. Most recently, she was the principal investigator on two studies assessing the extent and causes of the sexual abuse crisis in the Catholic Church in the United States.

Rev. Richard Vega is president of the National Federation of Presbyteral Councils and has been a priest and pastor in the Los Angeles Archdiocese for several decades.

Charles Zech, PhD, is a professor of economics at Villanova University, where he has taught since 1974. He also serves as the director of the Center for the Study of Church Management at Villanova. He received his BA in economics from St. Thomas University (MN) and his MA and PhD from Notre Dame University. He is the author or coauthor of 10 books on the topic of church management, including *Money Matters: Personal Giving in American Churches* (Westminister/John Knox, 1996), *Plain Talk about Churches and Money* (Alban Institute, 1997), *Why Catholics Don't Give . . . And What Can Be Done about It* (Our Sunday Visitor Press, 2006), *The Parish Management Handbook* (Twenty-Third Publications, 2003), *Lay Ministers and Their Spiritual Practices* (Twenty-Third Publications, 2003), *Listening to the People of God: Closing, Rebuilding, and Revitalizing Parishes* (Paulist Press, 2007), *Best Practices in Parish Stewardship* (Our Sunday Visitor Press, 2008), and most recently *Best Practices of Catholic Pastoral and Finance Councils* (Our Sunday Visitor Press, 2010). He is a regular presenter at the Annual Conference of the International Catholic Stewardship Council (ICSC) and at diocesan and parish stewardship days around the country. In 2008, the ICSC awarded him the Christian Stewardship Award. He has served as a consultant to a number of U.S. Catholic parishes and dioceses.

Index

About the Abnormal Psychology Series

Why do people do what they do? Why do so many engage in patterns of thought and behavior that are so troubling and often disturbing either to themselves or to others? Why do people act in ways that are destructive or not in their own best interest? Understanding abnormal behavior has been a perplexing challenge throughout the centuries. Furthermore, what is and what is not considered abnormal has changed a great deal over time. While we have learned much about the biological, psychological, and social influences on behavior and our notions of what is and what is not abnormal, we still have so much to learn.

In addition to understanding abnormal psychology, a further critical challenge is how to best diagnose disorders and treat them. While different perspectives for intervention have varied radically over the years, current and future research evidence helps us better focus our treatment strategies in ways that will result in better outcomes and, thus, be more successful.

Abnormal psychology impacts all of us. We all have experienced the stress associated with psychopathology among our friends, family, colleagues, and even strangers who have crossed our paths in life. We all could learn more about abnormal psychology: what it is, how to understand it, and how to manage it better.

The Abnormal Psychology Series attempts to help all better understand abnormal psychology in a thoughtful, scholarly, yet readable manner led by multidisciplinary experts in the field. These books will help readers secure a state-of-the-art understanding of what we know about a wide variety of problems in human thought and behavior that we consider abnormal, pathological, and destructive to self and others. An enhanced appreciation for abnormal behavior helps professionals, students, and lay readers appreciate the complexity of psychopathology but also offers hope that we can better understand, intervene in, and cope with these troubles. This knowledge can potentially make our community a better place in which those who struggle with abnormal thoughts, moods, and behaviors might find understanding, help, and hope.

Thomas G. Plante, PhD, ABPP (Series Editor)